2.50

The English Novel and Prose Narrative

Elements of Literature
Series Editor: Stuart Sim, Professor of English, University of Sunderland

'Elements of Literature' is designed to introduce students and researchers to the structural and methodological principles underpinning the main branches of literary study. Incorporating the very latest scholarship on issues of form and genre, the series offers exciting new perspectives that will further our understanding of how literature operates within its cultural context.

The first volumes in the series are:

The English Novel and Prose Narrative
David Amigoni

Poetry
John Strachan and Richard Terry

The English Novel and Prose Narrative

David Amigoni

Edinburgh University Press

© David Amigoni, 2000

Edinburgh University Press Ltd
22 George Square, Edinburgh

Typeset in Poliphilus and Blado
by Norman Tilley Graphics, and
printed and bound in Great Britain
by MPG Books, Bodmin

A CIP record for this book is available
from the British Library

ISBN 0 7486 1121 5 (paperback)

The right of David Amigoni
to be identified as author of this work
has been asserted in accordance with
the Copyright, Designs and Patents Act 1988.

Contents

Acknowledgements

I should like to thank Keele University for granting me a semester's sabbatical leave to complete this project, and my colleagues in the Department of English Language and Literature for covering for me in my absence. Special thanks to James McLaverty and Anthea Trodd, who, with heavy workloads to manage, generously read and commented on portions of the manuscript with characteristic acumen. I am indebted to Stuart Sim, first, for inviting me to embark on the project; and, secondly, for his efficiency and supportiveness in reading and commenting on the entire manuscript. Thanks also to David Walker for the loan of books and conversations about the novel. The anonymous readers appointed by Edinburgh University Press provided me with encouragement and constructive criticism at a helpful stage: I thank them. It has been a real pleasure to work again under the ever-considerate guidance of Jackie Jones. Above all, thanks to K, to whom the book is dedicated.

Preface: the scope of the book and how to read it

This book introduces students to the novel and prose narrative. For the most part, it works with case-study readings of novels which are, in my experience, widely and frequently taught. They are: Jane Austen's *Emma*; Samuel Richardson's *Pamela*; Charlotte Brontë's *Jane Eyre*; George Eliot's *Mill on the Floss*; Charles Dickens's *Bleak House*; Henry James's *The Spoils of Poynton*; H.G. Wells's *Ann Veronica*; Virginia Woolf's *Mrs Dalloway*; and Salman Rushdie's *Midnight's Children*. In other words, they are a selection of fictions dating from 1740 to 1980, which are explored in more or less chronological succession to illustrate the ways in which the narrative strategies of the novel have been subject to both change and continuity over the course of two and a half centuries, from the origins of the English novel in the eighteenth century to the postmodern and postcolonial novel in the late twentieth. In being considered in the final chapter and alongside *Midnight's Children* (1980), Laurence Sterne's eighteenth-century novel *Tristram Shandy* finds itself somewhat out of line: but readers who know anything about Sterne's wonderfully anti-linear novel will not be surprised at this. Moreover, the anti-linear nature of Sterne's narrative encourages a revised approach to the story of the novel in literary history. Generally, each novel is accorded its own itemised section (or sections) within a chapter. I have sought to use editions which are readily available.

In Chapter 4 I also demonstrate ways of reading two different kinds of short story from the late nineteenth and early twentieth centuries, an important transitional period in the history of fiction during which the short story became a genre acknowledged in its own right: the stories are Thomas Hardy's 'The Withered Arm' and Katherine Mansfield's 'The Garden Party'.

In being concerned with prose narrative as well as the novel, the book offers ways of reading non-fictional narratives which are coming to figure increasingly in students' programmes as the nature of literary studies itself changes. In Chapter 3 I explore ways of reading a nineteenth-century autobiography, Samuel Bamford's *Early Days*, and a nineteenth-century biography, Elizabeth Gaskell's *The Life of Charlotte Brontë*. In selecting these narratives, I hope to show how, first, Bamford's autobiography can help readers to think about the relationship between writing and class (Bamford is generally recognised as a contributor to a tradition of working-class male writing). And, secondly, in the case of Elizabeth Gaskell's biography of Charlotte Brontë, my aim will be to show how this work can be used in discussions of women's writing.

Of course, judgements are involved in making selections, and selections had to be made on the assumption that the average reader's principal study needs are still likely to be orientated towards the novel (which as a result remains the principal focus of the book). Consequently I should not like readers to assume that my readings of non-fictional prose narratives amount to a universal code for reading all autobiographies and biographies, different examples of which can be found from periods and contexts which, for reasons of space, I have not been able to tackle. My readings of non-fiction prose narratives offer broad principles to guide reading, backed up by examples, and are designed to act as starting points for further study. Of course, the same can be said for my readings of novels. Notes which follow the chapters point to sources for this further study, and additional information is provided in the annotated select bibliography. Where material is available in easily accessible anthologies and readers I have endeavoured to cite from these (whilst seeking also to refer to the original source).

One of the aims of this book is to provide students with a framework for thinking about the relationships between novels and other forms of prose narrative, in historical and cultural context, in the light of recent developments in literary studies. In addition, the book provides a basic introduction to recent critical positions which have had a major impact on the study of the novel, such as feminism, postmodernism and postcolonialism. It is important that a book such as this be a synthesis of established positions, and, within the bounds of accessibility, as up to date as it can be. As a consequence, it has been necessary to venture into some, at times, quite challenging conceptual territory. This is particularly the case in the second half of Chapter 1, where I elaborate a critical vocabulary that has emerged from the movements known as structuralism and poststructuralism, New

Historicism and cultural materialism; and in the second half of Chapter 2, where I consider debates about the origins of the novel which have been conditioned by these movements.

In the light of this, a word about how to read this book: if during the more abstract discussions the reader should happen to find the going tough, move on to the more detailed case-study readings in individual chapters, which I generally cite after making a conceptual point, and which amount to illustrations of the general conceptual point I am making. It could be helpful to move around the book, taking advantage of the sections and the cross-referencing. Then re-read the challenging section. Feel free to make choices: if the reader's immediate need is to find out how narrative in the novel works in principle and detail, turn to the beginning of Chapter 2 (where I use *Emma* as an exemplary novel narrative).

Literary study without concepts is not an option. Wherever possible I have provided definitions of more specialised concepts, such as point of view, rhetoric, discourse, intertextuality, the implied reader, and free indirect speech, to name but a few. However, it is worth stressing that definitions in themselves are of limited use: my definitions are always located in the context of an interlocking argument, and this is as important as the definitions.

Introduction: straightforward discourse and novel transactions

1.1 Literature and non-literature?

This book is an introduction to the novel and prose narrative as elements of literature. 'Literature' is a complex term. It can be used to describe a range of linguistic techniques and strategies which generate, for instance, a resonant image, or a sense of irony, or purposeful ambiguity, the effects of which would lead us to describe the writing which embodied it as 'literary'.

'Literature' is most often used to signify a valued tradition of writings, which is implicitly how it functions when we speak of 'English literature'. When I use the term in this work, I by no means reject that meaning: many of the works I use to illustrate this study are major contributions to English literature which have their status confirmed in the regularity with which they are taught in schools, colleges and universities. However, this implies that 'English literature' is inseparable from processes of selection, which are embedded in structures of power and prestige. So I shall also take note of this position, and, consequently, argue against a view of 'literature' which assumes that it is a knowable and immutable thing for all times and all people. Consequently, novels and prose narratives will have more than one relation to different meanings of 'literature'.

Reading the novel, and to a lesser extent the short story, in their relations to different meanings of 'literature' will be my principal focus. But I shall also explore the novel in relation to the biography and the autobiography: prose narratives which are classified as non-fictional, factual and often 'non-literary', and, yet, which can invite complex responses from readers. If the boundaries of 'literature' are, from an historical point of view, never quite settled, then 'non-literature' becomes a category which we cannot ignore. We will need a rather different kind of critical approach to draw out the full consequences of this point, which will be the overall aim of this intro-ductory chapter. To begin with, we should address the problem of prose which is, on the face of it, language which is rather less than 'literary'.

1.2   Prose

The *Oxford English Dictionary* (*OED*) defines prose as 'straightforward discourse' or 'the ordinary form of written or spoken language'. The ordinariness of prose makes it different from poetic language, which, at its most characteristic, is recognisable from the presence of rhyme or metre. This ordinariness is a strength from the perspective of communicative efficiency and flexibility. Prose is the medium I am writing in now, and it could equally be used to introduce readers to the use of computer software: 'This introductory section of the *Microsoft Windows User's Guide* provides a guide to the documentation – so you know where to find information about working with Windows.'[1] But this rather militates against the literary credentials of prose, a point recognised by the journalist Andrew Marr when reviewing *The New Oxford Book of English Prose* (1998): 'prose is such a general commodity that a real anthology of English prose is unthinkable. It would spread too widely, from computer manuals to *Sun* editorials, and would be unreadable.'[2] Marr's comment raises two questions that will concern us. The first relates to his sense of prose as a 'general commodity': if prose is so ubiquitous, why are certain forms of prose adjudged distinctive? The second question raised by Marr is that of readability: if an anthology of the totality of English prose would be so inclusive as to be unthinkable, what is it that makes some forms of prose more pleasurably readable and thus selectable than the variety found in computer manuals? One answer to that question must be: narrative.

1.3   Narrative

In fact, the majority of anthologised pieces in *The New Oxford Book of English Prose* are from either novels or short stories, forms cast in narrative. In 1752, the poet and critic Samuel Johnson reflected on why narrative is so captivating:

> No Stile of Conversation is more extensively acceptable than the Narrative. He who has stored his Memory with slight Anecdotes, private Incidents, and personal Particularities, seldom fails to find his Audience favourable. Almost

every Man listens with Eagerness to contemporary History; perhaps almost every Man has some real or imaginary Connection with a celebrated Character, some desire to advance, or oppose a rising Name ... He that is a Hearer in one Place, qualifies himself to become a Speaker in another; for though he cannot comprehend a Series of Argument, or transport the volatile Spirit of Wit without Evaporation, yet he thinks himself able to treasure up the various Incidents of a Story, and pleases his Hopes with the Information which he shall give to some inferior Society.[3]

Skilfully told stories give pleasure to their listeners. As Johnson indicates, narrative consists of 'Incidents' or events arranged into a story. These events are related by a 'Speaker', or narrator, and they are addressed to a 'Hearer'. The popular and nonspecialised nature of narrative is evident from the way in which 'Hearers' can themselves become 'Speakers' or narrators in turn. We will all, at some points in our conversational lives, be narrators in ways that will not lead us all to be poets. Johnson reflects on the ordinary, everyday status of narrative as a conversational genre – a genre is a regular (conventional) way of speaking or writing – which highlights similarities between this mode of communication and prose.

This book will explore the workings of written prose narratives which relate 'History' in the form of 'private Incidents' acted out in the 'personal Peculiarities' of 'Characters' either 'real or imaginary'. For whilst Johnson is reflecting on oral narrative, his terms account for the defining characteristics of written narrative genres such as biography and autobiography which narrate the lives of 'real' individuals. They also account for the 'imaginary' representation of characters and their histories in the novel, a narrative form which was rising to prominence in England when Johnson was writing in the mid eighteenth century (see sections 2.11–14).

It would be wrong to infer from this that all narrative is popular, conversational and prosaic: epic poetry of grand subject matter and sophisticated diction such as John Milton's *Paradise Lost* is woven in the 'volatile Spirit of Wit', but is still a narrative. At the same time, narrative does not require Milton's epic grandeur to endow it with artistic status. By the end of the nineteenth century certain English novels had come to use prose in remarkably sophisticated – indeed poetic – ways which made the ordinary and prosaic the basis for distinctive literary art, a theme which will be pursued particularly in Chapter 4. The general argument of this book is that it is important to see such developments in cultural and historical contexts: in sections 4.4–5 I explore the narrative sophistication of Henry James's fiction in relation to popular narrative forms such as the late nineteenth-century newspaper story. Having said this, we need to acknowledge that placing novels and prose narratives in social and historical contexts requires considerations which respect the specific characteristics of narrative.

1.4   Narrative in context: the novel, mimesis and poetics

Narrative is generally classified as a mimetic medium. 'Mimesis' is a term used to describe literary modes which aim to 'imitate' human thoughts, speech, action and the world in which they take place: drama and narrative would be more readily recognised as mimetic than would lyric poetry. Given the mimetic impulses of narrative, and Johnson's recognition of the way in which narrative presents us with 'History', it is understandable that students expect to study novels and short stories in ways which accentuate their relation to the worldly situations which they dramatise. For instance, readers may turn to Charlotte Brontë's *Jane Eyre* to experience the lot of an orphan and governess in the Victorian period. It would appear that such novels reflect their historical contexts almost transparently.

However, approaches to the novel and its contexts which assume that a narrative imitates or simply reflects the times in which it was made encounter obvious difficulties when confronted by certain narrative strategies. These challenging, self-conscious narrative strategies are explored in Chapter 5 through Laurence Sterne's *Tristram Shandy* (an eighteenth-century novel), John Fowles's *The French Lieutenant's Woman*, Paul Auster's *City of Glass*, and Salman Rushdie's *Midnight's Children* (twentieth-century novels). These narratives playfully expose the limits of mimesis. Although I shall argue that even playful, sceptical narrative strategies lead the reader back to worldly insights into societies and histories – in the case of *Midnight's Children* to colonial domination and its resistance – it will be important to demonstrate how these contexts have to be traced through narrative as a complex medium. This remains the case even when narratives appear to be transparently mimetic.

If we adopt a basic distinction between the form and content of narrative – roughly, content is what a narrative says or is about, form is how it says it – then poetics is a formal mode of literary study based on the systematic identification and analysis of the devices and patterns which deliver the 'how' of a narrative. Poetics is the essential starting point for analysing how narratives mediate their effects – even when that mediation amounts to a disavowal of narrative's capacity to reflect the world transparently. Sections 2.1–5 are a reading of Jane Austen's *Emma* which uses poetics to explain its narrative strategies by accounting for the elements of narrative in general, such as events, point of view, and character. This will help to explain why *Emma* is viewed as 'literary'.

But this raises another question: how do we trace social and cultural contexts in 'literary' strategies which did not come into the world ready-made, but which were themselves shaped by processes of historical and cultural change? These questions will lead us into a debate about the origins of the novel as a distinctive literary form developing in conjunction with specific social and cultural circumstances in eighteenth-century England. This is a literary-critical debate that has been in progress since the 1950s, and continues in the present. Sections 2.7–10 will answer these questions through a reading of Samuel Richardson's early novel *Pamela* which will be framed by the questions: what do we mean by a novel? Which genres and writing techniques were drawn together to produce it? As we shall see, *Pamela* is based on the familiar letter and the journal. A cultural and critical debate about literacy and the making of the self in the mid eighteenth century will be traced through the distinctive way in which Richardson's *Pamela* transforms these genres into a special kind of narrative.

1.5   The novel and prose narrative in literary-critical argument: formalism and old and new historicisms

This brings us to the importance of literary-critical argument. Writers of novels often wrote critically and reflectively about the narrative strategies they were shaping, a point that will be demonstrated in connection with Samuel Richardson and Henry Fielding in section 2.10; George Eliot in 3.12; and Henry James, H. G. Wells and Virginia Woolf in 4.7 and 4.14. Moreover, since the nineteenth century, novels have been reviewed and judged in literary periodicals (sections 3.4 and 3.7 will explore examples of these). These practices link the novel to the academic literary criticism which has been practised on the form for around one hundred years: it demonstrates that the nature of narrative was actively debated and analysed in its own time.

Whilst there are continuities between the critical writings of practising novelists of the past and more recent forms of literary criticism, it is also necessary to be alert to differences. The main difference is that, since the end of the nineteenth century, the novel has become a major object of academic study in schools and higher education, viewed as an embodiment of literary and artistic tradition. This was not necessarily the function it was 'born' to, or a reliable index of the esteem in which it has sometimes been held, as this chapter will later suggest. Nonetheless, in becoming a major object of literary and artistic tradition, increasingly sophisticated varieties of literary criticism have been developed to validate this view of the novel.

Literary criticism is a powerful shaping force in the study of literature, which has played, and continues to play, a central role in selecting what we read and how we read it. The initial forms of academic novel criticism to be formulated in the later nineteenth century were orientated towards historical study, in line with the general way in which English literature – a university discipline that barely existed before the end of the nineteenth century – was studied at that time. This approach emphasised the relationship between philology (the history of the language), the history of genre, and authorial genius in shaping a national literary tradition. Subsequently, the dominant modes of twentieth-century novel criticism have taken poetics as their orientation, emphasising the formal complexity of the novel (formalist approaches will be differentiated and discussed in more detail in sections 2.1–5).

Formalist approaches have generated rich insights, but also some drawbacks. In making distinctions between literary and non-literary narrative strategies – by, for instance, foregrounding the complexity of point of view in the novel – formal approaches have commented richly on a selection of important novels whilst remaining relatively silent on non-fictional prose narratives such as biography and autobiography. Consequently these formal approaches to the novel have offered only limited insight into the wider literary and cultural significance of prose narrative.

Biography and autobiography are complex narratives which can invite readers to think again about what we mean by 'literature'. Victorian examples of these prose narratives are a major focus of sections 1.8–11, where I offer ways of reading Elizabeth Gaskell's *The Life of Charlotte Brontë*, and the working-class autodidact Samuel Bamford's autobiographical *Early Days*. My approach to narrative is framed by a style of new literary-historical reading which looks for literariness in the supposedly non-literary, and the non-literary in literature. Such an approach can be aligned with such movements as poststructuralism, the New Historicism, and cultural materialism (as well as their feminist and postcolonial inflections): movements which have developed out of recent theoretical approaches to literary study.[4] The remainder of this chapter will provide a basic outline of the conceptual vocabulary which supports a new literary-historical approach, along with a discussion of its significance. The concepts of rhetoric, intertextuality, discourse and culture can provide readers with new ways of making literary-critical connections between novels and non-fictional narrative forms. At a deeper level they provide us with new ways of re-thinking the historically shifting relations between literary and non-literary writings as practices which are embedded in cultural and social relations.

Of course, new literary-historical approaches are not entirely new: one of the striking things about the conceptual vocabulary that will play a role in the more integrated approach to the novel and prose narrative I advocate is that an earlier version of it can be found at work in the 'old' historicism, which organised literary criticism prior to the ascendancy of formalism. We can observe this by returning to one of the first textbooks designed to introduce students to the study of the novel, in order to measure the simi-larities and differences between 'old' and 'new' historicisms.

1.6 Studying the novel and prose narrative: historicism, culture and rhetoric

Selden L. Whitcomb's *The Study of a Novel*, published in 1906 when the author was an associate professor of English literature at the University of Kansas, addressed the first generation of students to study the novel as an academic exercise. Whitcomb's approach was historicist in the sense that he saw the development of the novel running parallel to and reflecting the grand historical progress of civilisation: 'Every great movement in the history of fiction, though modified by race and nationality, is one phase of a general cultural episode in modern civilisation.'[5] Whitcomb clearly understood 'modernity' to be a process of change and transformation, and his evidence for the novel's links to this progressive movement were to be found in such grand constructs as civilisation, the race, the nation and culture. 'Culture', as Raymond Williams has pointed out, is a complex word with a wide sem-antic range, and we will encounter its different past and present meanings in what remains of this chapter.[6]

To begin with, Whitcomb supposes that the progress of civilisation is reflected in novels which, when taken together, constitute a major 'cultural episode' in that process. This was because the novel, for Whitcomb, reflected 'cultural life in general'. For Whitcomb, 'culture' shaped the specificities of race and nation, and the mimetic capabilities of the novel 'give one a more extensive picture of social culture than any other form of art' (p. 138). In making this claim he brought 'culture' and 'society' together in a way which was characteristic of nineteenth-century thought. Societies were conceived as historically developing organisms, made up of varied yet interdependent social classes and groupings. What distinguished these societies from one another was the distinctive pattern of 'culture' by which such societies lived, the term here embracing knowledge, belief, law, morals and customs. In this sense 'culture' was conceived anthropologically as a whole way of life (the impact of this conception of culture on George Eliot's novels will be examined in section 3.12). Not only could the novel reflect culture, it was formed from the expressive essence of culture: Whitcomb noted that the novel's 'medium of expression, language ... must always suggest some special type of cultural life' (p. 138). This was to be found in a detailed study of the novel, and his textbook opened with a close analysis of its distinctive narrative structures (events, episodes, story, plot, character, point of view) and their artistic effects. To this extent, Whitcomb's cultural historicism depended on formal analysis. Yet, he approached the question of form from a specific perspective.

Whitcomb wrote from the perspective of an American university system which placed a strong emphasis on 'comparative rhetoric' and composition (p. 218). Rhetoric is a discipline with ancient roots, concerned with analysing the construction of oral and written compositions in order to maximise their persuasive and affective powers on their intended addressees. Clearly rhetoric has a practical aim to advise writers on good, and not so good, ways of writing. Whitcomb's book regularly suggests compositional exercises which will assist in clarifying the rhetorical effects of particular modes of writing: 'Assuming that Silas Marner [in George Eliot's novel of 1860] was a real individual, recast the novel into the form of a biography' (p. 225). This is something that I put into practice, albeit on a less ambitious scale, when I rewrite passages of narrative in sections 2.2 and 4.12 to assess the workings of the originals. In section 3.10 I focus specifically on biography as a distinctively rhetorical form of writing.

The approach I adopt towards biography urges an appreciation of rhetoric as a significant critical tool with much broader implications. Formalist novel criticism in the twentieth century has, with some exceptions,[7] tended to neglect the role of rhetoric. But in the last decades of the twentieth century critics have rediscovered rhetoric, because it enables critical and analytical insight into the social and historical contexts within which particular forms of narrative have aspired to be persuasive and powerful. There are two consequences which follow from this: first, rhetoric encourages readers of narrative to widen their horizons beyond the novel, and to look at the workings of the novel in relation to other kinds of narrative (and non-narrative) material – I'll explore this in the following sections. Secondly, if we remember that rhetoric has a persuasive aim, then a rhetorical approach to narratives can highlight the way in which narratives have entered into contests to secure the attention of readers, or tell the truth from particular perspectives. Rhetoric can be seen as an index of the struggles that divide, fracture and fragment the historical process along the lines of gender, class and race. I'll explore these in more detail in the following sections: they will lead us to an accordingly modified understanding of 'culture'.

1.7   The novel and prose narrative: from 'literature' to 'intertextuality'

A defining feature of the novel is that it does not belong to any single genre, yet participates in all genres. Whitcomb's rhetorical approach to the novel acknowledges its borrowings from the conventions which distinguish other literary modes and prose genres. For instance, Whitcomb suggests that 'students of the novel might profit by plot analysis of [Thomas] Carlyle's *French Revolution*', a colourful and dramatic work of history published in 1837 (p. 48). Thus Whitcomb saw the novel as a 'complex, composite ... type' (p. 218) which was made up from 'literature itself'.

By 'literature' Whitcomb meant a vast field in which writings and generic conventions circulated. It included drama, which provided conventions for representing the speech, thought and action of characters. It also included the prose genres of the narrative history (such as Carlyle's *French Revolution*), which provided models for plotting the passage of time and processes of social change and continuity. The prose genre of documentary reportage provided models for writing about the observation of social life and manners on which the 'realistic' effects of novels often depend (different critical accounts of 'realism' will be traced in sections 2.12 and 3.12). The biography provided models for narrating the life-course of individual characters. Finally the essay provided models for narrative commentary and discussion (p. 171).

Whitcomb's approach to the derivativeness of the novel anticipates present-day approaches to what have come to be known as the 'inter-textualities' of narrative. These approaches are premised on understanding narrative as 'text', that is to say a tissue of interwoven writings. Thus 'intertextuality' is a concept which seeks to grasp the fact that a novel 'is not a self-contained, individually authored whole, but the absorption and transformation of other texts'.[8] The intertextualities of the novel and prose narrative will be a consistent focus of my approach, especially in Chapter 2, where I consider the eighteenth-century origins of the novel; Chapter 3, which considers the relation of the Victorian novel to contemporary bio-graphical and autobiographical narratives; and Chapter 5, which explores the complex intertextualities of late twentieth-century postmodern and post-colonial fictions (the absorption and transformation of Laurence Sterne's parodic eighteenth-century novel *Tristram Shandy* in Salman Rushdie's *Midnight's Children* in particular). In thinking about the significance of intertextuality, it is necessary to make links with the concept of discourse, and broader trends in present-day literary theory.

1.8   The novel and prose narrative as 'forms of discourse'

Whitcomb's approach addressed the different 'forms of discourse' that are woven together in the novel (p. 218). 'Discourse' is a term which links Whitcomb's book to present-day theoretical concerns, though in consider-ing these we shall need to trace some shifts in its meaning. 'Discourse' derives from the Latin *discursus*, which means to run to and fro: the OED tells us that some of the earliest sixteenth-century usages in English employ the term to describe, for example, the movements of the sun during its daily course across the sky. At around about the same time, 'discourse' was also being used to classify any spoken or written treatment of a subject. For Whitcomb 'discourse' describes an approach to the analysis of a novel's composite textual structure as it goes to and fro between a variety of genres, their linguistic conventions and implied social contexts. Late twentieth-century theoretical approaches to novel and narrative criticism continue to invoke 'discourse' in this sense. At the same time they have gone further in using the term to probe the linguistic, social and power relations that are embedded in a narrative's absorption of 'discourses'.

It is beyond the scope of this book to provide a detailed introduction to the terrain of literary theory which has transformed literary study in Britain since the mid 1970s.[9] It is possible to outline a general sense of the way in which it has transformed an understanding of the orientation of language in general, which has, in turn, had major implications for the language of the novel and prose narrative. The initial impetus for the turn to theory derived from Ferdinand de Saussure's early twentieth-century linguistics and its adoption by the continental European structuralist and semiotic movement of the 1950s and 1960s ('semiotics' is the study of signs).

What did Saussure and structuralism challenge? Selden Whitcomb wrote his 1906 guide to the novel in an intellectual climate which recognised language as a rhetorical medium, but a medium which individuals could freely use to refer to and express the things of the world, human states of mind, emotions and so forth. This made language an intelligible fact of nature. Whitcomb accepted that writers would struggle with the imperfec-tions of language in an effort to express their 'ideas and ideals'; but in the end they 'may take delight in calm obedience to the will of nature, as it appears in ... language' (p. 248).

In a radical departure, Saussure's linguistics argued that language does not work on the basis of nature, reference and expression. Instead, it works on the basis of convention, signification and difference. Saussure no longer started with a conception of the word, conceiving instead of the 'sign', arguing that signs generate meaning not because they refer to things; on the contrary, they have a completely arbitrary relationship to things. Signs generate meaning because of conventionally maintained relations of difference from one another within a self-contained structure ('la langue', or language).[10] This powerful, self-contained structure is something that humans are born into: language speaks, or writes, its users, rather than the other way round. In practice, this structural and semiotic theory of language breaks the natural 'fit' between language and the world which was always a possibility for pre-structuralist novel criticism. For the novel and narrative, this break means that its mimetic effects have to be seen as being derived from signification rather than reference and expression. If the novel imitates at all then it imitates the conventions of signification which structure language as a practice. Instead of imitating the things of the world, the novel imitates language structures.

These arguments have been extended by certain present-day theories of 'discourse'. One of the difficulties with Saussure's structuralist theory of language is that 'la langue' is assumed to be homogeneous and smoothly self-regulating. This is where theories of 'discourse' take Saussure's insights in directions which theorise language as a field fractured by complex social and historical conflicts.[11] Poststructuralist discourse theorists argue that 'la langue' is really an array of discursive practices, or specific domains of speaking and writing, which authorise and regulate social life and power relations.

Poststructuralist critics have started to re-read the novel in history in the light of discourse theory. Nancy Armstrong has argued that manners and morals of the seventeenth and eighteenth centuries were institutionalised in the discourse of domesticity, which became the object of Richardson's novel *Pamela* (see section 2.14). Discursive practices also authorise and regulate recognisably institutionalised knowledges, such as religion, philosophy, the law, medicine and science. These can be equally important to the novel: the authority of the discourse of scientific 'biology', which emerged only in the nineteenth century, is used decisively in H. G. Wells's novel *Ann Veronica* (1909) (see section 4.8). Over time the status, internal composition and relations between discourses change. Nancy Armstrong's reading of *Pamela* argues that its discourses of domesticity and sexual desire acquired considerable authority and power in the middle of the eighteenth century. By the time of H. G. Wells's novel, domesticity could no longer be assigned such authority (Wells's heroine has to escape its stifling suburban manifestation). In Wells's novel biology is the master discourse which assumes authority over the messy conflict waged between other competing social and political discourses, which the narrative dramatises through character types.

Discourses 'make' characters in novels and in life: they do this by marking out particular positions – so-called subject positions – from which individual subjects and collective interests can fashion identities. Accordingly, discourses construct evaluations of individual identity based on the social categories of masculinity and femininity (gender), class and social rank, and race and ethnicity. This is a particularly important point for the new literary-historical rationale in constructing links between novels, biographies and autobiographies. These emerged as important genres for absorbing and transforming discourses of subjectivity to articulate what Dipesh Chakrabarty has described as 'the public and private rituals of modern individualism'.[12] I noted in my brief discussion of Saussure that one of the implications of his theory of language is that language 'makes' the self. 'Literature' can be viewed as a discourse which can be drawn upon in these rituals of self-making. If we take 'literature' to be present in specific, prestigious uses of

language, we will see how the Victorian working‑class writer Samuel
Bamford uses 'literary' discourse in his autobiography to fashion an image of
himself as a 'cultured' individual (see section 3.9).

1.9   The novel and 'culture' revisited: 'culture' as learning, 'self‑culture', 'culture' as a field of conflict

Whitcomb's book was aimed at the first generation of students who were
beginning to study the novel as 'literature'. This brings us to another sense
of the novel's relationship to 'culture' which is implicit in Whitcomb's
project: 'culture' as the learned study of selected and valued objects which
could promote the moral and intellectual growth of an individual reader in
'self‑culture'. As I shall demonstrate in Chapters 2 and 3, novels such as
Richardson's *Pamela* and Brontë's *Jane Eyre* told powerful stories about selves
which were expected to enrich their readers morally. And yet, a certain
defensiveness in Whitcomb's tone indicates the difficulty he faced when
installing the novel in general as a valued and self‑improving object of study:
'it is no longer deemed necessary to apologise for fiction itself, but a detailed
study of its form is still quite generally proposed in apologetic tones' (p. vii).
Whitcomb's comment recognises the novel's quasi‑disreputable past during
which it had, in some incarnations, been vilified as trivial or downright
harmful to processes of 'self‑culture'.

Let us look at what was at stake in two examples of ways in which the
novel was seen to be harmful to 'self‑culture'. Because novels are classified
as fictions or made‑up stories, and because certain Protestant theologies are
distrustful of imitations and images, novels were anathema to some religious
sects, especially during the nineteenth century. However, the same sects still
subscribed to the benefits of 'self‑culture' through approved forms of read‑
ing. If novels were rejected, biographies and autobiographies – non‑fictional
narratives about 'real', exemplary individual lives – were considered to
be suitable.[13] Another example of the novel's perceived harmfulness was
articulated supposedly in defence of women readers of novels in the nine‑
teenth century, whose 'weaker minds' were deemed, in the gendered dis‑
courses of biological and psychological science, to be more susceptible to
damage under the influence of sensationally shocking narratives.[14] The
point to note about these examples of attempts to regulate the relations
between the novel and 'self‑culture' is that they judge the novel through,
on the one hand, discourses of theology and its distinctions between

divine truth and devious fiction; and, on the other, gendered science and psychology.

This brings us to the least immediately obvious, yet most important sense of the relation of the novel and prose narrative to 'culture'. This defines 'culture' as a field, actualised in print and book production, in which meanings are made and exchanged, and discourses clash and collide over contests between, for instance, the real and the fictional, high and low taste, convention and originality, and masculine and feminine identities. Novels can be open to challenge in this field by authoritative discourses which dismiss them as trivial or harmful. But novels can selectively absorb those authoritative discourses into their intertexts, as we shall see in *Jane Eyre*'s use of psychological discourse (section 3.5). Novels can also, as we shall see in sections 4.4–5, aspire to the higher echelons of the field by refining themselves into serious mediators of a refined artistic perspective on life. Or, indeed, novels can adopt a playful and parodic orientation towards cultural discourses (Chapter 5). Thus novels in England have been, since the eighteenth century at least, important participants in the field of culture, absorbing discourses into their narrative intertexts which rehearse and seek to resolve conflicts over contested values and meanings.

This way of seeing the novel needs to be blended with the very factors that grant novels their privileged position in the cultural field, which is based on the subjective investments and involvements that they invite of their readers. Novels engagingly dramatise conflicts over truth and value through stories about character formation and relationships in recognisable social settings, where the everyday materials of manners, morals, customs and beliefs seem to be like life itself. In other words, readers can generally seek the pleasurable surface presence of a mimetic 'picture of social culture', to use Whitcomb's words again. But this is an effect, an artfully constructed alibi to deflect from the contest of discourses that is being waged.

But the contest is never deflected completely. Certain narratives, for instance those I shall address in Chapter 5, insist that the reader recognises them for what they are: narrative discourses. And even in more transparent reading experiences, readers are often invited to negotiate complex linguistic or indeed 'literary' effects. Whitcomb noted that 'the interpretation of culture by the novelist often has a touch of irony, for the imagination sees manners in their relative values' (p. 138). Whitcomb recognised, importantly, that novelists can be active and critical interpreters of that which they represent, as is evident in the degree of ironic distance perceptible in even the clearest picture of manners or morals. If we remember that discourse signifies in order to produce the effect of mimesis, it follows that irony in the novel is produced by linguistic means; that is to say, the imitation and ironic framing or 'quoting' of voices and forms of discourse. This is a point that I shall demonstrate in section 2.6, when I analyse the narrative techniques of free indirect speech in Jane Austen's *Emma*; and section 4.2, where I analyse 'language images' in Charles Dickens's *Bleak House*. Both techniques invite complex literary responses, but the general point to emphasise is that these are shaped by the discursive contexts, and conflicts of culture, in which the novels participate.

For Selden Whitcomb the development of the novel in history coincided with periods of conflict: 'the novel has flourished most in periods of complex social life, when antagonistic currents of thought were meeting, giving rise to social, ethical and aesthetic problems' (p. 160). To that extent Whitcomb's view of the novel is close to that which has been formulated by an important twentieth-century Russian theorist and historian of the novel, M. M. Bakhtin. Bakhtin's view of the history of the novel will be discussed in more detail in section 5.6. Broadly, he conceived the novel as a dynamic form in continuous and active dialogue with the forms of language and discourse which struggled against one another at particular moments of social and cultural history.[15] The main difference between Whitcomb and Bakhtin, and other present-day critics who have moved broadly in line with the new literary-historicism, is this: for Whitcomb the novel was a reflection of social change and conflict, whereas for critics in the present the discursive intertexts of the novel and prose narrative are seen as active participants in shaping and negotiating these cultural conflicts – sources of power in their own right.

Notes

1. *Microsoft Windows: Version 3.1 User's Guide* (Microsoft Corporation, 1990–2), p. xix.
2. *Observer*, 20 September 1998.
3. Samuel Johnson, *Rambler* 188, in Mona Wilson (ed.), *Johnson: Prose and Poetry* (London: Rupert Hart-Davis, 1950), p. 266.
4. For a recent representative statement of what a new-literary approach amounts to, see Thomas O. Beebee, *Epistolary Fiction in Europe, 1500–1850* (Cambridge: Cambridge University Press, 1999), Chapter 1. For more detailed guidance to

the New Historicism and cultural materialism, see the select bibliography.

5. Selden L. Whitcomb, *The Study of a Novel* (London: D. C. Heath, 1906), p. 195. All future references to this text will be to this edition and given in parentheses in the main text.

6. For Raymond Williams's account of the meanings of 'culture', to which my discussion is indebted, see *Keywords: A Vocabulary of Culture and Society*, 2nd edition (London: Fontana, 1983).

7. The work of Wayne C. Booth, which will be described in more detail in Chapter 2.

8. See Stephen Heath, 'Intertextuality', in Michael Payne (ed.), *A Dictionary of Cultural and Critical Theory* (Oxford: Blackwell, 1996), p. 258.

9. An excellent starting point is Roger Webster's *Studying Literary Theory: An Introduction* (London: Arnold, 1990). For more detailed guidance, see the select bibliography.

10. For an accessible and lucid introduction see Terence Hawkes's *Structuralism and Semiotics*, New Accents (London: Methuen, 1977).

11. For a more detailed introductory account see Diane MacDonell, *Theories of Discourse* (Oxford: Blackwell, 1986).

12. Dipesh Chakrabarty, 'Postcoloniality and the Artifice of History: Who Speaks for Indian Pasts?', *Representations* 37 (winter 1992), 1–26, reprinted in H. Aram Veeser (ed.), *The New Historicism Reader* (London: Routledge, 1994), p. 341.

13. This was in part due to the authority of traditions of spiritual autobiography deriving in the main from the seventeenth century, in which powerful conversion experiences were recorded. Hagiographical traditions of biography recording the good works of an individual were also influential. For the nineteenth-century context see Richard D. Altick, *The English Common Reader: A Social History of the Mass-Reading Public* (Chicago and London: University of Chicago Press, 1957), pp. 122–3.

14. See Kate Flint, 'The Woman Reader and the Opiate of Fiction', in Jeremy Hawthorn (ed.), *The Nineteenth-Century British Novel*, Stratford-upon-Avon Studies (London: Arnold, 1985).

15. For a lucid and accessible introduction to Bakhtin's thought and his approach to the novel, see Michael Holquist's *Dialogism: Bakhtin and His World*, New Accents (London: Routledge, 1990).

2

The elements of narrative analysis and the origins of the novel: reading Jane Austen's Emma and Samuel Richardson's Pamela

2.1 The novel and formalist criticism

Jane Austen's *Emma* announced itself to readers in the following terms when it was published in 1816: EMMA: / A NOVEL / IN THREE VOLUMES / BY THE AUTHOR OF 'PRIDE AND PREJUDICE'.[1] This suggests a number of 'givens': that 'the novel' was an identifiable cultural institution, recognised by 'novel' readers; that certain authors were 'novelists' to whom readers would return because of prior performances (Jane Austen is not named, instead there is a reference to the earlier *Pride and Prejudice*); that readers would find a continuous narrative in the three separate volumes comprising the work. Two years before in a postscript to his novel *Waverley* (1814, published anonymously), Sir Walter Scott was able to write confidently of a 'contract' between reader and novelist.[2] If all of this points to the existence of a stable and knowing relationship between novelists and readers in the first decades of the nineteenth century, why is it that Percy Lubbock, over one hundred years later in 1921, should complain in an influential book entitled *The Craft of Fiction* of 'the want of a received nomenclature', or vocabulary, for the purpose of 'criticising the craft of fiction'?[3]

Lubbock's sense of a lack can be explained by the fact that he was 'inventing' a formalist novel criticism. Novel reading might be founded on an implicit contract, but criticism had to be explicit and precise. Lubbock's own preference for a critical vocabulary, centred on the question of narrative point of view, was derived rather selectively from his mentor Henry James, a late nineteenth-century novelist and critic whose legacy will be examined in sections 4.5–7. Lubbock argued that the novel, in order to be considered as good art, ought to be unified around a consistent narrative point of view (a concept which will be explored in section 2.5 below).

17

In claiming that there was no received vocabulary, there is a sense in which Lubbock was overlooking the intellectual past he could have built upon.[4] For instance, when John Colin Dunlop published his monumental *History of Prose Fiction* in 1814 (the same year as *Waverley*), he was attentive to what he called 'disposition', or narrative method, and, accordingly, to the fact that any explicatory summary would edit out the 'style and sentiments', or formal details, that made the way in which a 'subject' was treated in narrative distinctive.[5]

Dunlop approached his subject historically; he was interested in the 'genesis and genealogy of fiction'.[6] Lubbock's approach consciously swerved away from the problems of historical and cultural difference, and his invention of ahistorical, formalist criticism inaugurated a particular tradition of critical reading.[7] This has developed into an important approach to reading the novel. In the first part of this chapter, I shall look at the way in which this tradition can help readers to appreciate the narrative distinc-tiveness of Austen's *Emma*, a text that knew itself to be a novel. In addition to Lubbock I shall consider the work of Wayne C. Booth, Seymour Chatman and Shlomith Rimmon-Kenan.[8]

At the same time it is worth highlighting a sceptical note that Lubbock strikes when he observes that 'the literary critic, with nothing to point to but the mere volume in his hand, must recognize that his wish to be precise, to be definite, to be clear and exact in his statements, is hopelessly vain.'[9] In one sense, Lubbock conceived this as a state of affairs that his own approach would begin to rectify. However, as I will argue, something confirming the vanity of longed-for critical precision is manifest in the way that vocabulary is not at all settled between formalist critics themselves.

Lubbock's sceptical point raises an even more searching question: what kind of an object are we studying when we read a novel? According to Lubbock's way of reading, our task is to analyse singular works of narrative art. But it may be that we need to think about that seemingly autonomous text intertextually: that is to say, as a text which has absorbed and trans-formed other texts and discourses (see section 1.7). This will involve us in having to think differently about the construction of that category, 'the novel', which seems so settled from our hitherto limited exploration of Austen and Scott. The second half of this chapter will explore these questions in relation to Samuel Richardson's *Pamela* (1740) and other works which figure in the debate about the rise of the novel. This will involve a shift from one style of critical discussion to another: the chapter will begin with close reading, but will use this as a basis for a move to, first, more historical and then theoretical styles of discussion. The end of the chapter will return to *Emma* again to reconsider Austen's text in the new light shed by these styles of discussion.

2.2   Reading the form of narrative fiction: Jane Austen's *Emma*

In *The Craft of Fiction* Lubbock distinguished between stories which 'tell' their readers what to think, and stories which 'show' their readers actions or thoughts which invite the reader to make judgements on the basis of more active processes of sense-making and interpretation. He held the latter to be more artistically coherent and satisfying.

First, 'telling': in the opening paragraphs of *Emma*, the relationship between Emma and her governess Miss Taylor is described in the following way: 'the shadow of authority being now long passed away, they had been living together as friend and friend very mutually attached, and Emma doing just what she liked; highly esteeming Miss Taylor's judgement, but directed chiefly by her own' (p. 37). Here, the reader is told what to think about their relationship and Emma's tendency to do as she likes.

What if Jane Austen were to have written this in a different way? The effect of 'showing' can be assessed through experimental rewriting:

> Emma looked at her friend and could recall a distant time when it had been Miss Taylor's duty to exercise authority; Emma esteemed Miss Taylor's judgement as the very source of her own ability to discriminate confidently and act decisively in ways which, strangely, were often contrary to her former governess's.

This is angled more from Emma's perspective: although it is still written in the grammatical third person, Emma is realised as a dramatised centre of consciousness – the reader is in touch with her thoughts – confirmed by the way in which we seem to 'hear' something of the surprise in her voice ('strangely') from which we infer a lack of self-awareness. The reader comes to the same conclusion about the Emma–Miss Taylor relationship, and about Emma's forthright and excessive self-confidence which leads her to do what she wants: but the judgement is based on something that the reader has been 'shown' rather than told.

Lubbock's distinction between 'showing' and 'telling' is a useful introduction to some of the major issues that have preoccupied formalist critics of the novel. At the same time, later critics have found it wanting. In 1961 Wayne C. Booth pointed out in *The Rhetoric of Fiction* that it was unwise to rate 'showing' above 'telling' because the distinction was 'arbitary', in the sense that narrative is always told from some source or other. Rejecting Lubbock's concern with narrative unity and consistent 'method', Booth was more interested in the 'many voices' that an author uses to tell a tale effectively.[10] But a grasp of the way in which these 'many voices' are ordered requires a more detailed and elaborate account of narrative than Lubbock offered.

In his book *Story and Discourse* (1978), Seymour Chatman devised a model for anatomising the formal elements and relations of narrative; it aimed to provide the critical reader with a framework for identifying the 'many voices' and levels of meaning production at work in a narrative:

> real author...> (implied author -> narrator -> narratee -> implied reader) ...> real reader[11]

The elements within the parentheses ( ) are the most important aspects of this model. Thus, the activities of the real author and the real reader are constrained by a set of formal relations which are internal to the narrative. These internal relations will guide our reading of *Emma*, helping the real reader to identify, for example, when the implied reader is invited by the narrator to read some aspect of the story – received opinion, character speech, thoughts or actions – ironically. The model will also help to highlight some of the major terminological and conceptual differences between critics who have developed the formal approach. For although Chatman concluded his work by defending the precision, integrity and inclusiveness of his model, in practice critics have continued to argue about his terminology and categories, which would seem to confirm Lubbock's lurking scepticism about the quest for precision in vocabulary.[12]

Before embarking on a close analysis of the opening paragraphs of *Emma* – which will in turn lead us to ways of thinking about events, characterisation and point of view – we need to say an introductory word about the concept of the implied reader. An addressee is a rhetorical feature of all written discourse. In mentioning the 'critical reader' in the paragraph preceding Chatman's model, the discourse of this book inscribes the sort of reader who is implied by the development of its argument and choice of examples: someone who wants, or needs, to become skilled as a critical reader of the novel and prose narrative. The concept of the implied reader draws attention to the fact that any writing, whether imaginative or critical, is addressed to a reader who is assumed to have, temporarily at least, an investment in the means and ends of that writing. According to Wayne C. Booth in his classic account of the rhetorical means and persuasive ends of fictional narrative, and in which he devoted a substantial portion to the technical feats of *Emma*, control of the reader is the goal.[13]

2.3   Implied reader, real reader: narrator, implied author

The pact that is established between a narrative discourse and the reader implied in that discourse is central to effective fictional prose narrative. As you will see from Chatman's diagram, this pact has to be located in relation to the narrator, who imparts to the reader the 'contents' of the story: the events, the locations in which they unfold, and the characters affected. We can look now at the opening of *Emma* in full:

> Emma Woodhouse, handsome, clever, and rich, with a comfortable home and happy disposition, seemed to unite some of the best blessings of existence; and had lived nearly twenty-one years in the world with very little to distress or vex her.
>
> She was the youngest of two daughters of a most affectionate, indulgent father, and had, in consequence of her sister's marriage, been mistress of his house from a very early period. Her mother had died too long ago for her to have more than an indistinct remembrance of her caresses, and her place had been supplied by an excellent woman as governess, who had fallen little short of a mother in affection.
>
> Sixteen years had Miss Taylor been in Mr Woodhouse's family, less as a governess than a friend, very fond of both daughters, but particularly of Emma. Between *them* it was more the intimacy of sisters. Even before Miss Taylor had ceased to hold the nominal office of governess, the mildness of her temper had hardly allowed her to impose any restraint; and the shadow of authority being long now passed away, they had been living as friend and friend very mutually attached, and Emma doing just what she liked; highly esteeming Miss Taylor's judgement, but directed chiefly by her own.
>
> The real evils, indeed, of Emma's situation were the power of having rather too much her own way, and a disposition to think too well of herself; these were the disadvantages which threatened alloy to her many enjoyments. The danger, however, was so unperceived, that they did not by any means rank as misfortunes with her.
>
> Sorrow came – a gentle sorrow – but not at all in the shape of any disagreeable consciousness. – Miss Taylor married. It was Miss Taylor's loss which first

> brought grief. It was on the wedding day of this beloved friend that Emma first sat in mournful thought of any continuance. The wedding over and the bride-people gone, her father and herself were left to dine together, with no prospect of a third to cheer the long evening. (p. 37)

The reader implied here by the third-person narrator's opening description of Emma Woodhouse values good looks, cleverness, wealth and domestic comfort. The real reader – you, situated at a different point in history possessed of, in all probability, somewhat different social horizons to the implied reader of 1816 – may value these less than other things. But to read the novel appropriately, the real reader enters into the position of the implied reader. Actually, the implied reader is invited to look beyond these values by appreciating, at relevant points, a tone of playfulness and irony which relativises this limited scale of values in relation to wider, more generous possibilities. This tone is conveyed by the functions of the narrator in the use of words such as 'seemed'. The fact that Emma 'seemed to unite some of the best blessings of existence' implies a distance between appearance and reality. In discussing the role of the narrator as the authoritative and ironising source of the story, we shall also need to think about the role that is sometimes played by an 'implied author'.

The first point to make about the implied author is that it is a function which needs to be distinguished from the real author, Jane Austen. Wayne C. Booth has gone so far as to argue that the implied author is the real author's 'second self', though the idea of an authoritative 'shadow' function to the narrator is of more practical use in analysis.[14] An implied author as 'shadow' is most evident in narratives where we follow the guidance of a dramatised, unreliable narrator; that is to say a first-person narrator of limited understanding who has to some degree participated in the story being told. Thus in Emily Brontë's *Wuthering Heights* (1847), it is clear that Mr Lockwood's narration of the situation he walks into at the Heights is not reliable: his evaluation of Heathcliff as a 'capital fellow!' sits uneasily with Heathcliff's 'suspicious' and 'jealous' disposition.[15] It is as though there is, as the source of the latter adjectives, a 'shadow' function which, to correct Lockwood's effusive and unknowing dramatised first-person narration, 'establishes norms for the work', in Seymour Chatman's phrase.[16]

Shlomith Rimmon-Kenan is sceptical about the need to find an implied author in all narratives. Rimmon-Kenan prefers to distinguish between 'forms and degrees of perceptibility of the narrator in the text'.[17] In *Emma* the third-person narrator is highly perceptible, and explicitly involved in the process of establishing 'norms', so here the function of narrator and implied author have merged. In *Emma* the narrator moves between statements which invite inference, and statements which didactically state the conclusion which the implied reader has been invited to draw. As we have already seen, at the end of the third paragraph the narrator observes that Emma esteems Miss Taylor's judgement whilst she follows her own. Just in case the reader has missed the point the narrator then states the 'real evils' of Emma's situation: that the young Emma has had too much her own way, and that restraining authority has been absent from her upbringing. The norm that is established in these opening paragraphs is that individual judgement needs to be checked by a more sagacious authority. We might add that the third-person narrative voice is precisely the authority that Emma has been deprived of through the negligible presence of a self-absorbed father and a friend rather than a governess.

In addition to establishing 'norms', the narrator of *Emma* also performs the function which in some narratives may be performed by the implied author: that is, 'stacking the cards', to borrow again from Chatman. By this, Chatman means the function of shaping and clarifying the implied reader's dramatic expectations in the deployment of strategic words such as 'un-perceived'. The 'danger ... at present ... unperceived' points to a reversal not glimpsed by Emma, but which is now anticipated by the implied reader. The narrator in *Emma* establishes norms and stimulates an appetite for narra-tive and the events that it organises. According to this model, the implied reader is at least as enthralled by the pleasures of narrative anticipation as by morals and values.

2.4 Events: story and discourse

This brings us to a consideration of events. Without events, there could be no story for the reader to anticipate and follow. Rimmon-Kenan defines an event as, quite simply, something that happens and that can be summed up by a verb or the name of an occurrence.[18] The whole enterprise of ordering and making sense of events is made pleasurable and challenging by the fact that, contrary to superficial appearances, events in a narrative discourse are seldom presented to us in strict chronological order. An example from the first paragraph of *Emma* would be that in the narrator's recounting of events relevant to Emma's early life, we find out about Emma's sister's marriage before we are told of the death of the sisters' mother, though the latter is, chronologically, the prior event. Thus our conventional sense of time and sequence leads us to wish to reorder events. In making sense of events, the implied reader keeps moving between, to borrow terms from Chatman, the 'what' of the 'story' (the events comprising the story sequentially arranged) and the 'how' of the 'discourse' (their manner of being narrated).

The passage above ends with the event which inaugurates the main action, the marriage of Miss Taylor to Mr Weston. This is represented sparingly as an event that has just passed, so, simultaneously, we also need to think in a 'how' mode. Percy Lubbock would describe its manner of being registered as a 'summary' rather than a 'scene'; had it been a 'scene' we might have had a full account of the wedding, its social interactions represented in the dialogue or direct speech which is such a strong component of later significant 'scenes' in the novel, such as the ball at the Crown, Highbury, in Chapter 38.[19] This is characteristic of the flexible resources of prose narra-tive in its relations to the representation of events; the chronological duration of an event is seldom equivalent to the volume of narrative discourse allo-cated to it; after all, going back to the passage, twenty-one years of Emma's life pass in the space of five-and-a-bit shortish paragraphs.

But there is more to be said about this summary of Miss Taylor's marriage: it represents Emma's relationship to the event. Because Emma has lost by Miss Taylor's union, it is a source of mild grieving. We could plausibly argue that this summary performs an aesthetic function, blending the 'what' and the 'how' into a unity: its brevity conveys a mood which seeks to block out an event which has brought 'gentle sorrow'. The emptiness and loss which the union between others has brought to Emma are woven together to produce the basis for further development of the story. But the mean-ingfulness of that story depends on adopting a particular point of view. Point of view is a very important concept in the reading of narrative, made central, as we have seen, by the criticism of Percy Lubbock. When Lubbock laid down criteria for artistically successful fiction, he conceived it in terms of the unity and consistency of perceptual focus: in other words, which character sees what, and how that governs the reader's relationship to the story. This understanding of point of view will be an important one in analysing *Emma*, and I'll explore it in more depth in the next section, which will move beyond the passage we have been analysing to this point.

2.5   Character and point of view in *Emma*

Marriages — which legitimate sexual unions and order the transmission of property — convey certain connotations in drama and narrative; they are rooted in the ancient emplotments of romance and comedy. So a wedding that deprives Emma of companionship so early in a narrative creates an expectation of restitution, or the completion of Emma by means of another union. How is the implied reader's investment in this romantic and comic outcome, blended with the theme of individual judgement and authority, sustained by characterisation and point of view? It is largely the result of the construction of Emma's character and point of view.

E. M. Forster's influential *Aspects of the Novel* (1927) was in some sense a rejoinder to Lubbock's theory of fictional art. Forster — a novelist himself — makes a useful distinction between 'flat' and 'round' characters. Mr Woodhouse would be a 'flat' character, statically fixated on his hypochondria and domestic comfort; on the other hand, Emma would be a 'round' character, manifesting complexity and the potential for development. This is a useful distinction up to a point, so long as it does not encourage us to think that the property of 'roundness' inheres in particular characters who come to dominate a story by sheer force of 'personality'. Rather, 'roundness', or the effect of personality and complex selfhood, is something that is generated by the structural relations between various components of a narrative discourse, and the implied reader's investment in that process of structuration. How does this work?

In one sense, Emma is as predictably flat as Mr Woodhouse in that she comes to be associated with a finite number of traits: a drive to make matches and a sense of her own infallible powers of judgement. This is evident from the primary material for structuring character, the dramatised, mimetic discourse comprising Emma's direct speech: '"Everybody said that Mr Weston would never marry again ... Some people even talked of a promise to his wife on her death-bed, and others of the son and uncle not letting him go. All manner of solemn nonsense was talked on the subject, but I believed none of it"' (p. 43). Although Emma asserts her correctness in emphatic terms, the implied reader, reading Emma ironically from the perspective established by the narrator, may surmise that the possibility of a death-bed promise and intra-family conflict is more than 'solemn nonsense'. Emma is further 'rounded' by the rhetorical position adopted by Mr Knightley's direct speech in this exchange: Knightley suggests that Emma's 'success' in matchmaking is due to lucky guessing rather than 'endeavour'. Mr Knightley's speech does two things: first, it provides us with an alternative to Emma's perspective; and, second, it creates an expectation of development, that Emma will move beyond her own perspective. Knightley, who shares the narrator's attitude to authority, expresses the view that Emma will be completed when she comes to know the 'worthy employment for a young lady's mind' (p. 43). This sense of proper feminine worth is a recurrent topic of Mr Knightley's speech about Emma, as we see in Chapter 5, where he laments the fact that she consistently fails to follow through an improving programme of reading (pp. 65–6). We will return to the topic of literacy and appropriate feminine behaviour from a different critical perspective towards the end of this chapter.

The expectations of rounding and completion that are generated around the character of Emma are complemented by the fact that readers are presented with more varied means than direct speech and others' views of her for building a profile of Emma's traits and characteristics. In addition, the reader has a special relationship to Emma because of privileged access to Emma's 'inner life'. These are established for the reader through verbal formulations which register, first, Emma's point of view, and, second, Emma's private thoughts. This use of point of view and inner thought is quite fundamental to the workings of Jane Austen's narrative. In Wayne Booth's study of *Emma* in *The Rhetoric of Fiction*, Booth described these workings as Jane Austen's 'control of distance'. By this he meant that Jane Austen's narrator controls the reader's relationship to Emma's point of view on the events of the story very carefully, balancing closeness to and involvement in Emma's discourse – her direct speech, inner thoughts and so on – with a more distant and objectified assessment of the accuracy and validity of Emma's judgements.[20]

For illustration, it is helpful to look closely at the episode in which Emma encourages the *ingénue* Harriet Smith to reject the attentions of Mr Robert Martin, a tenant farmer, while simultaneously hatching her plot to match Harriet and Mr Elton, the young unmarried clergyman. Emma's point of view is established by the narrator in the sentence 'Emma watched her [Harriet] through the fluctuations of this speech, and saw no alarming symptoms of love' (p. 60). But in becoming aware that we are restricted to Emma's point of view, the implied reader is invited to 'peer beyond' the limitations of Emma's viewpoint. This is where more recent critics such as Genette and Rimmon-Kenan have argued that Booth's own work does not go far enough, and that a more nuanced concept than point of view is required, advocating in its place the concept of focalisation.[21] Focalisation distinguishes between who sees (Emma), and who speaks (the narrator). Readers can only 'peer beyond' using the words provided by the narrator (and/or implied author), and here the word 'fluctuations' helps us to do this: it suggests an uncertainty in Harriet's speech, the true significance of which Emma fails to appreciate, because its source is Harriet's dilemma in pleasing her new, powerful mentor at the expense of rejecting Martin's interest in her. The 'blindspots' in acts of focalising centred on Emma are further manifest when we are given access to Emma's 'inner thoughts'. As Mr Elton praises Emma's portrait of Harriet, Emma's inner voice thinks: 'Yes, good man! ... but what has all that to do with taking likenesses? You know nothing of drawing. Don't pretend to be in raptures about mine. Save your raptures for Harriet's face' (p. 71). Emma's 'inner thoughts' intimate just enough of what is going on 'outside' of them for the reader to conclude that Mr Elton is attracted to Emma rather than Harriet. In the gap that emerges between what Emma sees, thinks and predicts at the level of discourse, and what can be glimpsed in the wider context of the unfolding story, the implied reader follows a narrative based on a number of dramatic ironies, reversals of romance expectations, and the potential for moral transformation.

What are these ironies and reversals? In trying to make a match between Harriet and Elton, Emma fails to see that Elton wants Emma herself as a wife rather than Harriet. Second, in thinking that Frank Churchill is vying for her affections, and fearing that Mr Knightley is falling in love with Jane Fairfax, Emma fails to note that Frank and Jane are surreptitiously attached to each other (by contrast, Knightley sees this). Finally, in fearing that Mr Knightley is falling in love with Harriet, Emma comes to realise that she herself loves Mr Knightley. This reversal is brought home to her as a result of the picnic at Box Hill (Chapter 43), which represents the crisis and completion of Emma's moral transformation. Emma, playing to her audience by making a joke at the expense of the garrulous spinster Miss Bates, is castigated by Knightley, the authoritative keeper of the conscience of the community. Knightley reminds Emma that her joke was hurtful because Miss Bates 'is poor; she has sunk from the comforts she was born to ... Her situation should secure your compassion' (p. 368). This, in terms of values, is the biggest reversal of all in a narrative which began with a seeming celebration of youth, good looks, cleverness and wealth. The narrator's focus on Emma's inner thoughts and feelings here registers the scale of the moral earthquake: 'she was vexed beyond what could have been expressed – almost beyond what she could conceal. Never had she felt so agitated, mortified, grieved, at any circumstance in her life' (p. 369).

If the implied reader has negotiated the balance between 'closeness' to and 'distance' from Emma's evaluations in line with the various cues that are offered by the narrator and implied author, then the closure, or completion, of the story ought to be satisfying. The frustrated expectation of romance is satisfied by Emma's marriage to Knightley, whilst the marriage to Knightley is permissible because of Emma's own completion, and her having acquired a rounded sense of her powers and responsibilities in the community. The formal 'pleasure' derived from reading *Emma* resides in the reader having been inside Emma's limited perspective, whilst also being able to see around it. I said at the beginning of this formal reading of *Emma* that the opening paragraphs of the novel raise the issue of individual judgement through Emma's relationship to her governess, and that the direct speech and inner thoughts which construct Emma also present her as a figure who is proud of her independence of thought and judgement. In the light of this, the open-ing up of Emma's private judgement to the authoritative view vested in the narrator and Knightley could be seen as a triumphant aesthetic integration of form (the control of distance through focalisation) and content (a story about the dangers of unfettered individual judgement and its correction). This is, as I have suggested, pleasurable: but there is also an embedded moral, educational dimension to the implied reader's investment.

2.6   Limitations of the formal approach: social spaces and voices in narrative, from free indirect speech to social contexts

This approach to *Emma* is important because it helps us to read the formal properties of narrative in elaborate detail. We become skilled close readers if we follow this kind of approach, and that enables us to appreciate the complex aesthetic invitations that forms of narrative we call 'literary' offer.

But a reading of *Emma* may need to account for more than this. While the implied reader of this kind of narrative responds to formal elements and relations, we would have to acknowledge that even forms have histories which are, at some level, homologous to the power relations at work in society. It is important to remember that novels are strongly marked by the distinguishing discourses of class and gender that operate and discriminate in the social world. In the case of *Emma*, it is Mr Knightley – a high-born, male landowner – who, by integrating and reforming the relations between individual judgement, authority and romantic love, is pivotal to the implied reader's aesthetic satisfaction. And it is Emma, a high-status woman of the gentry class, who is the object of that reform. In moving beyond the formal approach we need to account for the impact that social categories have on our interpretation of the forms which construct the 'what' and 'how' of narrative.

For example, when Seymour Chatman discusses things and objects, or 'what' a narrative is about, in addition to events and characters he includes settings (basically, where the story takes place). But setting is not just some inert 'background': Chatman wants us to be aware that setting is always narrated, which is why he coins the concepts of 'story space' and 'the focus of spatial attention'.[22] The latter concept is especially helpful for thinking about the mediation of social values. In *Emma*, the story space is predominantly the village of Highbury, and the focus of spatial attention is on three properties and their owners, all of whom are from the gentry class: Hartfield (the Woodhouses), Randalls (the Westons) and Donwell Abbey (Knightley). As Chatman remarks, story space is always mediated by focalisation (so the question of 'what' is practically inseparable from questions of 'how'), and in *Emma* this provides a helpful way of highlighting the social discriminations which structure Emma's focus of spatial attention. This is where we need to make reference to the Coles, a socially ambitious family relatively new to Highbury: they come from a trading background and have accumulated wealth which makes them second only to the Woodhouses. Yet, they and their property are only conditionally admitted into Emma's focus of spatial attention; 'the Coles were very respectable in their way, but they ought to be taught that it was not for them to arrange the terms on which the superior families would visit them' (pp. 217–18).

We should note, however, that the narrative voice puts distance between itself and Emma's class-conscious haughtiness. It does this by subtly ironising Emma's condescending social attitude to the Coles by using a technique, when reflecting on Emma's subsequent visit to the family, that has become known as free indirect speech: 'she must have delighted the Coles – worthy people, who deserved to be made happy! – and left a name behind her that would not soon die away' (p. 239). While Emma is the focaliser it is the narrator who speaks, so the character is speaking indirectly rather than directly – except, it appears, in the emphatic remark after the slashes ('worthy people …'), which is in a markedly different register from the narrator's and is clearly Emma's direct and unappealing, self-regarding speech. As Rimmon-Kenan remarks, free indirect speech juxtaposes the language of the narrator and character and 'can assist the reader in recon-structing … attitudes towards … character'.[23]

Rimmon-Kenan interprets such blending and clashing of voices in the context of the formal relationship between narrator, character and implied reader, and whilst this is a valid starting point, it needs to be located in a particular context: that is, discourses about the countryside and social relations in southern England in the first decades of the nineteenth century, the extra-textual setting for Austen's work, and where Austen resided. In *The Country and the City* (1973), Raymond Williams argues that the formal sophistication of Austen's narratives subtly addresses the anxieties about a changing social structure in the countryside, brought about by the influx of new money derived from trading families (the Coles in *Emma*), and felt keenly among members of Jane Austen's traditional gentry class (of whom Emma herself is a representative).[24]

Viewed from this perspective, we may argue that the narrator is imagina-tively rehearsing and resolving inter-class tensions between new, wealthy tradespeople and the gentry through subtly ironic narrative devices: in the same way as Emma has to learn a more sympathetic attitude to poor spinsters like Miss Bates, the implied reader surmises that Emma ought to adopt more gracious and generous manners towards the Coles (precisely because Emma is their social superior; the narrator does not doubt that). This is a further indication that the establishment of norms in a novel is seldom a matter of simple assertion, but instead a complex rhetorical activity. Moreover, the norms or values that the implied reader is asked to negotiate through reading the narrator's account of the relations between heroine, characters and their settings are socially specific.

Social specificity is highlighted in Williams's work on the countryside context. This adopts a comparative focus which looks beyond Austen's novels about manners, to writers who represented the same countryside space and class tensions more explicitly, such as her near contemporary William Cobbett, the radical journalist and social observer. Cobbett com-posed non-fictional essays (*Rural Rides*, 1822–6, published as a work 1830) about worsening social conditions in the English countryside, travel narratives which construct a radically different focus of spatial attention – farms and villages in decline – and which seeks to persuade its reader of a need to reverse the new monetary, fiscal and capitalist system which permeates rural society.[25] Williams claims that Cobbett's social observations crafted conventions which would come to be used by novelists who sought to write about the interaction between different social classes after 1830 (we will analyse one such novelist, Charles Dickens, in Chapter 4).[26] Williams's cultural criticism asks us to consider the view that novels are forms of imaginative narrative which, though enormously important in themselves, exist in the presence and on the borders of competing and contrasting narratives.

This is our bridge to a discussion of the novel as an emergent cultural form embedded in history and diverse sources of prose narrative and social and cultural debate, for the novel is an institution which has been formed out of a complex cultural history. It can be argued that the novel has been the central developing institution in the long and contested revolution in language, literacy and reading that characterises the period since 1780; a point evidenced in the interest expressed in the form by the two major English schools of social and cultural criticism in the twentieth century, F. R. Leavis's Scrutiny movement, and Raymond Williams's cultural materialism.[27] In order to take an early snapshot of this history in the making I will turn to a text that is commonly regarded as being one of the first major novels in English, *Pamela* by Samuel Richardson, which was published over seventy years before *Emma* in 1740.

2.7   What happens in Richardson's *Pamela*?

Turning to *Pamela*, and comparing it with *Emma*, we will find a different reading experience. Pamela Andrews marries her master, the gentleman Mr B.; she is from a lower social class than Emma Woodhouse: she is a servant girl. Pamela's low status makes her path to marriage much more dangerous and disturbing. Following the death of Pamela's mistress, the sexually predatory intentions of the mistress's son towards her are soon apparent. After a number of attempted assaults, Mr B. gives way to Pamela's protestations in defence of her virtue; she is seemingly allowed to return to her parents. Instead, the coach in which she travels is diverted to her master's Lincolnshire estate, where she is held as a virtual prisoner by the grotesque Mrs Jewkes. In the journal which she begins in the new environment,

Pamela records her attempt to escape with the aid of Mr Williams, her master's clergyman, though this escape is foiled. Mr B. plots a sham marriage to entrap Pamela, though Pamela sees through this trick. Mr B. comes to respect Pamela's virtue and the pair marry legitimately. In the last phase of Richardson's 1740 version the local gentry, embodied in Lady Davers (Mr B.'s sister), accept the pair after expressing extreme hostility.

These are the 'events' of the narrative, so to speak. While I'll point to the way in which the critical vocabulary of formalism can highlight narrative similarities between *Pamela* and *Emma*, I'll also endeavour to explain the relationship between Richardson's narrative framework and debates about telling the truth in narrative, class, gender and literacy within an expanding print culture. This is not a matter of dispensing with formal analysis: rather, it is a case of embedding key aspects of it in a social and cultural context.

2.8   First-person narration and the epistolary form: the dramatised narrator, rhetoric and the narratee

Richardson's *Pamela* is narrated differently from *Emma* in so far as Pamela is a dramatised, first-person narrator who tells her own story in letters (the epistolary form) and a journal. This is the opening of her narration:

> *My dear Father and Mother,*
> I have great trouble, and some comfort, to acquaint you with. The trouble is, that my good lady died of the illness I mentioned to you, and left us all much grieved for the loss of her; for she was a dear good lady, and kind to all us her servants. Much I feared, that as I was taken by her ladyship to wait upon her person, I should be quite destitute again, and forced to return to you and my poor mother, who have enough to do to maintain yourselves; and, as my lady's goodness had put me to write and cast accompts, and made me a little expert at my needle, and otherwise qualified above my degree, it was not every family that could have found a place that your poor Pamela was fit for: But God, whose graciousness to us we have so often experienced, put it into my good lady's heart, on her death-bed, just an hour before she expired, to recommend to my young master all her servants, one by one; and when it came to my turn to be recommended (for I was sobbing and crying at her pillow) she could only say, 'My dear son!' and so broke off a little; and then recovering, 'Remember my poor Pamela!' And those were her last words! O how my eyes overflow! Don't wonder to see the paper so blotted! (p. 43)[28]

It is important to recognise that the first paragraph of Pamela's first letter is, above all, the opening of an elaborate act of story-telling. Pamela's letter performs a similar function to the first paragraph of *Emma*: the chronology of Pamela's story (upbringing, employment, training) is embedded in Pamela's epistolary discourse. This discourse reveals the central character's servant status whilst disclosing something of her origins: allusions to destitution and hardship indicate that Pamela comes from a poor but devout family. References to the skills she has been required to refine by her kindly and enlightened, but now dead, employer – account-keeping ('cast accompts'), needlework and, above all, writing – indicate that she has been raised somewhat above her station, a factor which imperils Pamela's chances of future employment. This sense of reversal is supported by key oppo-sitions: 'trouble' and 'comfort' create a tension in the first sentence, rather in the way that ideas of independence and authority create a tension in *Emma*. This, taken with the death of Pamela's mistress as the event which initiates the narration, generates expectations which will themselves, readers discover as they progress, be subject to reversal: what appears a source of comfort (Pamela's employment by the new master of the house) becomes a source of trouble.

What is the effect of the first-person epistolary form on reading? The terms that I have used in the analysis above point to the difference; in the opening paragraph of *Pamela* matters relating to the story are revealed, disclosed, alluded to, indicated: their significance has to be inferred. They could be said to be, to call again upon Lubbock's distinction, 'shown' rather than 'told'. Following Henry James's late nineteenth-century interest in the novel as a form of writing which, through point of view, could show the subtle movements and shades of human consciousness, Lubbock thought he could see in Richardson's fiction the germ of his own preference for narrative that would 'show a mind in action ... [and] give a dramatic display of the commotion within a breast'.[29] A good example of this occurs at the end of the first paragraph of *Pamela*: Pamela's grief at the death of her mistress is 'shown' to us in the ink blotted by her tears, an image of intense sensibility which apparently closes the gap between Pamela's emotional mind, her body, her written words and the reader.

Except that the gap is not closed, at least not on the basis of the reader's being 'shown' this. As we have already established, all narration is telling to a greater or lesser degree. 'Showing' the effects of Pamela's tears would require someone to sob over the wet ink of every 'Letter I' of the work as it rolled off the press. Instead Pamela is telling, or, as the rhetorically aware Wayne C. Booth would insist, actively persuading, her reader of the depth of her grief. Or, to be more precise still, Pamela, the narrator, addresses and seeks to persuade her parents – '*My dear Father and Mother*, ... Don't wonder to see the paper so blotted!' The parents may be said to constitute the text's narratees, addressees who intercede between the narrator and implied reader. The narratee features in Chatman's model of the narrative transaction, yet we had no cause to draw on this category when analysing *Emma*. This is because explicit narratees are not obvious in every narrative text. The narratee is obvious in *Pamela* in the sense that someone identifiable – and sometimes unidentifiable – is always being narrated to. Narratees are im/ portant to the rhetorical project that the text is performing for its implied reader.

What sort of a reader is implied, and what is the rhetorical project? The title page of the 1801 edition of *Pamela* retained much of its 'machinery' from the first edition of 1740 and is highly explicit in framing what will follow, and its reader is initially inscribed rather than implied:

> Pamela; / or, / Virtue Rewarded. / In a / Series of Letters / From a Beautiful Young Damsel to Her Parents: / And Afterwards in Her Exalted Condition, / Between Her, And Persons of Figure and Quality, / Upon the / Most Important and Entertaining Subjects / In Genteel Life / ... Published in Order to Cultivate the Principles / Of Virtue and Religion in the Minds of the / Youth of Both Sexes. (p. 27)

The inscribed reader is drawn from 'the Youth of Both Sexes' who are to be educated in the principles of virtue and religion. These principles will be conveyed through Pamela's letters to her parents, which, additionally, will impart knowledge of 'Important' and 'Entertaining' kinds relating to 'Genteel' society. The '*Truth*' and '*Nature*' on which these letters are founded is guaranteed by the 'Editor' of the volume in a subsequent 'Preface', and it is also claimed that 'an *Editor* can judge with an impartiality which is rarely to be found in an *Author*' because 'his *own* passions ... have been uncom/ monly *moved* in perusing it' (p. 31). Here, the editor is a self-styled reader rather than a writer, who makes claims for the truthfulness of the letters that follow precisely because he has read, collated and had his own sensibility touched by them. The idea of the power and influence of writing is per/ vasive throughout this framework.

We should pause here for a moment to recall the way in which *Emma* presented itself to its first readers, for the contrast is quite striking. As we saw at the beginning of this chapter *Emma* announces itself simply as 'a novel'. Part of what that assumes and implies was what we spent a good deal of space analysing, making its implicit framework and machinery explicit through the formal analysis of its narrative. In *Pamela* the machinery and framing devices remain explicit, informing the implied reader how power' ful the reading experience will be. Of course, *Pamela* is still a fiction, and Richardson was not an editor but an author more or less making it up. But this 'fact' is outside the frame we are considering in the same way as Austen's actual authorship was always a mediated concern in our approach to *Emma*, even when we became concerned with questions of her class. This detour into the explicit framework of *Pamela* takes us back to the point about Pamela narrating to narratees: those who 'feel' the power of Pamela's letters and journals in the story. The following analysis of the narratee will help us to link *Pamela* to cultural contexts and debates about truth and represen' tation in the 1740s; this will in turn lead to a discussion (sections 2.11–14) of some of the questions that motivate inquiry into the origins of the novel.

2.9   The narratee and writing as an 'event' in *Pamela*

Pamela alludes to her writing skill in her first letter to her parents, and there' after she writes copiously. Although Richardson thought that in having his character 'write to the moment' he was employing a technique which would capture the transparent, immediate reality of Pamela's subjectivity, many present'day readers find it unconvincing. The fact that Pamela has seem' ingly to spend every available minute – that is to say when she is neither being assailed by the libertine Mr B. nor in a swoon – writing about these assaults and collapses strains at their tacit assumptions about 'realism' in narrative. But there have been many 'realisms' in the modern history of prose narrative, as we will see in the chapters to follow. Often, a sense of what is convincing or 'real' is conditioned by over'familiarity with the smooth workings of a narrative framework such as we find in a novel by Austen. What needs to be questioned here is not the veracity of Richardson's text, but a rather rigid adherence to certain ways of handling the categories of analysis that have been presented to us by the formal tradition. As well as looking at events comprising the story which Pamela's epistolary discourse records, we should also look at Pamela's acts of writing as events in themselves which act upon their narratees.

Pamela's writings are presented as the source of two major 'conversions' in *Pamela*: Mr B. casts off his libertine ways and comes to honour Pamela's virtue, and Lady Davers sets aside her aristocratic pride and comes to accept the low-born Pamela as a legitimate marriage partner for her brother. It is in this sense that we have to see Mr B. and Lady Davers as narratees, or figures who read Pamela's letters and journal. There are numerous narratees in *Pamela*. Some are intended: Pamela writes for her parents. Some narratees are not intended: it is soon clear that Pamela's letters home are being intercepted and read by Mr B. Some narratees are confronted with conflicting accounts of the same story: when Pamela finds herself in the house of one of Mr B.'s tenant farmers (Letter XXXII) en route to Lincolnshire, she attempts to persuade her hosts – an audience consisting of the farmer, his wife and a daughter – of the truth of her story only to discover that Mr B. has already sent a letter containing a conflicting account to them. In this drama played out before a number of narratees, Pamela's story of her determination to protect her virtue against her master's sexual despotism wins the sympathy of the farmer's young daughter, but not the farmer, who remains on the side of patriarchy and landed authority. A drama of identification rooted in class, gender and generation, but weighted unquestionably towards sympathy for Pamela, is as explicit here as the narrative framework is about the conclusion that the implied reader should reach.

When landed authority itself becomes an unintended narratee, in the person of Mr B., he is moved to sympathy by Pamela's story: Mr B. tells Pamela that his overhearing her 'pretty chit-chat to Mrs Jewkes the last Sunday night' – presented to the reader as Pamela in a mode of confessional recollection (p. 238) – 'half disarmed my resolution [to rape her], before I approached your bed' (p. 251). It is expected then that when Mr B. does eventually get to become an authorised reader – Pamela grants him permission to read the letters and journals that she has sewn into her underclothing for secrecy and protection – he is converted by the story he reads, as he relates to Lady Davers: 'she may ... make as great a convert of you from pride, as she has of me from libertinism' (p. 443). Having been converted by another of Pamela's self-justifying narrations, Lady Davers also requests to read Pamela's letters and journals.

Of course, Pamela reports all of these events and testimonies of affect subsequently in either letters or her journal, the very papers that Lady Davers desires to read. At key points in the story, we are reminded of the massive inventory of writings, and the events and feelings they relate, that Pamela has accumulated (p. 316). Indeed, the whole narrative scheme requires that we are attentive to the frequency, or number of occasions, upon which the same events are renarrated and re-read by characters. This awareness of frequency is best conceived as a starting point for casting a much more productive light on the effects that Pamela's writings have on characters such as Mr B. and Lady Davers: in fact, rather than simply 'reporting' events, we could say that Pamela's letters and journal entries are events which help to determine the outcome of the story that at one level they are only supposed to record. Once this way of looking at a formal detail of narration – writing as an event which dramatises affect and influence – is acknow- ledged we can begin to reintegrate *Pamela* into debates about the role of literacy in reconstructing social and cultural authority in the mid eighteenth century.

2.10 *Pamela*, print culture and debates about genre: the familiar letter, criticism and 'the novel'

Richardson's text became a much-debated publishing phenomenon in the 1740s, and the interpretation of the character of Pamela, and the rhetorical function of her letters, were at the heart of a multi-faceted cultural debate about how the truth should be told in prose narrative. Richardson's purpose in representing the affective powers of Pamela's writing was didactic. But Richardson's didactic intentions were defined by an established but growing and internally differentiated 'print culture': that is to say, a growing trade in books and other printed matter. In addition to manufacturing editions of poetical works and dramatic texts, such as Shakespeare's, reinvented as classics which aimed to satisfy 'high' tastes, this print culture also produced reading material which aimed to satisfy the needs of new readers from an increasingly ambitious 'middling' social rank. These readers sought instruction and guidance in taste, civilised modes of behaviour and conduct. A self-educated man, Richardson was an exemplary contributor to this educative, enlightening domain of print culture in being a printer as well as an author. As Richardson himself acknowledged, *Pamela* was a consider- ably expanded version of two letters exchanged between a father and his servant daughter which had featured in a conduct book commissioned by booksellers. Organised around advice letters which were designed to instruct 'Country Readers' in the approved, urbane ways of putting things into words (to 'indite'), Richardson found himself increasingly composing the letters to instruct readers in 'how to think and act' as well, using as a basis the story of a servant girl which had 'some slight foundation in truth', and dramatising her voice and story through an imitation of the so-called familiar letter.[30]

One of the first novels thus came into being through Richardson's use of the familiar letter, an eighteenth-century prose genre. The most regular way of talking about the familiar letter at the time when Richardson was writing stressed its intimacy, and the way in which it granted access to the 'heart' of the person. This is certainly the way in which Richardson conceived of the familiar letter in *Pamela*: it was a window to her virtuous sincerity, and Pamela spoke the generic language of the familiar letter – of spontaneity, transparency of motive and truth – to assert as much. Richardson's view of the character he had created through his narrative method held that her virtue and integrity were transparently self-evident and truthful.[31]

Truth claims made in respect of the self-presentation of character in the familiar letter were scrutinsed and debated publicly in eighteenth-century print culture. As Thomas Keymer points out, the eighteenth-century critic Samuel Johnson was alert to the possibility that familiar letters were less transparent than they seemed: that is to say, they were addressed to a particular person, sought to effect a purpose, and thus constituted a rhetorical act of self-dramatisation to that end. Johnson formulated this rhetorical sense of the letter in his commentary on the artful letters of the poet Alexander Pope (written in the 1730s), which appeared in Johnson's biography of Pope (1781), another prose narrative genre (the characteristics of which we will examine in more detail in the next chapter).[32]

Johnson's sceptical reading of the familiar letter needs to be added to a discussion of Pamela's letters as events which effect the conversion of narratees such as Mr. B. and Lady Davers. For it provides grounds for an alternative reading of Pamela's performance in the genre. Indeed, such a reading was satirically aired in a debate conducted through the culture of print. Henry Fielding read Pamela's character sceptically when he wrote (anonymously) a parodic burlesque of Richardson's narrative framework entitled *Shamela* (1741). As the title implies, Fielding's narrative uses letters and journals to reveal a servant girl hypocritically manipulating her master's sexual desire for her in order to secure a marriage and social advantage (here 'writing to the moment' includes writing in bed with the man alongside). We need to be alert here to the way in which anxieties about class, gender and the power of literacy are implicit in Fielding's parody. In Richardson's narrative, letters determine as well as record a story in which a servant girl morally reforms a man of the gentry class, marrying him and thus rising in the social scale to his station. Literacy – Pamela's capacity to fashion an image of herself in narrative – is an agent in this process. Fielding's satire contests the moral legitimacy of Pamela's story and character, as well as asking questions about Richardson's narrative method, which placed no 'check' on his character's subjectivism. Fielding was using fiction to explore the question: how does one tell the truth in narrative?

Fielding pursued this question further in 1742 when he wrote *Joseph Andrews*, based on the ruse that Richardson's Pamela Andrews has a brother, Joseph, a footman who is equally determined to protect his virtue, this time against Lady Booby, a relative of Pamela's Mr B. Thus, Fielding contests Richardson's reading of gendered power relations in making Joseph the victim of a woman's sexual predatoriness. Fielding also contests Richardson's narrative of class elevation in the sense that the virtuous Joseph Andrews turns out not to be low born, but is instead the child of a gentle- man, switched by gypsies at birth.

In a preface to the work, Fielding attempted to categorise the form of writing that the reader would encounter. He calls it 'a comic epic-poem in prose'. In naming and practising this 'species' of writing, Fielding addressed an implied reader who was familiar with the gentlemanly study of classical literature and its schemes of generic classification. Fielding distinguished his production from the romance, the dominant form of European prose narrative in the seventeenth century: a courtly genre set conventionally in the distant past, concerning questing knights and their encounters with such fabulous entities as dragons and giants. In contrast to the aristocratic romance, Fielding's new species of writing was low and comic, representing 'persons of inferior rank'. In classifying his writing as an 'epic-poem in prose', Fielding was describing a form of non-metrical narration which could authoritatively frame, embed and comment upon the elements of narrative with which we are now familiar, namely 'action, characters ... and diction'.[33] The classical story-telling techniques of epic are brought to the low-life subject matter of prose.[34] Fielding makes the narrator of *Joseph Andrews* tell Joseph's story in the third person. In other words, the narrative voice is as authoritative as the one which we have seen at work in the later *Emma*; though Fielding's narrator is much more obtrusive, and confides in the reader through a first-person address. Modern readers, with the benefit of hindsight, have little trouble in recognising Fielding's 'comic epic-poem in prose' as a novel. In the course of this discussion of the intertextual relations that define its position in a debate, I have presented it as an instance of a 'genre in the process of coming into being' as Michael McKeon describes the origins of the novel in English.[35] Let us now move to a more theoretical style of discussion to consider some of the major positions in the debate surrounding this phenomenon, before reconsidering *Emma* in the light of the questions posed in this debate.

2.11   The debate about the origins of the novel

In looking at the novel as a 'genre in the process of coming into being' literary historians are confronted by, in the words of J. Paul Hunter, 'something unfocused, sprawling across genres and modes more or less indiscriminately'.[36] Although it is commonly agreed that *Pamela* and *Joseph Andrews* occupy quite an advanced and mature position in the process and were more 'codified' or organised experiments, we can still see their generic heterogeneity quite explicitly in their narrative frameworks.[37] As we have seen, *Pamela* was made from the familiar letter, the journal and the conduct book. But it also borrowed from a tradition of Protestant narratives record-ing personal trials and spiritual self-scrutiny, which were often adapted from journals and diaries.[38] I am resisting the term 'autobiography' at present for reasons which will be explained in the next chapter, where we will look more closely at the naming of self-writing as 'autobiography' in its nine-teenth-century context. Even so, it is clear that many of the prose genres over which these early novels 'sprawl' provide opportunities for representing the 'inwardness' of character.

There is an associated rhetoric of 'truth' at work in the narrative frame-works of *Pamela* and *Joseph Andrews* which makes them similar. We have seen that Richardson, in claiming the existence of an organising editor who has collated his character's letters and journals, and in so doing has dis-covered the truthfulness of the narrative they comprise, at least leaves open the possibility that the reader is reading 'real' history rather than a fiction. *Joseph Andrews* refers to itself as a 'true History' (Book 4, Chapter 16). Consequently there are similarities between these writings and the slightly earlier narratives by Daniel Defoe such as *Robinson Crusoe* (1719) and *Moll Flanders* (1722). Again, Defoe's narratives are generically heterogeneous, drawing variously upon the scientific travel journal, the criminal biography, and the confessional narrative of the penitent. His texts are also framed by complex editorial statements which position these narratives ambiguously between 'real' histories and fiction.

How have critics and literary historians sought to explain the differences between Richardson and Fielding, and the distinctive similarities that characterise the narratives of Defoe, Richardson and Fielding? This is where we need to look at accounts of the rise of the novel, where identifications of the point of origin are as varied as the formalists' arguments over the vocabulary of narrative criticism.[39] Perhaps it is most appropriate to say that the novel has come into being from multiple points of origin, culturally, linguistically, geographically, historically (a point I will return to in section 5.6). It is as well to be aware of this when focusing on the stories of origins at work in a given culture – in our case, a culture defined by English-language writing and speech. This in itself is complex enough: as the following accounts will show, cultures are sites of conflict and contestation which prose narratives internalise in the very process of making the form that has come to be recognised as 'the novel'.

2.12   The rise of the novel: Ian Watt and the tradition of formal realism

One of the most powerful and enduring accounts of the origins of the novel in English is Ian Watt's influential study *The Rise of the Novel* (1957). Watt argues that the English novel came into being in the eighteenth century and that Daniel Defoe, Samuel Richardson and, to a lesser extent, Henry Fielding were the significant innovators. According to Watt, Defoe and Richardson crafted prose narratives which absorbed 'the general temper of philosophical realism'.[40] 'Philosophical realism' was constituted principally in the empirical philosophy of John Locke, the seventeenth-century philosopher who held that the associations and ideas that enable thought and the discovery of truth are apprehended by the individual's senses; a philosophical position known as empiricism. According to Watt, this had a profound impact on the writing of prose narrative. Archaic narrative types such as the romance, with their elaborate diction, distant-past settings and fantastic happenings, were abandoned in favour of story lines which were set in the present or recent past, and were more spontaneous and inventive in the way that they represented, in plain prose, the practical and plausible situations that individuals confronted in their everyday lives.

The expanding eighteenth-century print culture served a growing reading public which was generated by a changing social structure. Accordingly Watt's thesis has a sociological dimension in that he linked the emergence of narratives about individuals to the rise of economic individualism. Daniel Defoe is a crucial figure, in that his narratives forge links between the individualist ethics of Protestant theologies and the forms of competitive, individualist, economic activity which came increasingly to structure every-day life.[41] It is in this sense that Watt presents *Robinson Crusoe* as a founding moment in the rise of the novel. Defoe's narrative, in which the narrator recalls his God-guided struggle to bring the island on which he has been shipwrecked under his mastery, appealed to a growing commercial middle class, for whom Crusoe's battle with his circumstances constituted an exotic refraction of their own struggle with a new, competitive, capitalist world.[42]

Such narratives made individual perception of a material world their organising principle. First-person narration was a feature of Defoe's *Robinson Crusoe* and *Moll Flanders*, and as we have seen, it is Richardson's choice in *Pamela*. Watt notes how this first-person perspective is made more palpable by the presence of Pamela's elaborate descriptions of domestic detail.[43] For Watt, narration which emphasises perception, the everyday world perceived, and the psychological movements of mind in the act of making sense of the world are at the basis of what he describes as 'realism of presentation'. Realism of presentation is, in turn, the cornerstone of Watt's construction of a tradition of narrative which initiates and propels the 'rise of the novel'. He calls this 'formal realism', which acknowledges the formal, conventional nature of a new way of mediating a middle-class world view, founded on the primacy of the individual.

Watt's argument can be used to think about the status of much earlier popular prose narratives. Let us take Thomas Deloney's *Jack of Newbury* (1597) as an example. *Jack of Newbury* was a story set during the reign of Henry VIII, which, from the perspective of its late sixteenth-century reader-ship, was relatively contemporaneous. Jack is a sober and industrious cloth-worker who marries his recently widowed employer-mistress: there are anticipations of *Pamela* and virtue being rewarded. The narrative recounts, in a plain style, Jack's business success, his obedience and usefulness to the king (he assembles a troop of men to fight the battle of Flodden Field), and the social recognition increasingly bestowed on him. This culminates in the visit of the royal household to a banquet at Jack's home. Although royalty makes an appearance, the focus is on labour and the everyday existence of common people. Yet, Watt's theory of 'formal realism', and the emphasis it places on conventions for representing complex individuality, leads us to recognise the differences between Deloney's narrative and the later narratives of Defoe and Richardson. In *Jack of Newbury*, the eponymous figure represents little more than an allegorical substitute for the virtues of paternalism, benevolence and loyalty, providing a point of continuity between the various episodes, as opposed to a character like Robinson Crusoe, who is individualised through first-person narration.[44] In spite of some novelistic qualities, *Jack of Newbury* does not fit into Watt's tradition, strengthening his claim about the foundation of that tradition in the eighteenth century.

The difficulty for Watt, however, is that at the very moment that he posits the emergence of this tradition, he is confronted by an example from the mid eighteenth century which does not quite fit: Fielding's novels, as we have seen, reject the subjective narrative method preferred by Richardson. Watt accordingly adjusts and expands his theory of formal realism by dis-tinguishing between 'realism of presentation' and 'realism of assessment', evident in Fielding's third-person narration which 'assesses' characters and events 'objectively'. By this means, Watt is able to assimilate Fielding into the tradition of formal realism, especially when he argues for the developmental role played by the later writings of Jane Austen, which combined 'into a harmonious unity the advantages both of realism of presentation and realism of assessment'.[45] This certainly accords with the formalist reading of *Emma* developed in section 2.5, where we noted the way in which the narration moved between Emma's limited focalisation and the narrator's more 'objective' overview. However, the difficulty with Watt's solution is that, even though he begins with a social and cultural focus, he concludes by viewing the development of the novel as a sequential, problem-solving activity concerned with form, in the sense that Richardson and Fielding between them generate a problem which Austen comes along later and solves, thus getting herself elected to the tradition. This view is in danger of losing sight of questions of social and cultural context, and of allowing a teleology (reading the end back into the beginning and regarding progress to that end as inevitable) defined by formal questions to take over.

2.13   Contested fields of cultural discourse and the rise of the novel: Lennard J. Davis and Michael McKeon

More recently Lennard J. Davis's *Factual Fictions: The Origins of the English Novel* (1983) has noted the problem of teleology in approaches which become centred on constructions of continuous traditions. In response, Davis constructs a history of the novel which is concerned to stress breaks, discontinuities and the thresholds which separate the fields of discourse comprising 'culture'. Accordingly, he resists explaining the rise of the novel as a consequence of the decline of the courtly romance: for Davis, novel and romance were radically different genres.[46] Having made this break, Davis argues that the origins of the English novel can be located instead in a seventeenth-century culture of 'prose narrative in print', which included printed news ballads, the forerunners of newspapers. This produced what Davis describes as a 'news/novel discourse', an unstable blend of factual and fictional narrative.[47] This helps to explain not only the generic mixture that we find in novels by Defoe, Richardson and Fielding, but also the sense of ambiguity that we encounter when these fictional texts refer to themselves as 'true histories'. Davis sees the ambiguities around the 'truth' status of early fiction as a consequence of its emergence from a complex field of discourse.

Michael McKeon in *The Origins of the English Novel* (1987) also locates the problem of the early novel's preoccupation with 'truth' within fields of discourse. McKeon pushes the origins of the English novel back into the early modern period (the sixteenth and seventeenth centuries), arguing that the writings of Defoe, Richardson and Fielding mark the culminating point of, and are in a sense produced by, a history of social conflict during which epistemological categories such as 'truth', and moral categories such as 'virtue', were refined and debated within and between fields of philo-sophical, scientific, theological and political discourse. For McKeon class relations and conflicts drove this process, and changing forms of prose narrative internalised the contests that were being waged. The 'literary' form which has come to be recognised as the novel internalised these contests in special ways: McKeon argues that 'the distinctive feature of novelistic narra-tive is the internalisation or thematisation of formal problems on the level of content'.[48]

How did this work? We have already seen how, from the perspective of Ian Watt, the late Elizabethan *Jack of Newbury* does not belong to the tradition of the 'formal realist' novel. McKeon's approach does not set aside the need for traditions; instead it broadens the focus by reconstructing a multiplicity of narrative (and non-narrative) traditions, and traces the dia-lectical interactions and conflicts that produced the novel. McKeon places Deloney's narrative in the context of a tradition of early modern stories about virtue which exalted the qualities of a particular class, in this case tradesmen. We noted how, given its theme of the virtuous figure who is rewarded with increased social recognition, *Jack of Newbury* seems to anticipate *Pamela*.

Yet, this is to admit a teleology which McKeon's approach resists. For McKeon, *Pamela* as a narrative that we have come to recognise as a novel was produced when the story about virtue came under subsequent intellectual pressure to tell itself 'truthfully' in a formally self-conscious manner, and to internalise that truth at the level of content (Mr B.'s 'conversion').[49] According to McKeon, the question of how to tell the truth in narrative had, by the mid eighteenth century, come to be contested by middle-class and aristocratic world views which placed themselves, respectively, at the opposite ends of two epistemological poles: naive empiricism and extreme scepticism. Richardson's choice of the familiar letter, and his claims for the 'truth' of Pamela's virtuous sentiments that it transparently represented, can trace its antecedents to a middle-class preference for the philosophy of naive empiricism. In turn, such naively empirical stories concerned with virtue were contested by an extreme form of conservative scepticism, evidenced in the 1740s as we have seen in Henry Fielding's parodic *Shamela*, and then more positively in his *Joseph Andrews*. Thus, McKeon presents an historical and theoretical interpretation of the social and discursive sources of the debate between Richardson and Fielding which we traced in section 2.10.

A consequence of this manner of tracing the debate is that it is difficult for us to read the novels of Richardson and Fielding without thinking of intertextual connections: not only between one fictional text and another, but also between fictional and non-fictional prose narratives and discourses. Moreover, fictional characters and the effects of 'realism' were not simply the artistic inventions of individual writers, but were produced out of embattled fields of discourse. This excursion into debates about the origin of the novel has the potential to alter radically the questions we ask when we read novels and prose narratives. Let us begin to return to *Emma* in the light of this new way of reading, approaching it by way of Nancy Armstrong's poststructuralist feminist thesis about the origins of the novel and its political role in constructing gendered subjectivity.

2.14   Gender and the rise of the novel: the domestic woman and the production of subjectivities

To what extent have critics recognised gendered discourses in their reconstruction of the early modern cultural conflicts from which the novel emerged? For the most part, their role has been investigated by feminist critics. An important strand of feminist literary criticism aims to recover for women a central place in literary history and to construct a tradition which challenges a male-dominated canon.[50]

Alternatively, feminist critics such as Ros Ballaster and Nancy Armstrong adopt aproaches which are less author- and work-centred, focusing instead on the cultural prevalence and power of discourses of gender and sexual desire.[51] For Nancy Armstrong, this introduces a different orientation to the history of the novel; as she argues in *Desire and Domestic Fiction* (1987), Defoe's *Robinson Crusoe* 'does not inaugurate the tradition of the novel as we know it', for the novel as we know it is preoccupied with relationships between men and women.[52] Whilst they are durable, desert-island stories have not proved to be as reproducible as stories about sexual desire. Romantic novels about men, women and sexual desire had to be told again and again in different ways, according to Armstrong, because they were at the root of an English political settlement which 'was accomplished largely through cultural hegemony'.[53]

What is meant by this? Armstrong's thesis about the rise of the novel as a cultural institution with important political consequences is alert to the contexts of early modern social conflict that McKeon's approach highlights. In common with Davis and McKeon, Armstrong's method is intertextual, or a 'foray into extraliterary territory as part of an effort to suggest how fiction might have worked with other, very different forms of writing to produce a new form of political power'.[54] In other words, the novel emerged out of a variety of narrative and non-narrative sources to become a cultural institution which absorbed and transformed the dangerous conflicts of society and politics into the microcosmic domestic world, the social and political conflicts being rewritten along lines of gender division. For Armstrong, the fact that *Pamela* is about a servant girl who marries the gentleman whose initial aim is her sexual conquest – a low-born expert in the domestic arts who converts a high-born gentleman from libertinism to romantic love and domestic responsibility – makes it politically charged. Armstrong argues that representations of the domestic woman had come, by the early eighteenth century, to exercise a considerable degree of power: the domestic woman and the space of the household were seemingly above the social conflicts generated by the religious and political controversies which had dominated the seventeenth century. The domestic woman was a role which became familiar to all literate classes through conduct books for women which codified gender differences (the different roles played by men and women) and appropriate modes of behaviour. Armstrong argues that these provided literate classes with 'a figure of female subjectivity, a grammar ... [which] awaited the substance that the novel and its readers ... would eventually provide'.[55]

At issue here is the production of selves in and through forms of discourse and reading. Armstrong works from the poststructuralist position, which argues that individuals acquire subjectivities which are constructed from discourse: in other words female subjectivities were fashioned from reading positions, which were inscribed in certain texts and discourses. Conduct books provided the woman reader with a model of subjectivity based on domestic propriety, which could refashion the woman reader into the domestic subject of male desire. Reading experiences such as *Pamela* utilised the basic 'grammar' of a conduct book – its culturally hegemonic figure of the domestic woman – whilst making it into a dramatic narrative which was both exciting and improving. Armstrong proposes that the novel reader was created as a political subject whilst reading a novel. This is, as we saw at the very beginning of this chapter, the basic premise behind the idea of the implied reader: we have to adjust our subject position when we enter into another world of narrative discourse. But Armstrong's argument is more historically and critically pointed than this: she asks us to see novel reading as a practice which developed in history, and out of a variety of sources which had political implications. Her argument asks us to think about why some reading positions have become more powerful than others in their capacity for forming and sustaining subjectivities. According to Armstrong, *Pamela* initiates a very powerful tradition in the English novel, not least in the way that it is about the production of a self through the possession of literacy.

Armstrong's reading of domestic ideology in *Pamela* stresses its place in the production of Pamela's self and the conversion of others. Pamela's virtue is based on her sensibility and the values of domestic propriety. But the innate virtue of Pamela's self has been, as we have seen, questioned by some readers (such as Fielding) on the basis of Richardson's chosen narrative method. Armstrong reads this positively: she argues that Pamela's self is actually a rhetorically performed subjectivity constructed out of writing skills. Indeed, Pamela's only weapon in her struggle with Mr B. is her written self. It is a self which Mr B. desires to read; and, as we noted in section 2.9, it is a self which converts Mr B.'s wayward masculinity to the domestic ideal once he has read it, a testimony to the power of the domestic ideal and its inscription in discourse.

2.15   Re-reading *Emma*: letters, standards and intertextual allusion

To what extent can Armstrong's thesis be used to read *Emma* as a narra-tive? Or, to broaden the question: does our excursion into historical and theoretical readings of the origins of the English novel offer any openings for the re-reading of *Emma*? As we noted in the first part of this chapter, a formal reading noted the artistic integration of content and form in Austen's narra-tive. The kind of approach adopted by Davis, McKeon and Armstrong disintegrates narrative into its social and cultural sources and contexts in order to understand its integretative power. Such an approach may be appropriate for 'early' novels which were characterised by seemingly clumsy frameworks, and which had no settled generic identity to speak of, but surely not for *Emma*, given its manifest artistic wholeness?

There are two points that we can advance to answer this; both come from Michael McKeon. First, we have seen how McKeon's approach to the emer-gence of the novel notes the way in which the novel is distinguished by the way in which content is internalised in the form of the narrative, a finding with which formalist approaches would be comfortable. But McKeon's thesis suggests that this characteristic is actually a product of historical dialectics. In other words, there is every reason to expect ourselves to be able to read culture and history in the content and formal arrangements of all novels. Secondly, McKeon notes that whilst it is true that early novels such as *Pamela* debate their cultural purpose and epistemological bearings through overt frameworks, or 'in the interstices of narrative itself', by Austen's time these explicit debates had been relocated to the periodical presses and into the discourses of 'fiction criticism' (of which more will be said in the next chapter).[56] The cultural function of the novel had not, however, changed.

Consequently, as Armstrong argues, *Emma* is a story about the refor-mation of subjectivity which draws upon the discourse of the domestic ideal. We noted in section 2.5 how Knightley wished for Emma to find 'worthy employment for a young lady's mind' (p. 43) and how in Chapter 5 he laments the fact that she consistently fails to follow through an improving programme of reading (pp. 65–6). The cultivation of domestic subjectivity is linked to literacy and reading, as in *Pamela*, though in Austen's novel it falls to the masculine Knightley to draw attention to the connection: Pamela's authority has passed to Knightley, and it is Emma who has to be regulated and reformed.

Armstrong argues that Jane Austen's fiction pursued a different line to Richardson's in its concern with 'the regulation of literacy and ... language'.[57] In *Emma*, literacy skills bring certain problems which contribute to the drama of the narrative, but which are managed by the narrator. Other prose genres are assimilated into the novel: Armstrong notes the part played by letters in the narrative, even though *Emma* is not an epistolary fiction in the way that *Pamela* is. In *Emma* some letters are represented as though in an epistolary fiction (Frank Chrurchill's letter at the end of the novel, for example). For the most part, however, letters are events which are reported by the narration: Frank Churchill's first letter is described in terms of the general reaction it provokes; Jane Fairfax's letter is reported when it is being read by her aunt, Miss Bates; most significantly, Robert Martin's letter proposing marriage to Harriet Smith is reported through Emma's negative commentary on its style. The issue that underpins these letters is one that never troubled Richardson in writing *Pamela* (though as we saw, it troubled his readers): what is the actual character of the person who has written these letters? Letters present interpretive problems in *Emma* which are intimately linked to the asymmetrical relations between status, writing, speech, gesture and personal worth that the novel explores. Frank Churchill writes an educated, stylish letter, but the sender is a deceiver; Robert Martin writes in a plain style which Emma takes to be an indication of his inferior status. Yet Knightley is on hand to point out the erroneous judgements that Emma makes, claiming that Martin's style is an indicator of self-assurance and good sense. Armstrong's point is that in the context of these problems the authoritative narrative voice, which we analysed at the beginning of this chapter, proposes itself as a standard of judgement and 'as a new standard for writing', which amounts to another perspective on the status of *Emma* as 'literature'.[58]

But Austen's fiction had to face down competition from other styles of fictional writing which were held to debase this 'standard'. Although conflict and debate between writers and their styles was an explicit feature of the emergence of the early novel, Jane Austen's realist novel of manners was in implicit competition with other traditions of fictional writing, particu-larly the gothic romance, a style of fiction which was was initiated by Horace

Walpole's anti-realist *Castle of Otranto* (1764). This style of narrative re-cycled many of the features of the romance tradition: stories were set in castles and ruined abbeys in foreign parts and in the distant past; they incorporated fantastic and supernatural elements such as ghosts and hauntings. The narratives conventionally emphasised the terrorising effects of these happenings on the raw feelings and sensations of the characters, who were usually young women incarcerated in claustrophobic space by libidinous male-master figures. The gothic was dismissed by Ian Watt in his account of the formal realist tradition as a 'fugitive literary tendency', yet this is to overlook its importance in its day: Walpole's *Otranto* is discussed by Dunlop in his 1814 history of prose fiction whilst Austen, who had published *Sense and Sensibility*, *Pride and Prejudice* and *Mansfield Park* by this date, is not.[59]

Austen wrote a parody of the gothic romance in *Northanger Abbey*. But resistance to the gothic also intrudes into *Emma* allusively and intertextually. Harriet Smith informs Emma that she is urging the sensible Robert Martin to read a novel which has enthused her, *The Romance of the Forest*. This was a novel of the gothic romance genre which appeared in 1791, written by the leading exponent of the genre, Ann Radcliffe, perhaps the best-known writer of the gothic romance in English. Set in seventeenth-century Catholic Europe, *The Romance of the Forest* was narrated in the third person. Yet, in common with many gothic narratives, it emphasised the intense feelings and sensibility of the focaliser-heroine (Adeline), both in her responses to nature and apparent supernatural happenings. *Emma*, as we have noted, is about the dangers of unfettered judgement. The point seems to be that Emma had better reform herself before she does any more damage to the already half-ruined and impressionable Harriet, spoiled by the wrong kind of novel.

The following chapter, which focuses on Victorian writing, will extend this exploration of the tensions between discourses of romance and realism and their relations to ideas about self-making. The chapter will also continue to discuss the intertextualities of the novel, specifically its relations to non-fiction prose narrative genres such as the autobiography and the biography.

Notes

1. Readers who are using the Penguin edition of the work will see a facsimile of the title page of the first edition; Jane Austen, *Emma* (Harmondsworth: Penguin, 1981), p. 33. All subsequent references to the novel will be to this edition, and will be given in parentheses in the main text.

2. Sir Walter Scott, *Waverley*, Everyman edition (London: Dent, 1979), p. 475.

3. Percy Lubbock, *The Craft of Fiction* (London: Jonathan Cape, 1921), p. 11.

4. Rather strangely, Lubbock made it sound as though no one had ever tried to think systematically about the workings of prose narrative: 'I have often wished that the modern novel had been invented a hundred years sooner, so that it might have fallen into the hands of the critical schoolmen of the seventeenth century' (*Craft of Fiction*, p. 22).

5. John Colin Dunlop, *History of Prose Fiction*, 1814, new edition, 2 volumes (London: George Bell, 1888), II, p. 546.

6. Dunlop, *History of Prose Fiction*, I, i.

7. Lubbock was keen to avoid the problems of historical interpretation: 'in these pages I speak only of the modern novel, the picture of life that we are in a position to understand without the knowledge of a student or scholar' (*Craft of Fiction*, p. 9).

8. See Wayne C. Booth, *The Rhetoric of Fiction* (Chicago and London: University of Chicago Press, 1961), Seymour Chatman, *Story and Discourse: Narrative Structure in Fiction and Film*, 1978 (Ithaca, NY, and London: Cornell University Press, 1993), and Shlomith Rimmon-Kenan, *Narrative Fiction: Contemporary Poetics*, New Accents (London: Methuen, 1983). See also the select bibliography.

9. Lubbock, *Craft of Fiction*, p. 11.

10. Booth, *Rhetoric of Fiction*, pp. 20, 16.

11. Chatman, *Story and Discourse*, p. 151.

12. Chatman, *Story and Discourse*, p. 264.

13. Booth, *Rhetoric of Fiction*, preface.

14. Booth, *Rhetoric of Fiction*, p. 138.

15. Emily Brontë, *Wuthering Heights* (Harmondsworth: Penguin, 1983), p. 45.

16. Chatman, *Story and Discourse*, p. 151.

17. Rimmon-Kenan, *Narrative Fiction*, pp. 87-9.

18. Rimmon-Kenan, *Narrative Fiction*, p. 2.

19. Lubbock, *Craft of Fiction*, p. 50.

20. Booth, *Rhetoric of Fiction*, pp. 239-60.

21. Rimmon-Kenan, *Narrative Fiction*, pp. 71-2.

22. Chatman, *Story and Discourse*, pp. 96-102.

23. Rimmon-Kenan, *Narrative Fiction*, p. 114. For a detailed discussion of the 'discovery' of the category of free indirect speech, see Roy Pascal, *The Dual Voice: Free Indirect Speech and its Functioning in the Nineteenth-Century European Novel* (Manchester: Manchester University Press, 1977).

24. Raymond Williams, *The Country and the City*, 1973 (London: Hogarth, 1985); see Chapter 11.

25. See Cobbett's ride from Winchester to Burghclere, 31 October 1825, especially his account of the village of Stoke-Charity, and his analysis of the causes of impoverishment; the address to the reader is forthright and

rhetorically powerful, and an implicit internal distinction in the address is observed between those who follow Cobbett's analysis, and those who continue to justify the system: 'Those, therefore, are fools or hypocrites, who affect to wish to better the lot of the poor labourers and manufacturers, while they ... uphold the system which is the manifest cause of it' (*Rural Rides* (Harmondsworth: Penguin, 1985), p. 266).

26. Williams, *Country and the City*, p. 112.

27. The phrase 'the long revolution' is Williams's, from his book of that title (London: Chatto and Windus, 1961). Williams's work follows from, and is a revision of, Leavis's somewhat reactionary account of English cultural tradition embodied in the novel, *The Great Tradition* (London: Chatto and Windus, 1948). Williams formulated his theory of cultural materialism in *Marxism and Literature* (Oxford and New York: Oxford University Press, 1977). See also the select bibliography.

28. Samuel Richardson, *Pamela; or, Virtue Rewarded*, 1740 (Harmondsworth: Penguin, 1980): all references will be to this edition – which is based on the 1801 edition of the novel – and will appear in parentheses in the main text.

29. Lubbock, *Craft of Fiction*, p. 152.

30. Richardson to Sinstra, 2 June 1753, in William C. Slattery (ed.), *The Richardson–Sinstra Correspondence* (Carbondale and Edwardsville: Southern Illinois University Press, 1969), p. 28. Richardson's advice manual, *Letters Written To and For Particular Friends, on the Most Important Occasions*, appeared in 1741.

31. See Tom Keymer, *Richardson's 'Clarissa' and the Eighteenth-Century Reader* (Cambridge: Cambridge University Press, 1992), pp. 18–19.

32. Keymer, *Richardson's 'Clarissa'*, pp. 11–12.

33. Henry Fielding, *Joseph Andrews* (Harmondsworth: Penguin, 1985), pp. 25–31.

34. Fielding parodies epic conventions as well; see for instance Book 3, Chapter 6.

35. Michael McKeon, 'Prose Fiction: Great Britain', in H. B. Nisbett and Claude Rawson (eds), *The Eighteenth Century*, Cambridge History of Literary Criticism, vol. 4 (Cambridge: Cambridge University Press, 1997), p. 238.

36. J. Paul Hunter, *Before Novels: The Cultural Contexts of Eighteenth-Century English Fiction* (New York and London: W. W. Norton, 1990), p. 16.

37. Hunter, *Before Novels*, p. 22.

38. For an account of this tradition see Hunter, *Before Novels*, Chapter 12.

39. The most recent contributor to this debate is Margaret Anne Doody's *The True Story of the Novel* (London: Fontana, 1998). See the select bibliography.

40. Ian Watt, *The Rise of the Novel: Studies in Defoe, Richardson and Fielding*, 1957 (London: Hogarth Press, 1987), p. 12.

41. Watt's work builds upon an historical sociology which has posited relations between the rise of Protestant religions in early modern Europe and the growth of capitalism; for instance, Watt cites Max Weber's *The Protestant Ethic and the Spirit of Capitalism* (*Rise of the Novel*, p. 64).

42. See Watt, *Rise of the Novel*, Chapter 3.

43. Watt, *Rise of the Novel*, p. 153.

44. Jack and his occupation as master cloth-maker 'to the great benefit of the commonwealth' is effectively allegorised in Chapter 5, which consists of a representation of the portraits hung in his house, all of which are of great men from history whose origins were from the humble worlds of work and craft. Digressive episodes in the narrative – of which there are many – are not focused on Jack at all. See *Jack of Newbury* in Paul Salzman (ed.), *An Anthology of Elizabethan Prose Fiction*, World's Classics (Oxford: Oxford University Press, 1987), pp. 313, 359–61.

45. Watt, *Rise of the Novel*, p. 297.

46. Lennard J. Davis, *Factual Fictions: The Origins of the English Novel* (New York: Columbia University Press, 1983), p. 40. Davis's insistence on this matter points to a history of usage whereby 'novel' and 'romance' were used virtually interchangeably until the end of the eighteenth century.

47. See Davis, *Factual Fictions*, Chapters 3 and 4.

48. Michael McKeon, *The Origins of the English Novel 1600–1740* (Baltimore: Johns Hopkins University Press, 1987), p. 266.

49. Although Deloney based *Jack of Newbury* on an historical figure, Deloney's framing statement is not concerned to demonstrate the 'truth' of his tale in the way that eighteenth-century novelists did.

50. See for instance Jane Spencer, *The Rise of the Woman Novelist* (Oxford: Blackwell, 1986), Janet Todd, *The Sign of Angellica: Women, Writing and Fiction* (London: Virago, 1989), and Dale Spender, *Mothers of the Novel* (London: Pandora, 1986).

51. Ros Ballaster, *Seductive Forms: Women's Amatory Fiction from 1684 to 1740* (Oxford: Clarendon Press, 1992), p. 11.

52. Nancy Armstrong, *Desire and Domestic Fiction: A Political History of the Novel* (Oxford: Oxford University Press, 1987), p. 29.

53. Armstrong, *Desire and Domestic Fiction*, p. 9.

54. Armstrong, *Desire and Domestic Fiction*, p. 35

55. Armstrong, *Desire and Domestic Fiction*, p. 60.

56. McKeon, 'Prose Fiction: Great Britain', p. 238.

57. Armstrong, *Desire and Domestic Fiction*, p. 98.

58. Armstrong, *Desire and Domestic Fiction*, p. 148.

59. Watt, *Rise of the Novel*, p. 290; Dunlop, *History of Prose Fiction*, II, pp. 576–7.

Bildung and belonging: studying nineteenth-century narrative and 'self-culture'

3.1   The bildungsroman

This chapter will explore ways of reading two important nineteenth-century novels: Charlotte Brontë's *Jane Eyre* (1847) and George Eliot's *The Mill on the Floss* (1860), both powerful stories about the development of individual women (Jane Eyre and Maggie Tulliver) in testing circumstances. The last chapter analysed the early nineteenth-century *Emma* in terms of the development of her character: Emma matures and acquires a sense of responsibility to match her cleverness. She marries, thus balancing the desire for self-determination with the demands of socialisation. Emma undergoes an education in the way that the mid eighteenth-century Pamela does not: in consequence we can say that *Emma* is an early English example of the bildungsroman.

'Bildungsroman' is from the German: 'bildung' means 'education' or 'formation', and 'roman' means – as it does in French – 'novel'. *Emma* can be seen as a 'novel of education' or 'formation'.[1] The novel credited with being the first bildungsroman, *Wilhelm Meister's Apprenticeship* by the German writer J. W. Goethe (1796), ends in Wilhelm's happiness and fulfilment as he marries and thus completes the formation of his character as an end in itself. Wilhelm's formation – the source of his happiness – has been shaped (and even recorded) by a community (the Society of the Tower). Clearly 'bildung', the representation of an individual's education, formation and development, would be inconceivable without a community within which the story of development unfolded. Franco Moretti's study of the bildungsroman argues that this became an important narrative form in nineteenth-century Europe, which 'held fast to the notion that the biography of a young individual was the most meaningful viewpoint for the understanding and evaluation of history'.[2] Moretti's definition indicates that in the nineteenth century this form of the novel, and in some sense the idea of history itself, was grounded in biographical assumptions. Consequently, in focusing on two important nineteenth-century novels, this chapter will also think about ways of reading those novels' intertextual relationships to cognate prose narrative genres such as biography and autobiography. Here the focus texts will be Elizabeth Gaskell's biographical *The Life of Charlotte Brontë* (1857) and Samuel Bamford's autobiographical *Early Days* (1847).

3.2   Biography and autobiography in the nineteenth century

Biography means 'life (*bios*) writing (*graphé*)': this was first coined as an English word in 1683 by the poet and critic John Dryden.[3] It thus influenced eighteenth-century novelists, even if they adopted a satirically antagonistic attitude to the genre, as Fielding did in *Joseph Andrews* (book 3, chapter 1: 'Matter prefatory in Praise of Biography'). Biography was in fact an ancient genre which had its origins in public orations uttered at the funerals of military or political leaders in classical Greek and Roman cultures. It involved a speaker narrating the person's career in military combat or public life. According to Bakhtin, these are the origins of 'biographical time'.[4] Biographical time sounds very like common sense, the time that it takes for a life to run its course from birth to death. But in practice it is always a cultural convention which selectively represents a particular configuration of events, time and space. Bakhtin makes the point that classical biography usually only included the events that comprised the individual's career and which bestowed the public identity: the biography of a commander would thus consist of a series of battles which would have occurred on battle fields. Such a biography would pay little attention to 'the time of a man's "becoming" or growth'.[5] Thus, the new emphasis on individual 'growth' and 'becoming' which distinguished the nineteenth-century bildungsroman took biographical and novel narratives representing the lives of men and women in new directions. This was closely linked to the movement known as Romanticism, which proclaimed a new, nature-centred aesthetic in celebration of the creativity, inwardness and developmental powers of the individual self; perhaps its most representative document being Wordsworth's *Prelude* (published 1850, but composed 1799), an autobiographical poem in the first person narrating the 'growth' of the poet's mind.

Accordingly, 'autobiography' was linked to this Romantic shift in mentality, even though self-scrutiny in prose was also a very ancient practice;[6] and, as we saw in the last chapter, some of the earliest English novels by Defoe were shaped by seventeenth-century Puritan narratives recording personal struggles and spiritual self-examination, adapted from journals and diaries. Of course, self-scrutiny in prose narrative continued to have important spiritual functions during the nineteenth century. But 'autobiography' is very much a nineteenth-century generic term and concept; its first recorded use occurs in 1809, by the poet and critic Robert Southey.[7] Although Jean-Jacques Rousseau is credited with writing the first recognisably modern, secular autobiography in France in the 1770s, he entitled his work *Confessions*, a term usually reserved, after St Augustine, for spiritual self-scrutinies addressed to God. The nineteenth-century concept of autobiography stressed a literary, expressive connection between *bios*, the story of a life course, and *autos*, the cultivated and autonomous self respon-sible for the act of narration which looks back to and reflects upon the 'developmental' path travelled. Autobiography was an indicator of 'self-culture', or an ethos of self-improvement which was an important strand of the nineteenth-century conception of culture (see sections 1.8–9). Auto-biography also lent itself to bildung-shaped narrative patterns and the cultural significance they attached to the formative stages of childhood and youth.

3.3   The viewpoint of youth: bildung in nineteenth-century history

Why was 'youth' granted such a privileged – but also, as we shall see, troubled – viewpoint on history at this time? The end of the eighteenth century and the beginning of the nineteenth was a period of great change, and communities found themselves in various states of transformation and upheaval.

The French Revolution broke out in 1789; its ramifications were felt socially, politically and culturally. As part of their determination to throw aside artificial convention, Romantic poets such as William Wordsworth enthused initially about the democratic politics of the Revolution, which aimed to liberate the individual by transforming the aristocratic structures of French society and government. However, society proved a very stubborn structure, and the violence into which the Revolution degenerated alienated many of its initial supporters.

The French Revolution was a watershed event: it initiated decades of conflict culminating in the European revolutions of 1848, and, in Britain agitation for democratic rights centred on movements such as Chartism. In the immediate aftermath of the French revolution European societies were transformed by Napoleon Bonaparte's continental wars, conquests and empire building. Given Napoleon's humble beginnings, breathtaking rise and relative youth, a biographical explanation of world history seemed irresistible: when the German philosopher Hegel saw the victorious Napoleon ride through the streets after the Battle of Jena in 1806 he thought that he saw 'the World Spirit on Horseback'.[8] Napoleon's biography had a profound impact on French narratives about the relationship between the young individual and society. The ambitious young peasant Julien Sorel, whose ultimately tragic life history is the subject of Stendhal's bildungs-roman *Le Rouge et le Noir* (*Scarlet and Black*, 1830), seeks his inspiration in Napoleon, who, Sorel cries, '"was most certainly a man sent from God for the youth of France"'.[9]

By contrast *Emma*, published in 1816 just one year after Napoleon's defeat at Waterloo, was sent for the youth of England. It is often noted that Austen's fiction ignored the French Revolution and the Napoleonic Wars. This is true in terms of surface detail, but Nancy Armstrong (see section 2.15) reads *Emma* as a narrative of self-formation which sought to bind 'youth' into a conformist cultural hegemony centred on the domestic values and writing standards of the rural English gentry.

We should also recall that in section 2.6 we looked at Raymond Williams's account of the social and economic contexts of the countryside settings of Austen's novels, which highlighted the great changes that rural England was experiencing in the early years of the nineteenth century, and which intensified the need to reaffirm gentry values. These changes were in part due to the demands on agricultural production brought about by the Napoleonic Wars, but these wars were only accelerating increased economic activity which had its roots in the Industrial Revolution which was re-structuring English society and culture. The consequences of this social restructuring had a major impact on the 'mission' of English fiction in the nineteenth century, as we shall see when we examine the work of George Eliot. Indeed, all of these changes generated a climate of debate in which the very processes by which individuals were 'made' were interrogated in both narrative and non-narrative, literary and non-literary discourses.

Clearly, nineteenth-century history was a turbulent phenomenon on which to maintain a 'viewpoint'. In reading the focus texts in this chapter, we will of course think about viewpoint or focalisation in ways established in section 2.5: Charlotte Brontë's novel *Jane Eyre* (1847) is a fictional drama-tised first-person narrative; the autobiography of the working-class radical Samuel Bamford, *Early Days* (1847), is also written in the first person. Elizabeth Gaskell's biography of Charlotte Brontë, *The Life of Charlotte Brontë* (1857), and George Eliot's realist novel *The Mill on the Floss* (1860) are third-person narratives.[10] Such grammatical and perspectival distinc-tions are important starting points. But in so far as they shape the reader's perception of the relationship between bildung and belonging, individual and community, it will be important to study these examples of genre and focalisation as forms of gender- and class-specific address which were em-bedded in and resonant of the contexts of instability and change. As we shall see, narratives about individual formation could evaluate history from very different viewpoints which stressed either a sense of accommodation with society, or a sense of alienation and self-division; and, often, a mixture of the two.

There is one other sense of belonging that we will need to bear in mind. Texts are intertextually complex tapestries of discourse which do not so much 'belong' to, but rather 'participate' in, genres, so that novels borrow autobiographical and biographical conventions, and vice versa. The lesson that we learned in looking at the origins of the novel can be used to read the novel and cognate forms of prose narratives from later periods where generic lines were ostensibly more clearly drawn. This in turn invites us to think about narratives as artefacts which perform – through, for example, choice of register, a strain of allusiveness – a sense of the way they 'belong' to, or more critically 'participate' in, the evaluations and discriminations that comprise culture. One of the major oppositions that we will chart in this chapter is that between realism and romance, which was (section 2.15) the source of Jane Austen's quarrel with the gothic romance. The use of 'realist' or 'romance' conventions will indicate, as we shall see, the narrative text's sense of its relationship to literary culture and, thereby, its mediated relation to the complex contests of meaning which comprise culture in the broader sense.

3.4   Reading *Jane Eyre*: the critical reception; romance and 'self-culture'

Before reading *Jane Eyre* it is necessary to say something of the literary culture into which it was received. When Thomas Carlyle presented his translation of *Wilhelm Meister* (see section 3.1) to an English-speaking audience in 1824 he was not hopeful of finding a mass of appreciative readers. Painstaking in its representation of a detailed sense of everyday life, particularly Meister's artistic education in the theatre, Goethe's narrative was deliberately slow in progression: 'Of romance interest there is next to none', Carlyle warned. However, for Carlyle this elevated Goethe's offering beyond the expec-tations of 'the great mass of readers, who read to drive away the tedium of mental vacancy, employing the crude phantasmagoria of a modern novel, as their grandfathers employed tobacco and diluted brandy'.[11] Novels of romantic incident, as Carlyle suggests, were thought to pander to the relatively low 'senses'; whereas the novel of education and formation appealed to 'thought' and could heighten the reader's own capacity for self-cultivation. We should bear these discriminations in mind when reading Charlotte Brontë's *Jane Eyre*, which has seldom been short of enthusiastic or even compulsive readers; many have read *Jane Eyre* 'for pleasure' before they are asked to study it academically. Indeed, the novel found many readers and generated debate upon publication in 1847.

In section 2.15, we noted Michael McKeon's point about the way in which, by the end of the eighteenth century, many of the explicit debates about truth and value in narrative had shifted location from fiction itself to the periodical presses and discourses of 'fiction criticism'. By 1847 there existed a highly developed system of reviewing which critically evaluated the multiplicity of writings, including fiction, in a whole variety of weekly and monthly periodical publications. Literary culture, and the discrimi-nations it imparted, were shaped, in large part, by middle-class periodicals in the nineteenth century.[12] Some contemporary reviewers of *Jane Eyre* were not slow to recognise the novel's distinctiveness and appeal when it appeared. The reviewer for the *Atlas* (23 October 1847) wrote the following:

> It is one of the most powerful domestic romances which have been published for many years. It has little or nothing of the old conventional stamp upon it ... but is full of youthful vigour, of freshness and originality, of nervous diction and concentrated interest. The incidents are sometimes melo-dramatic, and, it might be added, improbable; but these incidents, though striking, are subordinate

to the main purpose of the piece, which depends not upon incident, but on the development of character.[13]

If *Wilhelm Meister* was short on 'romance', not so *Jane Eyre*, which the reviewer describes as a 'domestic romance'. Reference to domesticity locates the novel in the tradition of domestic fiction (see section 2.14), whilst the presence of 'romance' and 'melo-drama' point to the novel's visible attach-ment to popular, sensational conventions. Romance in *Jane Eyre* is evident in two senses: first, at the level of plot, in the vicissitudes of Jane and Rochester's love story; and secondly, in the form of apparently supernatural incident, manifest in the uncanny happenings at Thornfield Hall. When Rochester quizzes Jane about the sighting which made the blood creep 'cold' through her veins, Jane's reply is derived from the gothic romance (see section 2.15); it reminds her of 'the foul German spectre – the vampire' (p. 311). These happenings prefigure the realist switch to melodramatic opposition that errupts between Rochester's incarcerated wife Bertha Mason, the fleshy, bestial monstrosity, and pure, spiritual Jane.

But as the reviewer notes, what distinguishes *Jane Eyre* is the way in which the novel participates in these sensational conventions whilst energizing them with 'freshness and originality', a distinctiveness generated by 'nervous diction', or a strikingly new narrative voice which exudes 'youthful vigour'. The emphasis on the narrative voice allows the reviewer to focus on the novel as one which foregrounds 'the development of character', a culturally higher goal, as we have seen. It is significant that this reviewer should introduce the idea of youth, the defining perspective of the bildungsroman: for *Jane Eyre* is the story of youth's progress, a displaced, alienated and rebellious orphan-child maturing into a young woman who becomes educated, supports herself by working as a governess, and marries the landed gentleman she has served in this role. As Elizabeth Rigby, reviewing the novel for the *Quarterly Review*, pointed out, this repeats *Pamela*; but *Jane Eyre* is a developmental story, and is narrated through a very different framework, drawing upon quite different discourses.[14]

3.5   Romantic autobiography and character classification in *Jane Eyre*

Jane Eyre is, as few will need to be told, a romantic heroine:

> I touched the heath: it was dry, and yet warm with the heat of the summer day.
> I looked at the sky; it was pure: a kindly star twinkled just above the chasm ridge.

The dew fell, but with propitious softness; no breeze whispered. Nature seemed to me benign and good; I thought she loved me, outcast as I was; and I, who from man could anticipate only mistrust, rejection, insult, clung to her with filial fondness. Tonight, at least, I would be her guest, as I was her child: my mother would lodge me without money and without price ...
My rest might have been blissful enough, only a sad heart broke it. It plained of its gaping wounds, its inward bleeding, its riven chords. (p. 350)

Jane is a romantic heroine in one sense because she is fleeing from the passionate temptation represented by Mr Rochester: a good example of this can be found in Chapter 27 as Jane wrestles with Reason, Feeling and Rochester's physicality (pp. 344–5). She is also a romantic subject in the sense that, outcast and alienated from corrupt, insincere society, she imaginatively embraces, and is embraced by, nature. She imagines nature to be benign and good; the heath is, symbolically, an earth mother which receives Jane as a child (in later paragraphs, Jane articulates a pantheistic view of nature and the universe; pp. 350–1). Finally, Jane's romantic identity is confirmed by the emphasis on the first-person 'I', which is a register of her intense subjectivity and tortured inwardness. The question that the narrative poses is: how does Jane 'become' this subject?

When we look at the title page of the first edition of *Jane Eyre* (the Penguin edition of the text reprints it) we see it reads JANE EYRE. / AN AUTOBIOGRAPHY / EDITED BY / CURRER BELL (p. 31). Even at the point where the novel was an established cultural institution we find, in eighteenth-century fashion, Charlotte Brontë's text pretending to be something it was not. As we saw in our discussion of *Pamela* (section 2.8), Richardson used the editor convention to frame Pamela's letters. But autobiographical conventions produce a very different style of narration to the familiar letter and the journal. And the language used by Jane as narrator-autobiographer is, as we will see, more varied than Pamela's language of sensibility.

Autobiographical narratives posit two subjects for the reader to interpret: the subject who enunciates the narration, and the one who is a character in the story told. The latter is a younger version of the former, the former the 'developed' outcome of the latter. The conventions which construct this sense of development are evident in Jane's narrative voice. We become aware of it in Chapter 4 when Jane recalls her night-time routine at Gateshead Hall: 'It puzzles me now to remember with what absurd sincerity I doted on this little toy, half fancying it alive and capable of sensation' (p. 61). The subject who enunciates the narration is in possession of mature judgement, which is a sign of development and growth.

It also enables the narrator to reflect on the differences between maturity and childhood; when the child Jane is quizzed by Mr Lloyd about her fear of ghosts, the narrating Jane comments that 'children can feel, but they cannot analyse their feelings; and if the analysis is partly effected in thought, they know not how to express the result of the process in words' (p. 56). This commentary articulates a theory of character-formation: it assumes that feelings (or sensations), thought, analysis and language are separate 'departments' of the person; and that thought, analysis and language – the language through which the story of one's early life can be narrated and analysed – develop over time, and are rudimentary in the child.[15]

This tendency to classify and objectify is further evident in Jane's reading of character, which borrows from the discourse of physiognomy, an ancient way of seeing reinvented as a 'science' of character in the late eighteenth century, which claimed to discern the moral and intellectual worth of people from their bodily demeanour, particularly their faces. Thus, when Jane first gets the chance to examine Rochester at close quarters she remarks, after commenting on his facial features, that 'His shape, now divested of cloak, I perceived harmonized in squareness with his physiognomy' (p. 151). Rochester attempts to read Jane in the same way just a few pages later. On meeting Mr Mason Jane detects 'something in his face that displeased' (p. 219); when the exhausted Jane lies 'torpid' beneath St John Rivers's gaze she hears him observe '"rather an unusual physiognomy; certainly not indicative of vulgarity or degradation"'. Jane's view of Mason's physiognomy invites the reader's wariness of this character; St John's words invite the reader to share a sense of Jane's uniqueness and moral worth.

The appropriation of this system of classification and knowledge by Brontë and other nineteenth-century novelists was pervasive. Jenny Bourne Taylor and Sally Shuttleworth have, in their valuable anthology of nineteenth-century psychological texts, been able to point to the very precise connections between the major textbooks of physiognomy, such as George Combe's *The Constitution of Man* (1828), and character description in Brontë's fiction.[16] But what is the broader significance of this? In section 3.3 I established a number of contexts for thinking about the significance of the individual in nineteenth-century prose narrative, including the French Revolution, the Napoleonic Wars and the Industrial Revolution. The French philosopher and historian Michel Foucault has argued that integral to these grand revolutions of democracy, reason and industrial efficiency was a less obvious, but no less profound, reorganisation of social institutions and the knowledges and practices which they disseminated (such as schools, hospitals, prisons, poor-relief houses and asylums). The aim of this re- organisation was to rationalise society by disciplining and scientifically objectifying human beings into individual 'subjects' bearing various social labels (pupils, patients, prisoners, paupers, lunatics, hysterics).[17] This was, so to speak, the obverse side of the nature-celebrating inwardness which fashions Jane's romantic subjectivity. Such discourses are negotiated during the making of Jane's self.

3.6   Space, time and subjectivity in *Jane Eyre*

The narrator juggles between genres in telling her story. As Jane says at the beginning of Chapter 10, 'this is not to be a regular autobiography: I am only bound to invoke memory where I know her responses will possess some degree of interest; therefore I now pass a space of eight years almost in silence' (p. 115). We established in section 3.2 the point that 'biographical time' is always a cultural convention; here the narrator's concern with the 'lessons' of self-culture delivered through autobiography is tempered by the implied author's recognition of the implied reader's anticipated pleasures, which call for Jane to be less of an autobiographer, more of a novelistic narrator, and character, and heroine. The implied author thus grants the narrative voice flexible powers, enabling Jane to be, at various stages, narrator, objectified character (see p. 323) and speaking heroine (see p. 344), as well as autobiographer. The point that we can make here is that Jane's subjectivity is being constructed and reconstructed as the narrative shifts from one focus of spatial attention to the next. Different phases of Jane's self- formation are narrated in the domestic space of Gateshead Hall, the institu- tional space of Lowood school, and the gothic space of Thornfield Hall.

At the beginning of the novel the orphan Jane has no legitimacy in the middle-class domestic space of the Reed household; she is branded a 'dependant' who is 'less than a servant' because she does not work for her keep (p. 44). These details highlight the extent to which a scene of 'everyday life', the middle-class household, has its familiarity stripped away and is shown to operate on the basis of moral and utilitarian classifications with exclusionary and disciplinary effects (we can contrast this with *Pamela*, in which everyday domestic space is also shown to be oppressive, but in

Pamela's case because of Mr B.'s seigneurial rights). Consequently, Jane Eyre recalls and objectifies her marginal status in the language of otherness: 'I sat, cross-legged like a Turk' (p. 39); 'like any other rebel slave, I felt resolved, in my desperation, to go to all lengths' (p. 44); and, locked in the Red Room and looking in the mirror, the narrator sees staring back an image 'like one of the tiny phantoms, half fairy, half imp' (p. 46). Using oriental and gothic discourses, and the language of tyranny and subjection, Jane constructs herself as an excluded and persecuted rebel-child, with no rights, only obligations which must be met to avoid incarceration in the institution of the poorhouse (p. 44).

Whilst Jane avoids the poorhouse, she is sent to Lowood Institution, the evangelical Mr Brocklehurst's charity school for orphans. Lowood is a school which is emblematic of Foucault's case for the disciplinary turn which characterised nineteenth-century institutions. Governed by the clock, passing time is marked by carefully regulated activities and surveillance: 'A chapter having been read through twice, the books were closed and the girls examined ... The play hour in the evening I thought the pleasantest fraction of the day at Lowood' (p. 86) .'Discipline prevailed', and girls sit erect in ranks, wearing brown uniforms, under the gaze of teachers (pp. 78–9). Punishment is meted out in public at Lowood, dramatised in Helen Burns's stoic endurance of corporal punishment, humiliation and victim-isation. Jane is subject to similar public punishment, but this is narrated in far from negative terms which make clear the inner resources that Jane draws from this episode:

> There was I, then, mounted aloft: I, who had said I could not bear the shame of standing on my natural feet in the middle of the room, was now exposed to general view on a pedestal of infamy. What my sensations were no language can describe; but just as they all rose stifling my breath and constricting my throat, a girl came up and passed me: in passing, she lifted her eyes. What a strange light inspired them! What extraordinary sensation that ray sent through me! How the new feeling bore me up! It was as if a martyr, a hero, had passed a slave or victim, and imparted strength in the transit. I mastered the rising hysteria, lifted up my head, and took a firm stand on the stool. (p. 99)

The glance that Jane receives – it is from Helen Burns – marks the transition from 'rising hysteria' to control of the sensations and the imposition of self-mastery. We can see then that this public punishment – measured and regulated in time ('"Let her stand half an hour longer on that stool, and let no one speak to her during the remainder of the day"') – is a formative event in the fashioning of Jane's subjectivity. Having been objectified and shamed as a 'deviant', she uses a discourse of heroism to fashion a liberating inwardness. As Foucault has argued, the objectification of individuals is just one side of the process he has mapped: techniques of self-'subjectification', usually shaped by narrative forms such as confessions and autobiographies, are important sources of resistance, as we see here.[18] It is notable that Miss Temple, the teacher with whom Jane identifies, encourages Jane to tell her life story for the first time at Lowood.

By contrast, gothic conventions are introduced to signify a crisis in the formation of Jane's subjectivity during the Thornfield Hall chapters, which bring the simultaneous discoveries of sexual desire for Rochester and the existence in the attic of her monstrous 'rival', Bertha Mason: both discoveries present individual imagination with unbridled opportunities. In the previous chapter (section 2.15) I briefly discussed the late eighteenth-century gothic 'revival' in fiction. Even though the heyday of the gothic romance was the 1790s, the form donated a repertoire of conventions which were recycled throughout the nineteenth century and beyond. The opening of Chapter 20 gives us a good instance of the effects of the gothic in *Jane Eyre*: the action takes place at night – 'sleep and night had resumed their empire' (p. 237) – by the light of the moon which streams in through the open blind; frightening and inexplicable sounds errupt from the house: 'terrified murmurs sounded in every room; door after door unclosed' (p. 235). Elsewhere in this central portion of the novel Thornfield's gothic decadence is further registered through Jane's experience of, on the one hand, Blanche Ingram's aristocratic disdain and, on the other, Rochester's cynicism and dark, ambiguous machinations.

And yet Jane's inwardness and self-control overcome this: as Rochester remonstrates with her, threatening violence as she makes to depart after the revelation of Bertha's existence, Jane narrates:

> I saw that in another moment, and with one impetus of frenzy more, I should be able to do nothing with him. The present – the passing second of time – was all I had in which to control and restrain him: a movement of repulsion, flight, fear would have sealed my doom – and his. But I was not afraid, not in the least. I felt an inward power, a sense of influence, which supported me. (p. 330)

Here time is presented as the drama of the moment, 'the passing second of time'. I noted in section 2.15 that the gothic places a strong emphasis on the immediate sensations of fear, desire and pain that characters experience. An example of this occurs in Chapter 17 when Jane's narration shifts to the present tense − 'He comes in at last; I am not looking at the arch, yet I see him enter' − and she records the 'pleasure' and 'agony' of desire as she gazes at Rochester (p. 203). But in the passage above the emphasis is on Rochester's loss of control, and it is Jane who can now exercise restraint upon others: though not by physical means; instead on the basis of her 'inward power, a sense of influence which supported me'. The precise significance of this will be discussed in section 3.7, but we can see why Elizabeth Rigby saw similarities between *Jane Eyre* and *Pamela*.

3.7   Where does *Jane Eyre* belong?

This question is double-edged, as we shall see. The simple answer, when we reply with reference to Jane's character, is with Rochester, of course. Jane may flee from Rochester and the shameful prospect of being his mistress, but she rejects the controlling, evangelical missionary zeal of St John Rivers to return to Rochester, who has become blind, crippled and widowed in her absence. As readers know, she marries him, and thus finds a sense of belonging. When we answer the question in relation to the novel and the conventions and discourses it deploys to create and cohere Jane's subjectivity, the reply is more complex. For Jane's 'development' and marriage negotiate a tension between gothic romance and domestic realism.

We have seen how the novel uses gothic conventions for narrating the fraught and embattled place of imagination and individual desire in the formation of Jane's subjectivity. The feminist critic Ellen Moers has argued that the conventions of gothic supernaturalism acquired significance as a discourse which nineteenth-century women writers used in their struggle to articulate a protest against their subordinate position in existing gender relations.[19] Such a protest is actually articulated by Jane, recollecting her sense of wanting more as she ascends, symbolically, beyond the 'haunted' attic of Thornfield: 'women feel just as men feel; they need exercise for their faculties ... they suffer from too rigid a restraint' (p. 141).

But Jane's continued cultivation of 'inward power' in the form of a 'sense of influence' (see section 3.6) signals an important stage in her development, for it marks her transition from romantic heroine to potential middle-class wife and domestic manager. In section 2.14 I sketched Nancy Armstrong's thesis regarding the significance of domestic discourse for the history of the novel and English cultural hegemony in the modern period. The idea of moral 'influence' was an extension of this: a nineteenth-century code for precisely this kind of delimited female power, which was supposed to tame and restrain the wild, competitive, worldly tendencies of the male through the civilising virtues of domesticity. It is the autobiographical character of the narrative which presents Jane's 'realist' domestic subjectivity as victorious over romantic individualism and gothic imagination, the final viewpoint which Jane casts on her own turbulent history and historical turbulence in general.

Feminist scholars and critics have, in recent years, made persuasive claims for *Jane Eyre* as a complex contribution to a tradition of women's writing.[20] At the same time, they have argued vigorously about its meaning. Whilst the novel does not make Jane subordinate to Rochester – the source of Rochester's worldliness, his physicality, is shattered, and Jane's inheritance makes her financially independent – there are still tensions. For instance, how is the monstrous Bertha Mason to be accommodated and explained by an inclusive feminist politics and its imagined community? Indeed, as Gayatri Spivak has argued from a postcolonial feminist perspective (post-colonialism will be explored in more depth in Chapter 5), Bertha's creole status 'naturalises' her monstrosity and marks the Eurocentric exclusiveness of the Western feminist project.[21] This is confirmed by the closing paragraphs of Jane's narrative, in which she reports, approvingly, of St John Rivers, now a missionary in India, 'hew[ing] ... down the prejudices of creed and caste' (p. 477). What is unacceptable for Jane herself is positively advocated for the subjects of empire.

We could say that present-day feminist criticism, itself a politically and intellectually complex field of debate, confronts in *Jane Eyre* a narrative which is discursively complex, nuanced, multi-layered and open to many interpretations. For some critics in the late 1840s it was not at all obvious that they were dealing with 'women's writing'; we need to recall that at this point readers only knew the author of *Jane Eyre* as 'Currer Bell', a name which could have been male or female.[22] Robert Lorimer in the *North British Review* remarked that 'Jane Eyre strikes us as a personage much more likely to have sprung ready armed from the head of a man, and that head a pretty hard one, than to have experienced, in any shape, the softening influence of female creation.'[23] Clearly this says much about gendered critical prejudices in the 1840s, but it was the case that in its allusions to 'millions ... in silent revolt against their lot' (p. 141), and its representation of Jane's famished begging as she flees from Thornfield (p. 355), the novel could be read as a radical address on behalf of the excluded and discontented everywhere.

Elizabeth Rigby's hostile review for the Tory *Quarterly Review* saw it precisely this way: instead of focusing on Jane's reaffirmation of the domestic ideal, Rigby saw Jane's viewpoint on history as one which arose out of the revolutionary social turbulence which marked the opening decades of the nineteenth century, and which reached a crisis point in 1848, the year of European revolutions (see section 3.3). For Rigby, *Jane Eyre* was an 'anti-Christian composition ... a proud and perpetual assertion of the rights of man ... We do not hesitate to say that the tone of mind and thought which has overthrown authority and violated every code human and divine abroad, and fostered Chartism and rebellion at home, is the same which has also written Jane Eyre.'[24] Rigby's hostility to subversiveness apparently owed something to the rumour passed to her by J. G. Lockhart, editor of the *Quarterly*: he had heard that Currer Bell, along with his brothers Ellis and Acton, were Lancashire weavers.[25] I want now to turn to the 1840s auto-biographical writings of Samuel Bamford, who was from Lancashire and was formerly a weaver. For in the nineteenth century, select working-class men recorded their viewpoint on history, and expressed the extent of their self-cultivation, through acts of autobiographical writing.

3.8   Reading Samuel Bamford's *Early Days*: the common narrative strategies of autobiography and novel

Samuel Bamford wrote two first-person narratives about his life: *Passages in the Life of a Radical* (1842), an account of Bamford's radical political activities and imprisonment for alleged treason following the period of post-Waterloo political agitation (1815–19); and *Early Days* (1847), an account of his childhood and youth in Lancashire. Given this chapter's concern with the bildungsroman, I shall focus on Bamford's *Early Days*.

I have demonstrated in my analysis of *Jane Eyre* some of the formal properties of autobiographical narration which generate signs of develop-ment linking past and present selves with varying degrees of coherence and continuity. We find similar strategies at work in *Early Days*. In an early episode, Bamford narrates the story of his impoverished mother's visit to her wealthy sister in Manchester, the rebuff she receives, and the long walk home to Middleton in the rain:

> The recollection of my heart-wounded, but noble-minded and forgiving mother, as she suffered under that trial, is still vividly before me; and never, I believe, will it be obliterated from my memory until consciousness remains. Ever

since I had the faculty for reasoning on these recollections I have cherished an unmitigatable contempt for mere money pride. (p. 31)

There are notable parallels with *Jane Eyre* here. The autobiographer accounts for his development into a political and moral radical through the image of his mother, who is excluded from a share in the fruits of the world because of middle-class pride. The narrator's mother has undergone a prejudiced 'trial', so that the episode is recollected in the kind of juridical discourse which is such a pronounced feature of the protests that pervade *Jane Eyre*: '"Unjust! – unjust!" said my reason' (p. 47). We can see why Elizabeth Rigby thought that *Jane Eyre* spoke in the common tongue of radical discontent.

There is also in this extract from *Early Days* an embedded associationist theory of character development which narrates the inevitability of the autobiographer's moral stance: the impression is powerfully inscribed on the mind, it becomes memory, and the developing faculty of reason sets to work on these recollections.[26] Clearly, nineteenth-century autobiographies and novels could draw on similar psychological and philosophical discourses when accounting for character-formation. What are we to make of this insight? How does it affect the authority of autobiography and its claims to 'truthfulness'?

3.9 'Reality is always romantic, though the romantic is not always real': the truth of autobiography

Autobiography is classified as non-fiction prose: the life it narrates or confesses to is that of the person who wrote it. Yet it is made of the same basic narrative material as the fictional novel (as noted in section 2.11, early examples of the novel as practised by Defoe presented themselves as truthful, confessional narratives). Accordingly, questions of veracity are often to the fore in the reading and discussion of autobiography. Autobiographers are usually the first to raise them: reflecting on the fact that his autobiography may emphasise the darker, more sombre episodes in his life, Bamford assures the reader that 'there may be some strong clouding here and there. There must be if truth and nature are adhered to, and from them we assuredly will not depart' (p. 51). At the same time as asserting the truth of his narrative, we can see from the quotation which heads this section (*Early Days*, p. 339) that Bamford conceded that there was also a 'romantic', or imaginative and figurative, dimension to this truth. Literary critics and cultural historians have, therefore, had to concern themselves with complex approaches to truth in autobiography.

In an attempt to devise a non-essentialist framework which might help to establish the 'truth' of an autobiographical text, the literary critic Elizabeth Bruss advocates a pragmatic, 'institutional' theory of the autobiographical genre. To this end she formulates a number of 'rules' which regulate the relationship between reader, text and autobiographer. One rule states that the existence of the individual who is autobiographer is independent of the text itself, and assumed to be susceptible to appropriate public verification procedures.[27] It is certainly the case that any reader of 1847 who went in search of the independent existence of Samuel Bamford would have had more success than a reader who sought out Jane Eyre: Bamford's social and political identity was in the public domain: he was, amongst other things, Manchester correspondent of the *Morning Herald*, and the writer Elizabeth Gaskell managed to locate him in order to deliver a volume of Tennyson's poems in 1849.[28]

But we cannot expect this rule to answer a different question. The question of Bamford's existence leaves aside the issue of the way in which Bamford's autobiographical text works to create effects of truthfulness. The impulse to verification that readers may feel is not so appropriate in this regard, even given Bamford's manifest desire to refer the reader to settings and objects in the community of Middleton:

> Beginning with the church, thou must know that externally it was in much the same state as at present. Internally, the chapel of the Asshetons would be somewhat different. The staircase mounting to that piece of 'pride' in a place of 'humility', the Suffield's pew, did not then cover up and obscure the grave-stone of Colonel Assheton, who commanded the Parliamentary forces of Lancashire during the Civil War of the Commonwealth. (p. 41)

This is very characteristic of Bamford's style in *Early Days*; in the way that relations of contiguity between objects are established in the quotation above, the autobiography begins with a genealogy which contextualises the narrator's place in the family history. It is very different from, for example, the first two paragraphs which open *Jane Eyre*, in which the action begins *in medias res*, and the isolation of the narrator is dramatised by contrasting use of pronouns ('we'/'I'). In addition, the grounds of Gateshead Hall figure incidentally as 'leafless shrubbery', creating the sense that place is subsumed into the barren, emotionally undernourished mood of the narrator (p. 39). For Bamford, place is described for itself, and its sense of actuality is created by a strategic 'that', which predicates 'Suffield's pew'. 'That' is an instance of what linguists call deixis, by which means the text employs a demonstrative to 'point' to something apparently outside itself. However, deixis is not necessarily an invitation to verify; its use at the beginning of George Eliot's *The Mill on the Floss* constructs a sense of immediacy with no extratextual reference: 'And this is Dorlcote Mill. I must stand a minute or two here on the bridge and look at it' (p. 55). Indeed, an excessive emphasis on verification misrecognises the reading relations into which we are invited. For deixis works together with direct address to the reader who is comfortable with archaisms; 'thou must know'. Bamford's address here implies a reader who belongs to his community and shares its sense of history: deixis rhetorically strengthens the imaginary bond. This anticipated identification is underpinned by what seem to be incidental details, but which are actually rich, and require a figurative interpretation grounded in culture and history. The fact that Colonel Assheton's tomb has been 'obscured' by the Suffield family's elevated private pew figuratively implies the view that the course of English history since Bamford's childhood has been dominated by the selfish creation of wealth, obscuring the Parliamentary victories of the Civil War which Assheton, in the name of liberty and the commonwealth, helped to lead; the archaic form of address to the reader perhaps indicates a romantic attitude towards a lost radical past which is being obliterated by a rapacious modernity.

Where does this leave the question of the truth of autobiography? Even though deixis is no guarantee of extratextual reference, we still have responsibilities to seek to contextualise realistic details which turn out to have a romantic inflection. For instance, Bamford's sense of his audience for *Early Days*, and his consequent use of direct address and deixis, may have been shaped by the knowledge that subscriptions were raised in the Manchester area to help towards the cost of publication; costs that were borne by the Londonbased but nationally networked commercial publishing house owned by George Smith in the case of *Jane Eyre*.[29]

Contexts are also linguistic, and can be inferred through textual details. Even if Bamford's autobiography casts a figurative inflection on its subject matter, this in no way diminishes the cultural significance that such subject matter imparts. Indeed, different emphases within ostensibly similar figurations can point to important social and cultural differences between a novel by a middleclass woman and an autobiography by a workingclass man. Thus, whilst Jane Eyre praises and validates the virtues of work and in dependence, it is Bamford's prose which describes in detail particular processes of work experienced in the course of a working life (see Chapter 25 of *Early Days*, entitled 'Warehouse Work Again'). And whilst both texts present the experience of love as being central to self-formation, they employ very different gendered conventions for narrating it. We saw in section 3.6 the place of the gothic in Brontë's *Jane Eyre*, and considered the gender politics it encoded for the nineteenth-century woman writer. By contrast, Bamford's *Early Days* contains a chapter entitled 'Love's Dawnings', and this key rite of passage in the narrative of self-formation takes its shape, language and intense introspective stance from Goethe's highly influential representation of male romantic love, *The Sorrows of Young Werther* (1774); 'I now became moody and melancholy, brooding over my ill success in courtship, and wondering how it happened that love like mine should go unrequited' (p. 181).

Non-fictional and fictional prose narratives consequently perform their sense of cultural belonging and alignment by virtue of the way in which they borrow conventions and idioms from different literary traditions. *Early Days* also weaves the supernatural into its narrative, but to rather different effect to that achieved by the use of the gothic supernatural in *Jane Eyre*. Bamford narrates in elaborate detail the superstitions and traditions of hauntings that surround Middleton, including one in which the presence of his mother's ghost is reported to him by his aunts. In its handling of this story, Bamford's autobiography announces a divided sense of belonging. Bamford represents his aunts' account of the sighting of his dead mother in direct-speech Lancashire dialect: '"I knew her the moment I set my een on her. Hoos comn fro' heaven, and hoo's gooin back theer"' (p. 146). Bamford represents his reply to the aunts by dramatising himself as a character in his own story. Addressing them through reported speech, he agrees with his aunts' sense of the 'haunting' quality of the place at which his mother's ghost has apparently been seen, but he does so in a register which implies a rather different kind of reader:

> 'Well, I cannot tell how it happens aunt, but I always feel so calm and soothed when at dusk I walk alone round the green, or sit on the bright grass under the trees. It seems as if I had all the company I desire: I can converse better with myself, as it were – can commune more deeply with my own feelings and thoughts in that lone spot than in any other ... I shall go there oftener.' (p. 147)

With its emphasis on the relationship between nature and solitary inwardness, Bamford's character speaks in the literary language of romantic sub-jectivity, much as we saw in the case of Jane Eyre in section 3.5. Figuratively, Bamford's autobiographical narrative has one foot in working-class Middle-ton, and another in Manchester's polite, literary culture. In a sense, literacy is a major subject in Bamford's life story (*bios*), and he narrates in some detail his self-education in reading. The literary language that Bamford has acquired provides a naturalistic sense of what it means to be haunted, which side-steps 'superstitious' belief in the actuality of the ghost. For Bamford, to be haunted is to commune and converse introspectively with the self. The 'journey' of self-education that Bamford has undertaken is performed at this moment, for to write in this way is an expressive sign of Bamford's cultivated and autonomous self (*autos*). However, this autonomous, solitary self is constructed through narrative: in practice the different registers and idioms of Bamford's autobiography suggest a viewpoint on his own life history which was divided between multiple sources of belonging.

3.10   Reading Elizabeth Gaskell's *The Life of Charlotte Brontë*: the rhetoric of biography

It is now commonplace to read *Jane Eyre* autobiographically: Jane Eyre's experience at Lowood appears to have its source in Charlotte Brontë's unhappy time at Cowan Bridge school in West Yorkshire. Yet, as I noted in section 3.7, following the initial pseudonymous publication of *Jane Eyre*, metropolitan literary intellectuals pondered rumours about the true identity of its author (it was rumoured that 'Currer Bell' was a male Lancashire weaver). For Charlotte Brontë's life to become public knowledge, it needed a biography: this was published in 1857 by Elizabeth Gaskell as *The Life of Charlotte Brontë*. Understandably, students of literature use biographies as tools, to be consulted as authoritative sources of scholarship. Biographers strive, on the basis of documentary and (where available) oral evidence, to reconstruct the chronological events comprising their subject's life and its meanings as accurately and dispassionately as possible. Elizabeth Gaskell's biography of Charlotte Brontë was researched and based on evidence.

Like autobiographies, biographies are narratives. Consequently, their transparency and objectivity can be demonstrated and accepted only to a point. As narratives, biographies are figuratively rich texts which are enmeshed with discourses of culture and, implicitly, participants in debates about the direction of culture. Elizabeth Gaskell's biography of Charlotte Brontë participates in a nineteenth-century cultural debate about the appropriateness of writing as a womanly vocation. As narratives, biographies represent characters and systems of evaluation made from the discourses also used by novels. For example, in Elizabeth Gaskell's *The Life of Charlotte Brontë*, discourses of physiognomy (see section 3.5) figure in the representation of character: in an extended description of Charlotte's appearance, the biographer recalls that her eyes gave access to inwardness 'as if some spiritual lamp had been kindled' (p. 76). It is the same physiognomical classification which accounts for her brother Branwell Brontë's character failings: 'there are coarse lines about the mouth, and the lips, though of handsome shape, are loose and thick, indicating self-indulgence, while the slightly retreating chin conveys an idea of weakness of will' (p. 146). In common with the first-person bildung narratives we have explored so far, Elizabeth Gaskell's biography narrates her subject's growth and development, taking childhood as the formative starting point: when Gaskell estimates an incident's 'effect upon the character of Charlotte Brontë', she urges the reader that 'we must remember that she was a sensitive and thoughtful child, capable of reflecting deeply, if not analysing truly' (p. 60). This is strikingly similar to the 'developmental' hypothesis in *Jane Eyre* which stated that 'children can feel, but they cannot analyse their feelings' (see section 3.5).

However, nineteenth-century biography often casts a quite different viewpoint on youth and formation because the motive for the writing resides in the subject's death. Readers are seldom allowed to forget that Charlotte is no more. The opening chapter, for instance, transcribes the inscription on Charlotte's gravestone; later on the biographer refers to the scrapbook of reviews of *Jane Eyre*, each review 'cut out and carefully ticketed with its date by the poor bereaved father, – so proud when he first read them – so desolate now' (p. 264).

The implied reader's response to this is shaped by a particular kind of address. So far in this chapter we have been reading first-person prose narratives, even though the narrator or autobiographer (fictive or actual) frequently narrates her or himself as a character in the story. In reading a biography – and even though therein we may read personal letters, or extracts from a journal – our response is shaped by a biographer; that is, a narrator who speaks of and for the memory of the central subject of the narrative in the third person. There is often a rhetorical purpose to this form of address, exemplified towards the end of Elizabeth Gaskell's narrative when she declares that 'to [the] Public I commit the memory of Charlotte Brontë' (p. 457). There are three points that we can pick up here which characterise biographical narrative: rhetoric, the invocation of memory, and the concept of the public, all of which are linked.

As we saw in Chapter 1, rhetoric has a persuasive function. Aristotle distinguished between three kinds of rhetoric: deliberative, forensic and epideictic. The first two were effective in the political and legal spheres respectively. The third, epideictic, was much wider ranging, classifying and codifying, for example, ways of articulating a panegyric, or encomium, or a funeral oration which emphasised to good effect the virtues of the person being spoken of (as we saw in section 3.2, for Bakhtin this kind of rhetoric generated the earliest forms of biography).[30] Rhetorical forms may of course be present in the novel and autobiography; indeed, Jane Eyre's address to the reader pleading the cause of the 'millions ... in silent revolt against their lot' (p. 141) could be categorised as a blend of deliberative and epideictic rhetoric. So too could Bamford's apostrophe to English labour in *Early Days*: 'Promote honest labour. Honour it wherever or however found. Have respect to the horny hand and the dewey forehead' (p. 210). In looking at biography, however, we are looking at a genre in which epideictic rhetoric, or the determination to persuade the public that the subject of the biography had led a good life, is a strong, framing presence.

It is significant that the subject's death and the memorial function of biography should be invoked in connection with public reactions to her writings, and the representation of private, family grief, for Gaskell's biography undertakes to make the private life of Charlotte Brontë known to the public. The first important modern biography in English was James Boswell's *Life of Samuel Johnson* (1791). Boswell's text was framed by the rhetorical impulse to defend and vindicate the memory of Samuel Johnson as a virtuous public man, in spite of his coarse and uncouth manner; and to claim for him the status of pre-eminent authority in literary culture. Victorian biographies of writers were at once justifications of the kinds of life that their subjects led, and assessments of their place in, and degree of belonging to, literary culture. Consequently, Elizabeth Gaskell works in the characteristic manner of the modern biographer after Boswell, commemorating Charlotte Brontë by showing to the public her character as revealed in private letters and testimonies of those who knew her. Charlotte Brontë's letters often take the form either of narratives or of journal-like exercises for self-exploration (see for instance pp. 163–4), which 'show her character' (p. 266) as Gaskell remarks.

But installing a character in the public sphere is a potentially controversial activity which shapes, and exploits, the specific rhetorical traits of biography. More specifically still, we have to acknowledge another manifestation of gendered domestic ideology as one of the factors that made a woman biographer's account of Charlotte Brontë as a private woman and public writer much more difficult to shape and place before 'the public'.

3.11   Biography, gender and the public position of the woman writer: negotiating 'realism' and 'romance'

I observed in section 3.7 that *Jane Eyre* has come to be seen as an important contribution to a tradition of women's novel writing. Elizabeth Gaskell's biography of Charlotte Brontë helped to promote it as such, in that it raised the question of the public status of the woman writer. The epigraph which Gaskell attached to the title page of her narrative clearly signifies this: it is from Elizabeth Barrett Browning's poem *Aurora Leigh* (1857) which was about a woman poet and had plot similarities to *Jane Eyre*. The lines: "'Oh My God, / – Thou hast knowledge, only Thou, / How dreary 'tis for women to sit still / On winter nights by solitary fires / And hear the nations praising them far off'". Ann Marie Ross has drawn attention to what may be described, following critics such as Elaine Showalter, as the gynocentric strategies and rhythms of novelistic narration which Gaskell – a significant woman novelist in her own right – wove into her memorial of another woman writer. Ross concludes that 'Gaskell viewed Brontë as a member of a "community of women" artists', which makes a strong claim about the terms of literary belonging that Gaskell asserts, jointly, for Charlotte Brontë and her own biographical account of Brontë's character-formation.[31] At the same time, the lines from Barrett Browning are about the constraints imposed on women by domestic confinement, and suggest something of the difficulty that Elizabeth Gaskell faced in writing a public account of the life of a woman who, imaginatively at least, sought to break with powerful social conventions.

I argued in section 3.10 that biographies are narratives which at some level rhetorically justify the moral lives of their subjects and, in the case of writers, make claims for their terms of belonging to literary culture. However, Elizabeth Gaskell, in justifying Charlotte Brontë's memory to the public, had to confront a domestic ideology which held that leading the life of a good woman was incompatible with being a writer. This ideology is set out clearly in Robert Southey's reply to Charlotte Brontë's request for a writer's advice on the vocation of writing, which Elizabeth Gaskell includes in her narrative: Southey opines that 'the more she is engaged in her proper [domestic] duties, the less leisure she will have for it [writing]' (p. 123).

This ideology frames the biographer's account of Charlotte Brontë's writing habits:

> Sometimes weeks or even months elapsed before she felt she had anything to add to that portion of her story which was already written. Then, some morning she would waken up, and the progress of her tale lay clear and bright before her, in distinct vision. When this was the case, all her care was to discharge her house-hold and filial duties, so as to obtain leisure to sit down and write out the inci-dents and consequent thoughts which were, in fact, more present to her mind at such times than her actual life itself. Yet notwithstanding this 'possession' (as it were), those who survive, of her daily and household companions, are clear in their testimony, that never was the claim of any duty, never was the call of another for help, neglected for an instant. (pp. 245–6)

We might note here that the authority for this account rests with the 'clear testimony' of domestic witnesses, so the biographer's rhetoric stresses evi-dence and actuality. This allows the biographer to negotiate the proscription on women's writing by domestic ideology. Charlotte Brontë was both a good, self-sacrificing domestic woman and a writer. But we need to look carefully at the terms that the biographer uses to describe Brontë's mental state when writing, because they carry resonant cultural evaluations: 'fic-tions' are 'more present to her mind ... than her actual life itself', which is tantamount to '"possession"'. In other words, Brontë was haunted by an imagination that was in tension with, even if it did not disrupt, the workaday world of domestic responsibility. The biographer is working with an opposition between 'romance' and 'realism'. These underpin the biographer's construction of the divisions and conflicts between the roles of domestic woman and romantic woman writer:

> Henceforward Charlotte Brontë's existence becomes divided into two parallel currents – her life as Currer Bell, the author; her life as Charlotte Brontë, the woman. There were separate duties belonging to each character – not opposing each other; not impossible, but difficult to be reconciled. (p. 271)

As in the case of Samuel Bamford, cultural conflict and tension divide the terms on which Charlotte Brontë belongs to a community.

This has led the feminist literary critic Deirdre D'Albertis to read Gaskell's biography of Charlotte Brontë as a comment on divisions which had broader implications for the direction and purpose of narrative itself, both fictional and non-fictional. According to D'Albertis, there is a funda- mental difference between Brontë and Gaskell as novelists: Charlotte Brontë's tendency to privilege introspective, tortured, romantic subjectivities was not shared by Elizabeth Gaskell, whose novels adopted an external viewpoint and sought to dramatise shared suffering, and thereby to spread sympathy in an imagined community, exemplified in *Mary Barton* (1848) and *North and South* (1855). Both novels narrate the social suffering brought about by industrial society and the conflict between social classes to which it gives rise; Gaskell's third-person narration seeks to represent the points of view of these classes and to generate understanding and sympathy between them. D'Albertis argues that 'If Brontë embraced the blending of narrator and heroine in her fiction, Gaskell … preferred the detachment and control exercised by the writer of others' lives.'[32] Gaskell's biography of the intro- spective Brontë can be read as enacting the triumph of Gaskell's convictions about the true value of narrative: its capacity to demonstrate the judgemental and sympathetic power of 'realism' over introspective 'romance'. This read- ing of Elizabeth Gaskell's *Life of Charlotte Brontë*, as a form of non-fictional prose narrative which implicitly contributed to a debate about the continu- ing refinement of the cultural functions of narrative at times of profound change, brings us to the novels of, arguably, the most important English novelist of the nineteenth century, George Eliot (Marian Evans).

3.12   Reading George Eliot's *The Mill on the Floss*: culture as 'incarnate history'

George Eliot's *The Mill on the Floss* was published in 1860. Set in the provincial England of the 1820s, it tells the story of the long-established Tulliver family, millers who possess but then disastrously are dispossessed of Dorlcote Mill by processes of change which the head of the family no longer understands. Its main drama is concerned with the youth, formation and tragic end of the brother and sister characters, the practical and un- imaginative Tom and the romantic, spontaneous Maggie; it is another example of the bildungsroman in which romance collides with realism. In many respects George Eliot's formal narrative practice resembles Elizabeth

Gaskell's (and indeed Jane Austen's), given its use of the third-person voice and its realist preference for the management of subordinate character voices to generate appropriate measures of 'sympathy'. In outline such practices are accounted for in Ian Watt's idea of 'realism of assessment', which he applied to the narrative methods of Fielding (see section 2.12). But by the middle of the nineteenth century, and in George Eliot's hands, realist fiction embraced more ambitious intellectual discourses and social aims, which were first articulated in Eliot's journalistic work.

It is in this context that we should read Marian Evans's 'The Natural History of German Life', a review of a book of German ethnography and sociology which appeared in 1856 in the *Westminster Review*, two years before she began to publish fiction under the name of 'George Eliot'. This review essay explores the role of artistic narratives in generating 'sympathy' and mutual understanding between disparate communities in the context of a rapidly changing society and class structure. For although the essay is about peasant life in central Europe, it begins by reflecting on the modernising phenomenon of the railways in Britain, which connected communities geographically whilst dividing them socially. The essayist notes that the word 'railway' would be likely to generate very different associations to people of different social classes, depending on whether they were working navvies who had built the structures, or middle-class people who used them for speedy travel (p. 260).[33]

The essay explores the 'character' type of the German peasantry, especially its unbending obligation to family ties, and 'its inveterate habit of litigation' (p. 272). These concerns indicate the extent to which the essay is under-pinned by a so-called 'anthropological' understanding of 'culture', or the total way of life of a particular community. This anthropological discourse about 'culture' became increasingly authoritative as the century progressed, in large part because of the emergence of scientific anthropological work on 'primitive' societies and the 'evidence' it yielded about evolutionary developments towards advanced civilisation.[34] At the same time, a strong sense of cultures and communities as 'incarnate history' was already established as yet another legacy of romanticism – particularly German Romanticism – and its interest in the archaic status of folk cultures. This helped to shape the highly influential period and historical romances of Walter Scott, known as the Waverley novels: *Waverley* (1814), in its account of Charles Edward Stuart's 1745 Scottish rebellion seen through the eyes of the young English soldier Edward Waverley, pitted the feudal culture of the

Scottish Highlands against the modernising forces of the eighteenth-century English state.

A similar sense of opposing currents in history is explored in 'The Natural History of German Life' when it alludes to the role of the peasantry in the German revolution of 1848 (see sections 3.3 and 3.7). The typical peasant's obstructiveness and suspicion is noted: 'His chief idea of a govern-ment is of a power that raises his taxes [and] opposes his harmless customs' (p. 276). However, modernising governments themselves were hampered by as blinkered and self-regarding a vision; 'seen from the windows of ducal palaces and ministerial hotels ... it was imagined that [the peasants] had a common plan of co-operation' – which, given the peasants' view of governance, was not the case at all (p. 278). This stress on limited points of view leads to the call for the establishment of an authoritative arbiter between the restricted points of view held by different social classes, and the essay appoints art – particularly narrative art – to this powerful role of 'awakening ... social sympathies' by 'amplifying experience and extending our contact with our fellow-men beyond the bounds of our personal lot' (p. 264). The essayist contends that 'a wise social policy must be based on the Natural History of social bodies', and the novel which observes 'real life', rather than stereotypical conventions evident in jovial peasants from the idealist, pastoral tradition, has an important educative role to play (p. 285).

As we move from Marian Evans's critical essay to the novel entitled *The Mill on the Floss* by George Eliot, we need to bear in mind that in 'The Natural History of German Life' language is conceptualised through its resistance to schematic idealisms, and consequently valued for the imaginative complexities it can produce by virtue of its historical 'anomalies and inconveniencies'(p. 283). We should not assume that George Eliot's theory of realism is based on a naive attachment to mimesis or reflection. *The Mill on the Floss* is a novel steeped in narrative complexities which demonstrates a dense engagement with, and reflexivity about, language and representation.

3.13   'Writing the history of unfashionable families': the workings of Eliot's 'realism'

The Mill on the Floss describes itself as a 'history of unfashionable families' (p. 385). It does so within a narrative framework which accounts for oppos-ing currents of history. First, vestiges of the kind of archaic peasant culture described in 'The Natural History of German Life' are present in the Tulliver family's constitution: family ties and obligations are paramount, and Mr Tulliver treats litigation as though it were 'the custom of the country' (and his failure to recognise the law as an impersonal system is the source of his family's catastrophic fall). Secondly, 'history' figures dimly as the distant but developing modern English liberal state of the 1820s, made present through allusions to the controversy surrounding its proposal to extend forms of social toleration such as Catholic Emancipation. These are historical currents which play upon the fears and Protestant prejudices of 'unfashionable' families. But these families have a perspective which the narrator wishes us to hear:

> Uncle Pullett sat by and listened with twinkling eyes to these high matters. He didn't understand politics himself – thought they were a natural gift – but by what he could make out, this Duke of Wellington was no better than he should be. (p. 133)

The dramatisation of limited points of view on historical progress is realised through focalisation which privileges 'unfashionable' social types such as Uncle Pullett, whose voice we hear through free indirect speech.

The 'hearing' of voices is important in *The Mill on the Floss*. The reader experiences the mimetic pleasures of direct speech: George Eliot, in common with Scott, Samuel Bamford and Elizabeth Gaskell, uses direct speech as an opportunity to incorporate stylised dialects other than standard English in order to create a more authentic sense of ordinary life, as in this exchange from the beginning of the novel between Mr and Mrs Tulliver, who are discussing Tom Tulliver's future education:

> 'You mustn't put a spoke i' the wheel about the washin', if we can't get a school near enough. That's the fault I find wi' you, Bessy: if you see a stick i' the road, you're allays thinkin' you can't step over it. You'd want me not to hire a waggoner, 'cause he'd got a mole on his face.'
>
> 'Dear heart!' said Mrs Tulliver in mild surprise, 'when did I iver make objections to a man, because he'd got a mole on his face? I'm sure I'm rether fond o' the moles, for my brother, as is dead an' gone, had a mole on his brow ...'
>
> 'No, no, Bessy; I didn't mean justly the mole; I meant it to stand for summat else; but niver mind .... It's an uncommon puzzling thing to know what school to pick.'
>
> Mr Tulliver paused a minute or two, and dived with both hands into his breeches' pockets as if he hoped to find some suggestion there. (pp. 57–8)

The reader is invited to acknowledge a hierarchy within this exchange; Mrs Tulliver's prosaic and family-centred world view is contrasted with and subordinate to Mr Tulliver's figurative, outward-looking, problem-solving assault on the world. But at the apex of the hierarchy is the 'omniscient' narrative voice, which objectifies both speech and speakers, and knows more about the chracters than they can ever know of each other, or indeed themselves; Mr Tulliver does not know that the act of digging his hands into his pockets betrays his utter loss as to how to proceed with planning Tom's education, but the narrator's commentary does.

Tom's formation is a topic of discussion between others – he is absent – and the framework for his formation is haphazardly cobbled together by family and community: Tom is not present at his own cultivation, and those who plan it are mired in narrowness and ignorance. George Eliot's narrative voice becomes a highly sophisticated device for tracing the webs within which Tom's development is imagined and temporarily stunted. Chapter 3, in which Tulliver consults the auctioneer Riley about Tom's education, and Riley responds by recommending the services of Stelling, a young clergyman to whom he is related, is a good example of the strategies of the narrative voice.

The reader discovers, from Riley's direct speech, that he has a family of unmarried daughters to keep, and that he is consequently short of cash (p. 69). However, the stark interpretation – that the self-interested Riley will benefit financially from the recommendation of Stelling – is coloured in shades of grey by the narrator. In a long commentary (see pp. 75–7), the narrative voice ironically, yet sympathetically, traces the dimly conceived rationale behind Riley's advice. Riley, we are told, is acting both self-interestedly and without secure foundation for his recommendation; he may indirectly be rewarded for the recommendation but knows nothing of Stelling's suitability. And yet, it is more important for the narrator to trace how he hides that from himself and others through his sense of self-importance and the family and community obligations which shape his sense of self. The narrative voice comments reflexively on its 'findings', and on its own refusal of melodramatic oppositions between guilt and innocence, and evil and good motives: 'Plotting covetousness and deliberate contrivance in order to compass a selfish end, are nowhere in abundance but in the world of the dramatist' (pp. 74–5). Thus, negative allusions to 'artificial' dramatic modes help to define the narrative voice's sense of its access to the 'realistic' representation of motive and action.

The narrative voice is at the apex of a hierarchy of character discourses, whilst managing their various relations of authority. The reader is invited to be sympathetic to the ignorant and self-important such as Riley, yet this does not protect these characters from the narrator's irony. By contrast, as heroine, Maggie's discourse is valued more than the discourse of any other character. If Tom's education is decided by others, Maggie's formation is dramatised for the reader through the detailed representation of her inwardness. In the first books of the novel, Maggie's romantic childhood inner world is rendered in rich detail. But unlike the effect of a Charlotte Brontë novel, inwardness is not permitted to stand as an authoritative viewpoint by itself, for it requires some external perspective from which to be judged. After the family's fall, Maggie Tulliver's 'enthusiastic' inner spiritual craving for the religious writings of a medieval monk, Thomas à Kempis, is presented as the best, but still severely limited, inner life that a gifted young woman such as Maggie can cultivate in intellectually and socially straitened circum-stances. These circumstances have presented her with 'shreds and patches of feeble literature and false history' but no sense, as the narrator teaches, 'of the irreversible laws' which form, 'through generations of painful toil', morals, religion or 'culture' in its anthropological sense (p. 381).

In making this judgement clear to the reader the narrative voice confronts the topic of irony, which is directed in more or less gentle doses towards certain of the characters. This commentary on irony is characteristic of George Eliot's realism in that it initiates a discourse which invites the reader to grasp a whole web of social relations:

> In writing the history of unfashionable families, one is apt to fall into a tone of emphasis which is very far from being the tone of good society, where principles and beliefs are not only of an extremely moderate kind, but are always presupposed, no subjects being eligible but such as can be touched with a light and graceful irony. But then, good society has its claret and its velvet carpets, its dinner-engagements six weeks deep .... But good society, floated on gossamer wings of light irony, is of very expensive production; requiring nothing less than a wide and arduous national life condensed in unfragrant, deafening factories, cramping itself in mines, sweating at furnaces, grinding, hammering, weaving under more or less oppression of carbonic acid ... This wide national life is based entirely on emphasis – the emphasis of want, which urges it into all the activities necessary for the maintenance of good society and light irony. (p. 385)

In this passage, the narrative voice begins in an almost self-admonitory manner: unfashionable topics, such as Maggie's poorly cultivated inner life, lead one to write, regrettably, in an unfashionable style which offends the canon of taste as defined by 'good society' and its preferred tone of 'light

irony'. 'Tone' makes the reader aware that 'good society' is based on preferred idioms, thus implicating literature and literacy in what becomes its
polemic. For there is irony here at light irony's expense, and it arises out of
the way the narrative voice constructs an opposition between surface
appearances and understanding in depth. The only depth to be found in
good society is in the volume of dinner engagements to which it is committed. This in turn is contrasted with depth of understanding, which is
vested in the narrative voice's knowledge of the increasingly industrialised
labour of ordinary working life, on the basis of which national life is
reproduced and resourced. The steps from Maggie's frustrated inner life to
the harsh material conditions of national life which perpetuate its frustration
are a good example of Eliot's realism. But that broadening of social
understanding and sympathy which that realism invites was simultaneously
an interrogation of received modes of writing and speech.

3.14   Testing 'self-culture': 'eddication' and the role of the reader in Eliot's realism

Contrasting gendered experiences of formation or bildung produce a
central irony on which *The Mill on the Floss* turns. Tom is subjected to a
masculine 'eddication' in classics and geometry for which he has no
aptitude, and this actually stifles his formation. He is only liberated,
ironically, after the family's fall, which requires him to develop practical
entrepreneurial skills: Tom makes enough money to enable the family to
purchase the mill again. In contrast Maggie, who is bright, bookish and
intellectually curious about Latin, is denied access to the very education that
would enable her to flourish and develop, because of gender. As dutiful
daughter she is confined to the home after the family's fall, fitfully sustains her
inner life through the self-renunciating doctrines of Thomas à Kempis,
becomes a governess but, unlike Jane Eyre, fails to marry the wealthy man
(heir to a trading fortune). Instead she disgraces herself in the eyes of her
community by seeming to elope with him. She returns, only to drown along
with Tom in a dramatic flood as the river Floss bursts its banks.

Is this a satisfactory story? Some readers have thought not, but then the
narrative voice draws attention to the language that characters have used for
shaping Tom and Maggie's lives into stories. Having been committed to the
inappropriate pedagogic supervision of the Rev. Mr Stelling, Tom flounders
dismally under the regime of instruction instituted by the *Eton Latin*

Grammar. The narration reflects on Tom's difficulties, using Stelling as a focaliser:

> Mr Stelling concluded that Tom's brain being peculiarly impervious to etymology and demonstrations, was peculiarly in need of being ploughed ... it was his favourite metaphor, that the classics and geometry constituted that culture of the mind which prepared it for the reception of any subsequent crop.

Stelling articulates the powerful nineteenth-century theory of the classics as the highest source of 'self-culture', and Stelling's choice of a metaphor from crop-husbandry clearly illustrates the origins of this 'organic' theory of character growth.[35] At this point, the narrator intervenes ironically to challenge this metaphor:

> I say nothing against Mr Stelling's theory: if we are to to have one regimen for all minds his seems to me as good as any other. I only know it turned out as uncomfortably for Tom Tulliver as if he had been plied with cheese in order to remedy a gastric weakness which prevented him from digesting it. It is astonishing what a different result one gets by changing the metaphor! Once call the brain an intellectual stomach, and one's ingenious conception of the classics and geometry as ploughs and harrows seems to settle nothing. (pp. 208–9)

The narrator reflects on the radically different ways in which the formation of character can be described. But there is also an acknowledgement of the power of language – not just Latin, but language about Latin, justifying its worth – in forming practices that are commonly held to shape character. What is more, the reader is asked to acknowledge a challenge to it.

'Realist' narration may be complex, striving for a truthful understanding of the world; but as George Eliot's use of it illustrates, it has a very clear sense of the social conventions that its preferred representations are shaping themselves against. The implied reader's habitual recognition of conventions for describing educational progress is challenged by a change of metaphor, and this suggests something important about the dynamic and educative reading relations in which Eliot's narrative imagined itself to participate. The problem that this addressed was theorised by the journalist and man of letters George Henry Lewes – George Eliot's partner – in his scientific theories of sensation and mental association. In *The Physiology of Common Life*, which was written while George Eliot was working on her own narrative representation of common life in *The Mill on the Floss*, Lewes confronts the problem of forms of speech which have become habitual and non-reflective: 'We utter, as meaningless expletives, phrases which originally cost us trouble to learn.'[36] There has been a tendency for some strands of recent criticism to argue that Eliot's realism effectively pacifies its readers, didactically shoring up received ideas.[37] In historical context, viewed in relation to Victorian theories of mental activity and reception, it can be argued that Eliot's narratives sought to enter into dynamic, educative but interrogative relations with readers and their reserves of cultural knowledge.

Significant novel writing is invariably innovatory in the ways in which it can absorb, whilst testing, the boundaries of genres and received forms of discourse. In Eliot's innovative fiction writing, 'art' was conceived as a vehicle which would mediate a higher social lesson. In the next chapter we will move towards an account of a different kind of innovatory energy in the practice of fiction: one in which the shaping and integrative power of 'art' is proclaimed as an end in itself. However, our critical practice will need to remain aware of the social contexts within which such proclamations were made.

Notes

1. Although it is not the best example of the form in Austen's work; that is probably either *Pride and Prejudice* or *Mansfield Park*.
2. Franco Moretti, *The Way of the World: The 'Bildungsroman' in European Culture* (London: Verso, 1987), pp. 3, 227.
3. See *OED*, and John Dryden, *On Dramatic Poesy and Other Critical Essays*, Everyman, 2 vols (London: Dent, 1964), 2, pp. 1–13.
4. M. M. Bakhtin, *Dialogic Imagination*, trans. Caryl Emerson and Michael Holquist (Austin: University of Texas Press, 1981), pp. 130–46.
5. Bakhtin, *Dialogic Imagination*, p. 141.
6. See the famous example of the Roman emperor Marcus Aurelius (AD 121–80), whose *Meditations* begin with an account of the virtues he has learned to imitate from his family teachers, and then branches into more general philosophical reflections on the practice of living.
7. See *OED*: 'this very amusing and unique specimen of autobiography', *Q.Rev.*, 1, 1809, 283; the *OED* 2nd edition has located an earlier, more tentative use: 'it is not very usual in English to employ hybrid words partly Saxon and partly Greek; yet *autobiography* would have seemed pedantic', *Monthly Review*, 2nd ser., XXIV, 1797, 375. This process of venturing and then drawing back from a neologism is perhaps indicative of the way in which new words enter into circulation. Clearly Southey did not 'invent' the word.
8. Hegel, 13 October 1806, in Joseph Hoffmeister (ed.), *Letters*, 4 vols (Hamburg: Felix Meiner, 1961), I, p. 120, cited in Martin Travers, *An Introduction to*

Modern European Literature: From Romanticism to Postmodernism (London: Macmillan, 1998), pp. 4, 249.

9. Stendhal, *Scarlet and Black*, trans. Margaret Shaw (Harmondsworth: Penguin, 1953), p. 110.

10. A note on editions used in this chapter. Charlotte Brontë, *Jane Eyre*, Penguin English Library edition (Harmondsworth: Penguin, 1966), ed. Q. D. Leavis, follows the third edition of 1848. Samuel Bamford's *Early Days* is vol. 1 of a two-volume edition entitled *Passages in the Life of a Radical and Early Days*, ed. Henry Dunckley (London: T. Fisher Unwin, 1893). Elizabeth Gaskell, *The Life of Charlotte Brontë*, World's Classics Edition, ed. Angus Easson (Oxford: Oxford University Press, 1996), follows the third edition of 1857. George Eliot, *The Mill on the Floss*, ed. A. S. Byatt, Penguin English Library edition (Harmondsworth: Penguin, 1979), follows the first edition. Bamford's *Early Days* is the only one that is, sadly, out of print (though Oxford University Press published an edition of *Passages* in 1984). References to the texts will be given in parentheses.

11. Johann Wolfgang von Goethe, *Wilhelm Meister's Apprenticeship and Trials*, trans. Thomas Carlyle (London: Chapman and Hall, 1890), translator's preface to the first edition, p. 5.

12. Although it may sometimes be difficult to get access to the originals, the study of the critical reception of nineteenth-century fiction has been assisted enormously by the series published in the 1970s, entitled 'The Critical Heritage', which issued volumes devoted to the reception of the work of particular authors. In sections 3.4 and 3.7 I shall draw on the selection of reviews reprinted in Miriam Allott (ed.), *The Brontës* (London: Routledge and Kegan Paul, 1974). Allot's volume also contains a useful record of reviews of Elizabeth Gaskell's *The Life of Charlotte Brontë*, which will be discussed in sections 3.10–11, itself an important moment in the reception of Charlotte Brontë's work.

13. Allott, *The Brontës*, pp. 67–8.

14. Allott, *The Brontës*, p. 108.

15. For a study which exemplifies this approach see Sally Shuttleworth, *Charlotte Brontë and Victorian Psychology* (Cambridge: Cambridge University Press, 1996).

16. Jenny Bourne Taylor and Sally Shuttleworth (eds), *Embodied Selves: An Anthology of Psychological Texts* (Oxford: Clarendon Press, 1998); see pp. 29–41 for Combe's classificatory system and the way in which it figured in Charlotte Brontë's *The Professor*, written 1846, published 1857. Karen Chase has explored the place of physiognomy and phrenology in Charlotte Brontë's fiction in *Eros and Psyche: The Representation of Personality in Charlotte Brontë, Charles Dickens and George Eliot* (New York and London: Routledge, 1984).

17. See Michel Foucault, *Discipline and Punish: The Birth of the Prison*, 1975, trans. Alan Sheridan (Harmondsworth: Penguin, 1991).

18. See Paul Rabinow's introduction to his *Foucault Reader* (Harmondsworth: Penguin, 1984), pp. 10–11.

19. Ellen Moers, *Literary Women*, 1976, intro. Helen Taylor (London: Women's Press, 1986), Chapter 5, 'Female Gothic'.

20. The classic studies are Sandra M. Gilbert and Susan Gubar, *The Madwoman in the Attic: The Woman Writer and the Nineteenth-Century Literary Imagination* (New Haven, CT: Yale University Press, 1979), and Elaine Showalter, *A Literature of their Own: British Woman Novelists from Brontë to Lessing* (London: Virago, 1978).

21. Gayatri Chakravorty Spivak, 'Three Women's Texts and a Critique of Imperialism', *Critical Inquiry* 12:1 (1985), pp. 243–61.

22. Patsy Stoneman has traced the process by which *Jane Eyre* was incorporated into a field of mid century debates and discussions between women novelists and critics about 'the woman's novel'; the other principal channel of appropriation was the stage melodrama: see Patsy Stoneman, *Brontë Transformations: The Cultural Dissemination of 'Jane Eyre' and 'Wuthering Heights'* (Hemel Hempstead: Prentice Hall/Harvester Wheatsheaf, 1996).

23. Allott, *The Brontës*, p. 116.

24. Chartism was a major British political protest movement of the 1830s and 1840s; Rigby's review appeared in December 1848, a significant year in Chartist agitation; Allott, *The Brontës*, pp. 109–10.

25. Allott, *The Brontës*, p. 26; see Clement Shorter, *Charlotte Brontë and Her Circle* (London: Hodder and Stoughton, 1896), pp. 348–9.

26. For associationist theories of character development, see Bourne Taylor and Shuttleworth, *Embodied Selves*, pp. 73–101.

27. Elizabeth Bruss, *Autobiographical Acts: The Changing Situation of a Literary Genre* (Baltimore and London: Johns Hopkins University Press, 1976), pp. 10–11.

28. Elizabeth Gaskell, letter to John Forster, 7 December 1849, in J. A.V. Chapple and Arthur Pollard (eds), *The Letters of Mrs Gaskell*, 1966 (Manchester: Mandolin, 1997), pp. 94–5.

29. See Martin Hewitt, 'Radicalism and the Victorian Working Class: The Case of Samuel Bamford', *Historical Journal* 34:4 (1991), 873–92; Hewitt reports that the *Manchester Courier* called for subscribers on 15 May 1847 (p. 876).

30. The best general history of rhetoric as a system is Brian Vickers, *In Defence of Rhetoric* (Oxford: Clarendon Press, 1988); see esp. Chapter 1. A very useful book on the applicability of rhetoric to literary study is by Dick Leith and George Myerson, *The Power of Address: Explorations in Rhetoric* (London: Routledge, 1989).

31. Ann Marie Ross, 'Honoring the Woman as Writer: Elizabeth Gaskell's *Life of Charlotte Brontë*', *Nineteenth-Century Prose* 22.2 (fall 1995), pp. 25–38.

32. Deirdre D'Albertis, '"Bookmaking out of the Remains of the Dead": Elizabeth Gaskell's *The Life of Charlotte Brontë*', *Victorian Studies* 39:1 (autumn 1995), pp. 1–31, 18.

33. References are to the text of 'The Natural History of German Life' which appears in Rosemary Ashton (ed.), *George Eliot: Selected Critical Writings*, World's Classics edition (Oxford and New York: Oxford University Press, 1992).

34. See E. B. Tylor, *Primitive Culture*, 1871. Charles Darwin's *The Origin of Species*, although seemingly narrowly focused on an argument about the evolution of biological species, had an enormous methodological impact. It was published in 1859, just one year before *The Mill on the Floss*.

35. These origins have been traced in Raymond Williams's philological study of the word 'culture' in English; see his *Keywords: A Vocabulary of Culture and Society*, 2nd edition (London: Fontana, 1983).

36. George Henry Lewes, *The Physiology of Common Life*, 2 vols (London: William Blackwood and Sons, 1859–60), II, pp. 58–60, quoted from Bourne Taylor and Shuttleworth, *Embodied Selves*, pp. 87–8.

37. Colin McCabe elaborated the case against George Eliot in the first chapter of his book about James Joyce, entitled *James Joyce and the Revolution of the Word* (London: Macmillan, 1978); Catherine Belsey extended it in her *Critical Practice* (London: Methuen, 1980). Both books made important contributions to the development of a poststructuralist literary critical practice. For a good, lucid introductory account of the intellectual aims of these poststructuralist critiques of George Eliot, see the entries on Belsey and McCabe by Antony Easthope in Stuart Sim (ed.), *The A/Z Guide to Modern Literary and Cultural Theorists* (Hemel Hempstead: Harvester Wheatsheaf, 1995).

Innovative stories and distinctive readers

4.1 The art of prose narrative

In 1842, the American writer and critic Edgar Allan Poe explained why he conceived of the short 'prose tale' as a distinctive form of art: 'The tale proper, in our opinion, affords unquestionably the fairest field for the exercise of the loftiest talent which can be afforded by the wide domains of mere prose.'[1] On the one hand there are the 'wide domains of mere prose': as we saw in section 1.2, prose – straightforward discourse – is defiantly ordinary. On the other hand there is the tale, a condensed narrative which asks to be handled by the 'loftiest talent', or authors who can exploit its artistic potential. This has been achieved when the sensitive reader experiences a 'unity of effect or impression' which is more usually encountered during the reading of the densely stylised and patterned discourse of poetry. Thus, the best kind of prose tale can achieve a unified, poetic effect, whilst it can treat a much wider variety of subject matters than poetry (prose still traverses a 'table-land of far vaster extent').

Poe's statement accounts for the aesthetic energy of certain kinds of prose narrative, and the effects of this energy on the reader. As such it offers a gateway to this chapter, which will explore ways of reading artistically self-conscious trends in novel writing and fictional prose narrative – including the prose tale or short story – in the nineteenth century and early decades of the twentieth century. It will explore how and why such narratives were shaped into distinctive and innovative forms of art.

But first we have to negotiate a question: have not the narratives that we have explored so far transformed the 'straightforward discourse' of prose into artefacts of distinctiveness? Of course, novels and narratives from given periods settle upon conventions which can easily become formulaic; but as the last two chapters have demonstrated, from the period of its English origins the novel has always had the potential to embrace innovatory energies, borrowing from other genres of prose narrative and non-narrative discourse, and in the process demonstrating a capacity to generate 'new' forms of expression, as the name 'novel' suggests. But in the last decades of the nineteenth century and early decades of the twentieth century, select novelists self-consciously rejected their inherited traditions of realism and became radically experimental. Accordingly the period has been viewed as 'transitional', and the artistic phenomenon which the transition heralded has come to be known as 'Modernism'.

'Modernism' as a literary-historical category was constructed in the 1950s in an attempt to create a homogeneous artistic and intellectual movement out of tremendous historical diversity.[2] Noting this, I shall use the term 'experimental' to describe narratives by writers such as Katherine Mansfield and Virginia Woolf, writers who are generally referred to as 'Modernists'. In steering a path through this diversity, the discussion will distinguish between the various sources of innovation and distinctiveness in narrative art. These sources will include the emergence of poetically inflected prose styles; increasingly self-conscious critical reflections on the form and scope of storytelling, in particular the emergence of the short story and its relation to the novel; narratives which foreground the voice and subjectivity of characters whilst rejecting the authoritative impositions of a realist narrator; and the emergence of a culturally distinctive implied reader who is, above all, a close reader. The texts we will focus on are Charles Dickens's *Bleak House*; Henry James's *The Spoils of Poynton*; H. G. Wells's *Ann Veronica*; Thomas Hardy's story 'The Withered Arm', and Katherine Mansfield's story 'The Garden Party'; and Virginia Woolf's *Mrs Dalloway*, as well as a selection of critical texts by James, Wells and Woolf. The discussion will be framed by a context which we have been tracing since Chapter 2: social and cultural modernisation and the development of new popular reading experiences which intensified the struggle to produce 'distinctiveness'.

4.2   Charles Dickens's *Bleak House*: reading the estranging poetry of prose

From one point of view, Charles Dickens is a Victorian novelist. Because Dickens addressed the social transformations of the early and mid-Victorian periods through his powerful and widely read fictions, he was seen as a figure who entertained an homogeneous middle-class readership whilst pricking their collective social conscience.[3] From a later point of view Dickens was seen as a transitional figure: in the 1920s the novelist and intellectual Percy Wyndham-Lewis claimed that Dickens's earliest novel (*Pickwick Papers*, 1837) displayed a level of stylistic and narrative innovation that anticipated Modernism.[4] *Bleak House* (1852–3) is a challenging novel to read because of its narrative and stylistic complexity. How are we to read, but also contextualise, such complexity?

Dickens constructs a labyrinthine mystery story; *Bleak House* is the first English novel to boast, in Mr Bucket, a police detective character. The multi-plot story gradually reveals a web of connections between a maze-like law case in Chancery (Jarndyce and Jarndyce), illegitimacy, and a multitude of characters inhabiting a wide range of places and social roles, from country estate-dwelling aristocrats (Sir Leicester and Lady Dedlock) to urban social outcasts (Jo, the crossing-sweeper). In its attempt imaginatively to grasp a whole society the novel employs a complex narrative framework, comprising two discrete methods of narration. First, there is the illegitimate Esther Summerson's first-person past-tense narration. Secondly, there is an omnipresent (able to move freely between characters and situations) third-person narrative voice, which creates a contrasting effect of immediacy by telling the story in a tense known as the historic-present (in which the verbs are all present tense, though the actions to which they refer are past, in common with all narrated acts).

With this latter method of narration, Dickens is able to generate some arresting and indeed estranging effects. Here, the omnipresent narrative voice focalises through Jo the crossing-sweeper, and the topic of the passage is 'strangeness':

> It must be a strange state to be like Jo! To shuffle through the streets, unfamiliar with the shapes and in utter darkness as to the meaning, of those mysterious symbols, so abundant over the shops, and the corner of streets, and on the doors, and in the windows! To see people read, and to see people write, and to see the postman deliver letters, and not to have the least idea of all that language – to be, to every scrap of it, stone blind and dumb! It must be very puzzling to see the good company going to the churches on Sundays, with their books in their hands and to think (for perhaps Jo *does* think, at odd times) what does it all mean, and if it means anything to anybody, how comes it that it means nothing to me? To be hustled, and jostled, and moved on; and really to feel that it would be perfectly true that I have no business here, or there, or anywhere; and yet to be perplexed by the consideration that I *am* here somehow, too, and everybody

overlooked me until I became the creature that I am! It must be a strange state, not merely to be told that I am scarcely human (as in the case of my offering myself for a witness), but to feel it of my own knowledge all my life! To see the horses, dogs, and cattle, go by me, and to know that in ignorance I belong to them, and not to the superior beings in my shape, whose delicacy I offend! Jo's idea of a Criminal Trial, or a Bishop, or a Government, or that inestimable jewel to him (if only he knew it) the Constitution, should be strange! His whole material and immaterial life is wonderfully strange; his death, the strangest thing of all.[5]

The first point to note is the historic present tense of the passage, which is most visible in the contrast between the infinitive form of the verbs which describe Jo's life in the present (to shuffle, to see, to think, to feel), and the fact that the narrator knows of Jo's death. Otherwise, the strangeness consists in the effects that are rendered in seeking to represent a mind or consciousness from which the conventional structuring devices of socialised consciousness – social and familial relationships, literacy and the memories that relationships, reading and writing help to shape – are absent, as in Jo's case. We should note an important transition from the third person to the first person, which is marked by the sudden intrusion of Jo's distinctive, colloquial idiom upon the narrator's voice: 'how comes it that it means nothing to me?' What is estranging about this transition is that Jo's idiom then recedes, and Jo's place in a world without knowledge and meaning – closer to the perspective of beasts than humans – is described in a gram⁄matically correct and idiomatically conventional public voice, predicated by a subjectivity, the 'I', which society withholds from Jo ('to be told that I am scarcely human').

It may be argued that Dickens, in contrast to Scott, Bamford, Gaskell and Eliot, who project character voices through non⁄standard dialects (see sections 3.9, 3.13), here reneges on the challenge to represent Jo's voice, subjecting an outcast character to the norms of a middle⁄class public voice. But elsewhere in the novel (and throughout his works) Dickens excels at styling characters through forms of direct speech which are distinctive, idiomatic, and symptomatic of their lives, as in the case of the minor but much⁄buffeted Phil Squod: '"let 'em throw me. They won't hurt *me*. I have been throwed, all sorts of styles, all my life!"' (p. 423). So Dickens's strategy in the passage above is calculated to make the reader work in a particular fashion. The key to that fashion is well described by Bakhtin, who has explained it with reference to 'language⁄images', or parodic representations of authoritative forms of language use.[6] The institutions of the law, the church, and governance are parodied, and summed up in the narrator's ironic reference to the English Constitution as an 'inestimable jewel'. The status and condition of Jo mean, of course, that it is anything but.

Consequently, we can develop a more productive interpretation: in reading about a figure who cannot read, for whom shop signs are mysterious symbols, readers are invited to reflect on their understanding of the mysterious symbols at work in the novel, which in turn may cast an estranging light on the familiar signs and objects that comprise the fabric of social and material life. This is confirmed in the very first paragraph of *Bleak House*, which opens with an urban street-scene where the street is hard to recognise:

> London. Michaelmas term lately over, and the Lord Chancellor sitting in Lincoln's Inn Hall. Implacable November weather. As much mud in the streets, as if the waters had but newly retired from the face of the earth, and it would not be wonderful to meet a Megalosaurus, forty feet long or so, waddling like an elephantine lizard up Holborn Hill. Smoke lowering down from the chimney pots, making a soft black drizzle with flakes of soot in it as big as full-grown snowflakes – gone into mourning, one might imagine, for the death of the sun. Dogs, indistinguishable in mire. Horses, scarcely better; splashed to their very blinkers. Foot passengers, jostling one another's umbrellas, in a general infection of ill temper, and losing their foot-hold at street corners, where tens of thousands of other foot passengers have been sliding and slipping since the day broke (if this day ever broke), adding new deposits to the crust upon crust of mud, sticking at those points tenaciously to the pavement, and accumulating at compound interest. (p. 49)

In one sense, this opening declares a commitment to realism: the coordinates of space (London, the Inns of Court, Holborn Hill) and time (November and, for the law, the professional time of terms) seem to promise precision and clarity. Yet the defining feature of the time-space configuration that Dickens actually constructs is captured in the adjective used to describe dogs in the mud: 'undistinguishable'. Though precision is half promised by one level of signification, readers find themselves in an impressionistic blur where linearity is frustrated, an effect in part created by single words followed by stops: 'London.'; or sentences without verbs: 'Implacable November weather.'. The images rendered with greatest clarity – the waters receding from the face of the earth, and the dinosaur waddling up Holborn Hill – are the most fantastic and, in the context of a London street, unlikely.

We should also note the workings of metaphor in generating the meanings attached to grim, prosaic features of the city. Metaphor is present when meaning is created by the substitution of one sign or 'thing' for another sign or 'thing' which is similar to it. Accordingly the descending smoke which contributes to the effect of darkness and the blurring of boundaries is represented in a complex way. The properties of soot – its shape and colour – are signified by not merely one, but two substitutions. First, its moving shape is substituted for something which is 'like' it, yet also its opposite; the white snowflake. Secondly, having been compared to something white, the actual blackness of soot is visualised through funereal clothing which is mourning the death of the sun, and, by implication enlightenment. Similarly, the mud piling up at street corners is seen metaphorically in that it is substituted for an image drawn from the discourse of finance: it is, like invested money, 'accumulating at compound interest'. The forcing of a connection between muck and money is, in terms of the wider architecture of Dickens's novel, instructive: the purpose of the complex story is to enlighten the reader, revealing the connections between privilege and poverty.

How are we to explain these stylistic features? In the preface to *Bleak House* Dickens stated that his aim was to reveal the 'romantic side of familiar things' (p. 43). This is another version of the realism-and-romance opposition which we traced through Chapter 2. But Dickens is using the opposition to conceptualise the act of looking at a familiar object in an effort to see it in a different, or, to borrow a specialised critical term coined by Victor Shklovsky, 'defamiliarising', fashion.[7] As our analysis of the opening passage of *Bleak House* suggests, Dickens 'defamiliarises' through a convention-breaking approach to grammar and syntax, but also metaphor. Metaphoric substitution, as the linguist Roman Jakobson has argued, is the dominant linguistic characteristic of poetry. As part of the same argument he claimed that prose tends to be characterised by the workings of metonymy, a related figure of speech which creates meaning by associating one sign with another on the basis of familiar contiguities of time and space (November is contiguous in time to the end of Michaelmas term, Holborn Hill is contiguous in space to Lincoln's Inn Hall).[8] The prose of the novel is made distinctive by stylistic features which generate innovative, poetic effects: the language of prose attains a symbolic density.

These effects cannot be divorced from the space that Dickens is representing: the city of London. *Bleak House* is not exclusively an urban fiction, for Dickens's novel asks the reader to grasp imaginatively the social networks which bind city and country together. But it was the urban environment

which intensified many of the most disturbing, yet, given that a growing
majority of the population were urban dwellers, familiar experiences of mid
nineteenth-century modernisation: poor living conditions, over-population,
traffic, anonymity and crime. It is significant that Dickens defamiliarises the
urban scene, rendering familiar things through unfamiliar symbols, thus
setting before his readers an estranged way of seeing which, as we have seen,
is also dramatised in Jo the outcast crossing-sweeper. We need to bear in
mind that Dickens's novel aims to capture the reader's conscience, as in the
rhetorical address by the omnipresent narrator at Jo's death: 'Dead, your
majesty. Dead, my lords and gentlemen ... And dying thus around us every
day' (p. 705). Consequently, estranging stylistic effects in Bleak House are
localised and subordinated to this moral purpose.

To this end they jostle with recognisable popular techniques of representation, such as melodrama, which dramatises domestic secrecy and its revelation through gesture and posture, as in the moment when the glance of the
closed and distant Lady Dedlock, secret mother to the illegitimate Esther,
meets the glance of Lawyer Tulkinghorn, who knows her secret: 'for an
instant the blind that is always down flies up. Suspicion, eager and sharp,
looks out. Another instant; close again' (p. 527). Clearly, Dickens uses
both innovative techniques which challenged the reader into establishing
meanings, based on metaphors and language images; and established and
conventional forms of meaning construction, such as rhetorical addresses
and melodramatic stagings between characters. The limits of Dickens's
willingness to 'defamiliarise' that which was familiar and comforting to the
domestic sensibilities of his readers is perhaps marked by the closure of his
novel: the married Esther is installed with her doctor husband in a visually
quaint and conventional 'cottage, quite a rustic cottage' (p. 912).

4.3   'Reading' in context: journalism and fiction

To understand the transitions that shaped experimental trends in the novel
and prose narrative in the later nineteenth century, it is helpful to place
Dickens's stylistic medley and its mid Victorian readership in context.
When the first edition of Bleak House appeared in volume form, Dickens
boasted that: 'I believe I have never had so many readers as in this book. May
we meet again!' (p. 43). How could Dickens claim a readership for a book
that was only just published? The readers to whom Dickens refers read the
book in serialised format. Whilst readers of today purchase Bleak House as a

unified object, the novel was initially published in nineteen individually issued parts, between March 1852 and September 1853. Dickens did not submit a completed novel manuscript to a publisher; as the most recent number was appearing on the streets, Dickens was busy writing the following instalment.

This is just one of the features of the diverse publishing practices of mid Victorian literary culture which secured large readerships through quasi-journalistic techniques. The connections between novel writing and journalism in the nineteenth century were extensive. We have seen how Marian Evans was a journalist before she became 'George Eliot' the novelist (see section 3.12). Dickens also trained as a journalist: he worked first as a Parliamentary reporter, and when an established novelist he also edited the weekly magazines *Household Words* and *All the Year Round*. We saw in section 3.4 how Victorian periodicals played an important role in reviewing novels and forming canons of taste. Increasingly, periodicals gave over space to the publication of serialised fiction: *Household Words* and *All the Year Round* carried serial versions of certain of Dickens's novels: *A Tale of Two Cities* appeared in *All the Year Round* in 1859. Moreover, journals became sites where fictional and non-fictional narratives exchanged and reworked representations of social life: in a piece of investigative journalism for *Household Words* Dickens followed a police detective through the streets of London, and this was used as the basis of some of the writing for *Bleak House*.[9] 'Sensation fiction' was a popular and important genre in the 1860s, anticipated by *Bleak House*. This genre traded on stories of divorce, bigamy and domestic violence, which were being made public as a result of legal reforms and the new styles of reportage which were established to render them into narrative.[10] Wilkie Collins's *The Woman in White* (1859–60) and Mary Elizabeth Braddon's *Lady Audley's Secret* (1861–2) were melodramatic novels of suspense and secrecy which commanded large readerships. Indeed, through these networks Victorian readers could consume the variety of the world, delivered to them through novelistic and journalistic prose narrative forms which often overlapped.

In practice, Dickens's stylistically complex yet enormously varied narratives successfully exploited the new apparatuses of publication and circulation. These developments helped to shape a new and reactive aesthetic self-consciousness in the theory and practice of the late nineteenth-century novel.

4.4   Nuggets for the masses: newspaper stories

Mid nineteenth-century journalistic energy presaged a newspaper revolution in Britain in the later nineteenth century. In the 1880s and 1890s mass circulation newspapers such as Alfred Harmsworth's *Daily Mail* were founded. The popular 'New Journalism' of these decades advertised itself as providing immediate access to the 'real'. As T. P. O'Connor stated in the first editorial of the *Star*, a London evening paper founded in 1880:

> In our reporting columns we shall do away with the hackneyed style of obsolete journalism; and the men and women who figure in the pulpit or the law courts shall be presented as they are – living, breathing, in blushes or in tears – and not merely by the dead words they utter.[11]

In its commitment to the dramatisation of people and events, newspaper techniques in the 1880s and 1890s became, as John Stokes has remarked, 'analogous to those of fiction', because 'the "story" became the basic molecular element of journalistic reality; a structured nugget of information – the basic unit through which the reader was to be presented with events.'[12]

Let us take a closer look at an example of the narrative structure of a characteristic 'nugget of information', a story taken from the *Illustrated London News* from 4 February 1899. The topic of the story – a disputed claim to the legitimate inheritance of a title and a country house – carries resonance in relation to the novel we will examine next, Henry James's roughly contemporaneous *The Spoils of Poynton* (1897). The *Illustrated London News* was, by this date, an established weekly newspaper, having been founded in 1842 with a national and international mandate ('a complete record of all the events of the week, at home, abroad or in the colonies') addressed to the 'RESPECTABLE FAMILIES OF ENGLAND'.[13] Ground-breaking at its inception, the *Illustrated London News* continued to innovate by being one of the first newspapers to move from engraved illustrations to black-and-white photographs to illustrate its stories.

For example, a story about the rivalry between Viscount Hinton and his half-brother W. J. L. Poulett is illustrated by a portrait of Poulett, and two commanding perspectival views of the disputed Hinton House and grounds (see Figure 1), which construct for the viewer an authoritative gaze on the 'real' objects around which the drama of the story turns:

> The rival claimants to the Poulett peerage have done with 'interviews', and their case must be left for settlement to the lawyers. The elder claimant, Viscount Hinton, who has made his living lately as an organ-grinder, and whose claims

THE ILLUSTRATED LONDON NEWS, Feb. 4, 1899.—161

THE HON. WILLIAM JOHN LYDSTON POULETT,
Eldest son of the late Earl Poulett's third marriage.

HINTON ST. GEORGE, THE SEAT OF EARL POULETT: LOOKING EAST.

HINTON ST. GEORGE, CREWKERNE.

Figure 1. The Poulett rivalry, *Illustrated London News*, 4 February 1899, p. 161

have elicited considerable popular sympathy, was the son of his father's first wife, and was born six months after the wedding ceremony. The younger claimant, the Hon. W. J. L. Poulett, a son by his father's third wife, was born in 1883, and had the late Earl's recognition as his rightful heir. The dispute turns on a question of legitimacy, as to which neither lawyers nor doctors in England appear able to agree. Meanwhile, Viscount Hinton has become an object of much curiosity in the vicinity of Henry's Buildings, Clerkenwell, where the organ-grinder is already proudly spoken of by his fellow-tenants as 'the noble Earl'. The tenants on the family estates at Hinton St. George, near Crewkerne, await events as placidly as does the rest of the public. Hinton House, in Somer-setshire, dates from the time of Henry VII. The garden front was designed by Inigo Jones. The park extends to about six hundred acres. (*Illustrated London News*, 4 February 1899, p. 161)

How does this work as a 'story'? As in a narrative discourse that we may find in a novel, we can transform the surface ordering of events into a chronology, beginning with the Tudor origins of the contested estates and house, succeeded by the birth of Viscount Hinton ('the organ-grinder') six months after his parents' marriage, followed by the later birth of the younger, and recognised, half-brother the Hon. W. J. L. Poulett. Even though 'factual', the topic of the story turns on devices which were central to the construction of many fictional narratives in the second half of the nineteenth century. Illegitimacy was used as a plot device in both *Bleak House* (Esther is the illegitimate daughter of Lady Dedlock) and *The Woman in White*. In addition, the prospect of the elevation of the 'organ-grinder' to privilege, which appeals to 'popular sympathy', echoes narratives of class trans-position concerned with the discovery of true origins and the restoration of lost rights. This is a staple novel plot: it is present in *Jane Eyre* (Jane's inheritance of her uncle's fortune) and extends at least as far back as the 1740s in Fielding's *Joseph Andrews*.

This particular newspaper story is governed by a register which seeks to minimise the dramatic and sensational: 'popular sympathy' is subordinate to the arbitration of professional authority (doctors and lawyers) and tenants on the Hinton estates are awaiting the outcome 'placidly'; the 'public' is invoked to suggest that this is the general, but also appropriate, response. Different newspapers construct different versions of the 'public' in accord-ance with their preferred code of behaviour and values. Even so, the power of the 'New Journalism' is evident intertextually at the opening of the story, when it is reported that 'The rival claimants to the Poulett peerage have done with "interviews"', or the advancement of their respective claims through disclosures about themselves. The interview was a prose genre developed and popularised by the 'New Journalism'. Based on a recorded encounter between a journalist and a famous or controversial subject, it was one of the techniques used for eliciting and representing, in line with T. P. O'Connor's aim, the 'living, breathing' truth about the subjectivity under scrutiny. The rhetoric of such truth-divining techniques often depended on conventions of characterisation which were analogous to those found in the frameworks organising realist novels. An interview with Mark Twain, for example, recorded that the rich ornamentation found in his house was 'no mere extraneous accumulations such as any man of wealth might create, but a gradual and organic outgrowth of the owner's mind which gives you a delightful peep into the inner recesses of his character'.[14]

Clearly, such 'nuggets of information' were stories with complex structures and intertertextual resonances. It is important to remember, though, that in its mandate to record the life of the nation and its empire, a newspaper comprised a collection of such nuggets. For instance, the story about the Poulett legitimacy contest is situated between stories about the price of rail travel for the working class in London, and the annual dinner of the Playgoers' Club. Other matters of interest in the early months of 1899 reported by the Illustrated London News included the launch in Belfast of the then largest ship in the world (the White Star liner Oceanic). In addition, there were numerous stories from the geographically dispersed colonies comprising the empire. This led to grand claims couched in imposing metaphors: as one late nineteenth-century editor put it: 'A newspaper, like society, is an organism which has a soul as well as a body. Its sustenance is drawn from the four quarters of the globe. Its nerves run in delicate fibres over two hemispheres.'[15]

These claims were not universally accepted. The American writer Ralph Waldo Emerson commented on the power of the popular newspaper, 'which does its best to make every square acre of land and sea give an account of itself at your breakfast table'; a power at once expansive and, as Emerson implies, too easily consumed and consequently reductive.[16] This dissatisfaction with the newspaper and the consumerist culture of modernising societies which it embodied was shared by Henry James, an American writer who settled in England in the 1870s. James is, as we established in Chapter 2, a central figure in the history of novel criticism in English. In the later years of the nineteenth century James forged an aesthetically innovative approach to the novel, which challenged reductive and indiscriminate approaches to reading through the production of narratives marked by stylistic complexity. To explore this we will look at *The Spoils of Poynton* and James's theory of the novel.

4.5   Reading the 'sacred nugget': distinctive narrative art in James's *The Spoils of Poynton* and its 'Preface'

The Spoils of Poynton is a story about a young woman, Fleda Vetch, who is required to act as an intermediary between two disputants: the widowed Mrs Gereth and her son, the engaged and soon to be married Owen. It is, consequently, a novel about class and taste distinctions. The mother, who embodies English aristocratic values and tastes, despises the son's fiancée, Mona Brigstock, who will displace the older woman from Poynton, the Gereth family's Jacobean country house: this is anathema to Mrs Gareth because the Brigstock family represent 'new wealth' and new, more populist, tastes. Mother and son are consequently in dispute over possession of the historic artistic treasures housed in Poynton ('the spoils of Poynton').

The Spoils of Poynton was first published serially in a periodical (the *Atlantic Monthly*, 1896), where it was entitled *The Old Things*. However, its transformation into *The Spoils of Poynton* is symptomatic of James's ambition to convert the novel into a self-conscious and distinctive art form. He achieved this in part by furnishing the later 'New York' editions of his novels with prefaces in which the critical prose is as stylised and symbolically resonant as the prose of the novels. Moreover, critical prose and novel narrative taken together situate James's critical project in a field of cultural debate, as we shall see in sections 4.6 and 4.7.

In the 1908 preface to *The Spoils of Poynton*, James self-consciously reflects on the means by which he encountered and artistically transformed the raw material of the story, selecting it from a snippet of society gossip overheard at dinner, 'a mere floating particle in the stream of talk' (the story was based on an actual incident from life), and turning it into a 'tiny nugget, washed free of accretions and hammered into a sacred hardness'. James constructs a key binary opposition between 'Life' which is characterised negatively by 'inclusion and confusion', and 'art' which is, in positive contrast, 'all discrimination and selection' (p. xxxix).[17] According to this opposition, the confusion and inclusiveness of 'Life' may be found in a novel by Dickens, or a Victorian popular newspaper, to their detriment (James described English Victorian novels as 'loose, baggy monsters').[18] James's story, on the other hand, is seen metaphorically as a 'hardened' golden nugget of sacred artistry.

By linking 'art' with hardness James is here challenging received ideas about material objects and the means by which they are conventionally represented. *The Spoils of Poynton* is, of course, about splendid objects and a contest for their possession. James acknowledges the 'heroic importance' of these objects, and recognises the way in which they might have been represented by writers renowned for their skills of visual realisation, such as the influential mid nineteenth-century French realist novelist Honoré de Balzac. However, the objects are not, as readers of the novel have discovered, carefully delineated (p. xliii). James refuses the verisimilitude of visual description that we can find in Dickens (Esther's charming rustic cottage), and which the *Illustrated London News* generated by photography. James explains how he came instead to realise the objects at the centre of the novel impressionistically: their collective effect is conveyed to the reader almost spectrally as 'the shimmer of wrought substances [which] spent itself in the brightness' (p. 38). James is concerned with a unity of narrative effect which gives his story nugget a 'sacred hardness': to achieve such unity objects have consistently to be seen through a 'weight of intelligent consciousness'. In this instance, the consciousness is that of the artistic Fleda Vetch, who is, to use our term, the narrative's focaliser (pp. xlvii–xlviii). The preface to *The Spoils of Poynton* highlights the value of Fleda's 'intelligent' inward 'appreciation' of exterior things and objects. Such an 'intelligent' mode of appreciation is, James contends, actually fundamental to the processes of active discrimination and selection that distinguish 'art' from the chaos of 'Life'. How does this work in the scheme of the novel?

4.6   James's narration and the discriminating reader

James undoubtedly took the novel in new directions, but in some respects, *The Spoils of Poynton* is a novel which continues to work with the familiar machinery of Jane Austen's early nineteenth-century novel of manners. Like *Emma* (see section 2.5), James's novel is based on restricted vision, scheming, mild deception, misunderstanding, self-delusion and the dramatic irony that such a combination of elements produces.

It is helpful to sketch these elements. Mrs Gereth identifies the materially impoverished but aesthetically sensitive Fleda as a person of taste and artistic sense, who appreciates the 'spoils' that she is to lose to her son and his fiancée,

Mona. Fleda stands by Mrs Gereth's 'cause' in the dispute, interceding on her behalf in an attempt to persuade Owen to forgo his legal right to the treasures. Mrs Gereth has illegally appropriated the treasures from Poynton and taken them to the cottage to which she has been banished. In taking Mrs Gereth's side, Fleda finds herself becoming attracted to Owen, whose relationship to Mona is foundering because of the dispute; in an about turn, Fleda responds to Owen and vows to help him to get the treasures back. But Fleda also senses that Owen is becoming attracted to her. She thus finds herself on the horns of an ethical dilemma: in acting to save Owen's relationship with Mona, Fleda finds herself pursuing a goal which is contrary to her own interests, in that an opportunity for her to become mistress of Poynton seems to arise. James's story is thus a finely tuned 'little drama', as he says in the preface, about the ethics of possession, influence and action.

What makes the story distinctive is the dense narration which employs conventions that we are now familiar with, whilst technically refining them to produce a unity of effect which demands attentive reading. The narrative technique is broadly analogous to Austen's in *Emma*: it is third-person which regulates the reader's distance from the dramatised focaliser: although we consistently 'see' through the perceptions of Fleda's 'subtle mind' (p. 8), what she perceives is articulated by an impersonal narrative voice which offers additional comment to and sometimes upon Fleda herself. But beyond this, James strives for complexity in the way in which he exploits the limits of his focaliser's knowledge by creating interpretative challenges for the reader.

Thus, at the point at which Owen appeals to Fleda for her help in persuading his mother to return the 'spoils', the reader is confronted with an apparent revelation:

> he stood there with his hand on the knob and smiled at her strangely. Clearer than he could have spoken it was the sense of those seconds of silence.
>   'When I got into this I didn't know you, and now that I know you how can I tell you the difference? And *she's* so different, so ugly and vulgar, in the light of this squabble. No, like *you* I've never known one. It's another thing, it's a new thing altogether. Listen to me a little: can't something be done?' It was what had been in the air in those moments at Kensington, and it only wanted the words to be a committed act. The more reason, to the girl's excited mind, why it shouldn't have words; her one thought was not to hear, to keep the act uncommitted. (pp. 67–8)

Owen appears to articulate his growing attraction to Fleda and his alienation from Mona's vulgarity. But this is a complex passage. Despite the inverted commas which appear to mark Owen's direct speech, this speech is framed by the narrator's account of, first, 'seconds of silence' which create a 'sense' which is 'clearer' than speech; and, second, 'the girl's excited mind'. It is not clear on first reading, but on re-reading this passage the reader is invited to infer that the moment is silent and enigmatic, but that Owen's speech is being 'imagined' in Fleda's head: it is worth pointing out here that elsewhere in the narrative, we see Fleda imagining herself as though in a scene from a novel (p. 37). But the passage uses this moment of difficulty as a foundation for the construction of additional interpretative questions. The narrator reports that Fleda sees a connection between speech and action, which suggests that if a thought is committed to words, then an act has thereby been committed. Conversely, if there are no words, then there is no committed act, and Fleda with her moral scruples – she does not want to act on Owen's behalf having been cast in the role of a rival to Mona – hopes that the 'sense' of the moment will not be committed to words 'to keep the act uncommitted'. And yet, the 'sense' has been committed to words in what we could describe as the narrator's representation of Fleda's inner speech. Even though 'imagined' it has become an act, and it does influence Fleda's capacity for action and judgement.

This passage dramatises the complexity of Fleda's subtle, subjective dilemmas. As for Owen's thoughts, the unity of effect maintained by Fleda's position as focaliser means that they remain an enigma: at the very moment at which Owen is about to inform Fleda of the identity of 'the one person on earth I love' he is interrupted, and the reader does not find out who this is (p. 115): but he marries Mona and installs her at Poynton.

Mrs Gereth returns the 'spoils' to Poynton believing, mistakenly, that Owen has married Fleda. In a final dramatic twist, the 'spoils', and Poynton, are consumed in a fire. But Fleda has already learned that the true value of the spoils does not reside in their materiality but instead in their impres-sionistic, ghost-like haunting of memory, a so-called 'fourth dimension' (p. 172). We can see then that the values of inward aesthetic appreciation and judgement espoused in James's preface are dramatically upheld in the resolution of the story. The reader who appreciates this lesson is the dis-criminating and sophisticated one that the dense and challenging narration implies.

This reader is also implied in 'realistic' details which actually have the force of resonant symbols, or details which signify beyond the surface comedy of manners which seems to contain them. James's opposition between 'art' as discrimination, and 'Life' as inclusion and confusion, is at work in 'realistic' details which are integral to the evaluative schema of the novel and its wider cultural resonances. Houses symbolise values, modes of perception and taste in *The Spoils of Poynton*. Poynton is aristocratic and old, and is represented through a discourse of discriminating aestheticism: when Mrs Gereth and Fleda perceive it, the treasures and the fabric of the house together create an impression of wholeness and harmony. On the other hand, Waterbath, the home of the wealthy and sporty Brigstocks, is associated with modernisation: it is symbolised by 'the acres of varnish, something advertised and smelly, with which everything was smeared' (p. 4). It is notable that the varnish of Waterbath symbolises all-inclusiveness – there are acres of it covering everything – and self-advertisement. To move from the novel to wider currents in 1890s culture and society for a moment, we find James using this symbolic scheme to read the 'gross defacement of London' during preparations for the popular celebration of Queen Victoria's Diamond Jubilee in 1897: he abhorred 'the miles of unsightly scaffolding between the West End and the City, the screaming advertisements'.[19] James's novel may affirm an aesthetic mode of reading and appreciation at the level of form and content, but this involves rejection as well as affirmation. The Brigstocks are explictly associated with newspaper and magazine culture: on their first visit to Poynton, Mona and her mother bring a new women's magazine – 'quite new, the first number' (p. 18) – as a gift, which Mrs Gereth comically but symbolically flings back at the party when they are leaving. A certain kind of easy and accessible culture is rejected here.

At this moment of transition in the history of the novel, readers' skills and alignments were being assigned to sharply differentiated cultural domains, the high-prestigious and the low-popular, a point which is articulated clearly in the novelist Joseph Conrad's reaction to *The Spoils of Poynton*. He praised its 'delicacy and tenuity', but when he thought of the 'man in the street' trying to read it he recoiled with the kind of nameless horror that he was later to reserve for Mister Kurtz in *Heart of Darkness* (1899), his own dense and challenging imperial narrative about the mind's encounter with the impenetrable:

> I imagine with pain the man in the street trying to read it! And my common humanity revolts at the evoked image of his suffering. One could almost see the globular lobes of his brain painfully revolving and crushing, mangling the

delicate thing. As to his exasperation it is a thing impossible to imagine and too horrid to contemplate.[20]

The innovative novel is a delicate organism being crushed by a machine (the man in the street is one of the masses). As we shall see, images and metaphors map the terrain of this new division.

4.7   Contesting 'The Future of the Novel': Henry James's 'delicate organism' and H. G. Wells's 'right to roam'

James wrote a number of essays on the novel. In this section I shall focus on two, 'The Art of Fiction' (1884) and 'The Future of the Novel' (1899). Later H. G. Wells wrote on 'The Contemporary Novel' (1911). Between these positions we can, at this moment of transition, trace a debate about the future and scope of fictional prose narrative. This was a debate conducted through images of machines, organisms, floods and roaming explorers, which addressed a wider question: how should narrative be written and read in the context of the currents of change and modernisation which charac-terised late nineteenth-century societies? This question beats a path to formal experimentation with both the novel and the short story.

James's position was to invoke self-conscious narrative art as a mode of thoughtful, individualised (or at least minority-led) responsiveness to wide-ranging social changes. James's concern with 'The Art of Fiction' in the 1884 essay is in part a response to the novelist Walter Besant, who had written an essay of the same title. Besant advocated a journalistic view of the function of the novel, arguing that it should aim to entertain a wide readership; be realist in the sense that it should absorb contemporary social questions into its story; and be reformist in its aim to generate sympathy in resolving them. In many respects this was a populist late nineteenth-century extension of George Eliot's 'aesthetic of sympathy' (see section 3.12). For Besant, 'sympathy is that sentiment which is destined to be a most mighty engine in deepening and widening the civilisation of the world.' As John Goode observes, this makes the novel 'a sparking-plug, an engine to ignite an engine'.[21]

In his account of the art of fiction in 1884, James implicitly refutes the engine metaphor, emphasising instead the primacy of organic form: 'A novel is a living thing, all one and continuous, like any other organism, and in proportion as it lives will it be found, I think, that in each of the parts there is something of each of the other parts.'[22] James's view of the formally integrated literary novel as a 'sensitive organism' is in stark contrast to his sense of 'the failure of distinction, the failure of style, the failure of knowledge, the failure of thought' which characterises the bulk of popular stories and novels.[23] In 'The Future of the Novel', James envisions this bulk as a deluge: 'The flood at present swells and swells, threatening the whole field of letters, as would often seem, with submersion.' Establishing this context helps us to see James's theory of the novel as a reaction to the commercial networks which dominated literary culture. His protest was directed at the modern fiction 'industry', which 'put into circulation more volumes of "stories" than all other things' aimed at 'schoolboys' and women.[24] James was reacting to an upsurge of interest during the 1880s and 1890s in adventure stories and romances (following the great popular successes of H. Rider Haggard's African imperial adventure *King Solomon's Mines*, 1885, and Robert Louis Stevenson's pirate romance *Treasure Island*, 1883).[25] For James these popular trends signified that 'we are ... in the presence of millions for whom taste is but an obscure, confused, immediate instinct.' Observing that a 'community addicted to reflection and fond of ideas will try experiments with the "story"' which would secure a future of continuous innovation for the novel, James feared for its future in England.[26]

What was H. G. Wells's opinion? There is a tendency to view their respective positions in this debate about the future of the novel in the light of Wells's declaration that 'I had rather be called a journalist than an artist.'[27] This makes James sound like the artist, and Wells the hack champion of those mind-numbing acres of ephemeral newsprint. In some respects, however, Wells and James articulate quite similar views of the novel. Both held that novels needed to challenge readers by breaking with conventions and forms which flooded the fiction market. In 'The Contemporary Novel' Wells attacked dominant tastes by satirising a middle-class male-gendered reader named 'the Weary Giant', who – appropriately for a giant – is unthinkingly addicted to popular escapist romances after a hard day at the office.[28] Moreover, both Wells and James were of the view that, potentially, the subject matter of the novel was limitless given that, in a changing society, manners were themselves evolving.[29]

The main point of contention between James and Wells was their different attitudes to narrative form and method. James's insistence on 'organic' formal coherence, unified around 'centres of consciousness', was not shared by Wells. For Wells the novel is:

a discursive thing; it is not a single interest, but a woven tapestry of interests; one is drawn on first by this affection and curiosity, and then by that; it is something to return to, and I do not see that we can possibly set any limit to its extent. The distinctive value of the novel among written works of art is in characterisation, and the charm of a well-conceived character lies, not in knowing its destiny, but in watching its proceedings.

There are two elements to Wells's claims for the 'distinctiveness' of a novel. First, there is the representation of character development. Second, there is the claim that the process of character development is best realised in recog-nising that the novel is 'a discursive thing', or 'a woven tapestry of interests'. In many respects, Wells's theory of the novel resonates strikingly with present-day critical interests in the relation between cultural discourse and its woven, textual manifestation in the novel (see sections 1.7–8). Wells's theory is well captured in his defence of the novel's 'right to roam' through a multi-plicity of contemporary discourses and 'interests' that will comprise testing grounds for its characters.[30]

4.8   Reading H. G. Wells's *Ann Veronica*

Wells practised 'the right to roam' in his controversial novel *Ann Veronica* (1909). This third-person narrative traces Ann Veronica Stanley's social and sexual awakening from her frustrated and restricted life in her father's house in a new suburb of London, to her affair with and marriage to Mr Capes, a writer and scientist. Ann Veronica's development is a result of the novel's 'roam' through a constellation of conflicting late Victorian dis-courses and interests which represent a society in transition. Consequently, Ann Veronica's progress is woven from her battles with repressive Victorian patriarchy in the person of her narrow-minded, middle-class father; her education in domestic rebellion and Fabian socialism derived from the Widgett family; her rejection of idealistic late Romantic bohemianism in the person of Mr Manning; her seduction by and rejection of male sexual hypocrisy in the person of Mr Ramage; her attraction to and rejection of late Victorian feminist discourses and the political struggle for female suffrage in Miss Miniver; and her embrace of the authoritative discourses of biological science, social Darwinism and sexual selection (or 'romance') in the person of Mr Capes. Wells's narrator leaves the reader in no doubt about the social authority of biology in the context of discursiveness:

The biological laboratory had an atmosphere that was all its own. It was at the top of the building, and looked clear over a cluster of inferior buildings ... The supreme effect for Ann Veronica was its surpassing relevance; it made every other atmosphere she knew seem discursive and confused.

Whereas James pared his stories down to aesthetically unified 'nuggets', Wells revelled in the discursiveness of his stories. It would be inconceivable for the reader of *The Spoils of Poynton* to encounter Fleda Vetch's conscious‐ ness ruminating on the 'reconstruction of the methods of business, of econ‐ omic development, of the rules of property, of the status of children, of the clothing and feeding and teaching of everyone': but, prior to the character's recognition of the authority of biological science, Wells's roaming narrator makes Ann Veronica worry about precisely these things, in these very precise terms, even though Ann Veronica allegedly experiences them as 'a clamorous confusion of ideas for reconstruction'.[31]

Wells's argument in 'The Contemporary Novel', and his practice in novels such as *Ann Veronica*, were motivated by a conviction that the novel was abrogating its social mission. In many respects, Wells was restating the argument for 'the aesthetic of sympathy'. In pinpointing a cause for this loss of direction and purpose, Wells singled out a trend in the theory of fiction. He argued – with James in his sights – that attempts to define the novel around questions of narrative method and technical refinement were mis‐ placed. Such efforts were most appropriately addressed to another fictional prose narrative form, the short story, which, by definition, was unified rather than discursive.[32] Wells's argument points to the emergence of 'the short story' in this period of literary transition, and the way in which certain trends in short story and novel writing started to develop in technical unison. We will explore these issues in the concluding sections of this chapter. We shall also see that Wells's affirmation of the 'discursive' novel came to be contested by these very trends. I noted above the way in which Ann Veronica's immersion in the 'clamorous confusion of ideas' for social reform is actually represented very neatly by the narrator, the topics of debate being packaged into delineated topics of discussion. When the experimental novelist Virginia Woolf looked back critically on 'Edwardian novelists' such as Wells from the perspective of the 1920s, she argued that their novels suffered from an excess of detail and discursiveness. Moreover – and this was especially damaging to Wells and other Edwardians such as Arnold Bennett, who defined the novel around the practice of character construction – Woolf argued that discursiveness and detail drowned out the voices of their characters. As we shall see, the representation of voice in fictional prose narrative is a crucial issue, and developments in the short story helped to make it so.

4.9   The short story

In the preface to *The Spoils of Poynton* Henry James reflected on a moment of indeterminacy during the imaginative gestation of his story: 'The thing had "come", the flower of conception had bloomed ... yet ... my idea wouldn't overstrain a *natural* brevity. A story that couldn't possibly be long would inevitably be "short".' So James's sense was that when he first started to write his story for magazine publication (as *The Old Things*), he was writing a short story. However, as he wrote the instalments, his story appeared to need greater expansiveness until he came to regard it as 'the poor little "long" thing' (xliv). *The Spoils of Poynton* is marked by an economy and condensed brevity that distinguishes it from many of its novelistic predecessors and contemporaries. James's self-conscious anecdote points to questions relating to the relationship between the short story and the novel. Of course, James sees this problem from the perspective of the writer in the process of composition. However, the problem was a significant one for critics and readers as well: critics in the period came to reflect upon 'the short story' as a distinctive genre in its own right.

In practice, short fictional narratives were a long-established part of the nineteenth-century publishing landscape. In the earlier part of the century writers generally referred to these narratives as 'tales', a term which has its origins in a root word which signified oral discourse in a number of Northern and Central European languages (see *OED*). As we saw at the beginning of this chapter, it was in 1842 that the American novelist, poet and critic Edgar Allan Poe first reflected upon the prose tale, arguing that it is characterised by two properties: first, it can be read at one sitting, and second, the reader experiences a unity of effect (see section 4.1). This theory was, in effect, recycled in 1884 when the American critic Brander Matthews coined the term 'short-story' (idiosyncratically hyphenated) for a British audience: his account of the genre, which stressed the principle of 'unity of effect', was derived from the earlier ideas of Poe.[33] It is notable that Matthews was theorising the aesthetic effects of the short story in the same year as Henry James published 'The Art of Fiction', when the novel itself was being theorised as an organic unity through aesthetic criteria.

It could be said that this period witnessed a transition from the 'tale' to the

aesthetically sophisticated short story. Terms for explaining this transition
have been suggested by the critic Eileen Baldeshwiler, who, in sketching
a history of the genre, distinguishes between epical and lyrical varieties
of story. The epical foregrounds dramatic incident and story: the 'what' of
narrative. The lyrical – a generic term conventionally associated with poetic
form – foregrounds states of mind at particular moments: the 'how' of
narration (see section 2.4).[34] We can explore the appropriateness of these
terms in relation to two contrasting short stories by Thomas Hardy and
Katherine Mansfield. Analyses of these stories will show this to be a useful
distinction, though, ultimately, it does not do justice to demands which the
complex handling of voice places on the reader. More recent critics such as
Clare Hanson and Dominic Head have come to regard short fiction from
this period as a genre which played an important role in re-educating
readers' attention to narration itself.[35] But this new focus of attention was
recognised by Robert Louis Stevenson in 1884 when, in response to Henry
James, he claimed that literature 'so far as it imitates at all …, imitates not
life but speech; not the facts of human destiny, but the emphasis and the
suppressions with which the human actor tells of them'.[36]

4.10   Thomas Hardy's 'The Withered Arm': the epical tale

Thomas Hardy completed his story 'The Withered Arm' in 1887; it was
published in 1888, first in *Blackwood's Magazine*, and then in Hardy's own
collection of *Wessex Tales* (1888).[37] The use of 'tales' in Hardy's title is
significant, for 'The Withered Arm' can be categorised as an epical fiction
in so far as plot and incident are central to the unity of effect.

Rhoda Brook, a milkmaid, lives with her illegitimate son. Neither is
acknowledged by the man who has caused Rhoda to 'fall', Farmer Lodge,
who marries a beautiful young woman, Gertrude. Rhoda sends her son to
look at his father's new wife, and on the basis of the report that she receives
constructs a vivid mental image of the woman. One night she experiences a
visitation from an 'incubus' or phantom which attempts to squeeze the life
out of her: the incubus is seen by Rhoda as an aged and degenerate image of
Gertrude. Rhoda resists by grasping the arm of the invader and flinging
its whole body to the floor. A sense of horror is the unifying effect which
compels further reading.

The next day Rhoda is visited by the actual Gertrude, who has come
to the cottage to offer charity to Rhoda's son, whose impoverished state

Gertrude has observed. In response to inquiries as to her well-being, Gertrude discloses that she has a problem with her arm, which is mysteriously becoming painful and withered, with the outline of fingermarks upon it. As Gertrude physically degenerates and is unable to conceive a child, her relationship with Farmer Lodge deteriorates in proportion to the worsening condition of her arm. In desperate need of a solution which conventional medicine cannot provide, she visits a 'conjuror', who magically reveals to her the obscure image of the person who wishes her harm; whereupon Rhoda and her son exile themselves from the community. Six years elapse, Gertrude's arm continues to worsen, and she pays another visit to the 'conjuror', who advises her that the only remedy is the 'turning' of her blood, and this can only be effected by her touching the warm corpse of a man killed by hanging. Gertrude discovers that a hanging is to take place at nearby Casterbridge: the condemned is a young man. During the public execution she gains access to the prison with the help of the hangman and is in the process of touching the corpse when a shriek breaks out behind her: it is Rhoda and Farmer Lodge, who have come to collect the body of the executed young man, who turns out to be their illegitimate son. Rhoda flings Gertrude against the wall by her arm; her blood 'turns', but too much, and she dies within three days.

Horror and the macabre are clearly unifying effects, but it is within an 'epical' structure of events that the more subtle unifying dramatic ironies of recognition (anagnorisis) and reversal (peripeteia) are generated. Gertrude recognises that her husband is the former lover of Rhoda and father to her child, and that she has displaced Rhoda and is the target of Rhoda's bitterness. The source of the recognition – the identity of the corpse – is also the source of the narrative reversal: for that which Gertrude believed would restore her turns out to be the cause of her destruction.

The events which generate this concluding moment are rooted in discourses of, first, the supernatural, exemplified by the incubus; and, second, superstition, exemplified in the figure of the 'conjuror', and the rumours in the community that Rhoda, as a 'fallen' woman, has witch-like powers. The supernatural and superstition link the rural world of the story to the archaic associations attached to the 'tale' as a genre. Representations of rumour and gossip privilege oral methods of communication: the narrator states that there was only one newspaper serving the community, and that word-of-mouth communication was the most effective means.[38] One would not want to take this too far – after all, Hardy's is a highly literate and written text – but there is a sense in which the narrator's style draws upon gestures associated with traditional, oral methods of story-telling. Walter J. Ong has pointed to ways in which narrators from oral traditions rely on patterns, repetitions and props to keep a narrative memorised and on track, and we can perhaps discern an element of this in the way in which Rhoda's son has to make two visits to form an impression of Gertrude, and Gertrude has to make two visits to the 'conjuror', which is reminiscent of the structures of repetition often found in folk tales.[39] As this suggests, and despite snatches of direct-speech dialogue which we associate with character construction, characters in 'The Withered Arm' are more like functions of the plot than psychologically complex subjects: the son is never much more than a function, an agent who is the cause of the two meetings of the two women characters (as impoverished boy and as corpse).

4.11   Katherine Mansfield's 'The Garden Party': the lyrical story

If we turn now to Katherine Mansfield, we find a very striking contrast. 'The Garden Party' was published in 1922. Like 'The Withered Arm', 'The Garden Party' concludes with its central character, Laura Sheridan, in the presence of a corpse. As we see from her reaction, death and sleep are seen from what may be described as a poetic standpoint:

> There lay a young man, fast asleep – sleeping so soundly, so deeply, that he was far, far away from them both. Oh, so remote, so peaceful. He was dreaming. Never wake him up again. His head was sunk in the pillow, his eyes were closed; they were blind under the eyelids. He was given up to his dream. What did garden parties and baskets and lace frocks matter to him. He was far from all those things. He was wonderful, beautiful. While they were laughing and while the band was playing, this marvel had come to the lane. Happy ... happy. ... All is well, said that sleeping face. This is just as it should be. I am content.[40]

The events that lead to this conclusion all take place on the same day: they involve the Sheridans, a middle-class family, preparing and hosting their annual garden party. The accidental death of a local working-class man occurs on the same day. When Laura Sheridan, adolescent daughter, learns of this she calls for the party to be abandoned, but her family overrule her. After the party and on the suggestion of her mother, Laura pays a charitable visit to the dead man's family. There is, then, no intricate plotting, and we can see that all of the main elements of the story are present in Laura's concluding moment of insight: the garden party and its superficial pleasures, the dead man in whose presence her realisation takes shape, the charitable basket that Laura takes as a token of sympathy.

It is the lyrical prose in which these elements are embedded which is significant. We have already observed the extent to which death and sleep figure poetically as interchangeable states. There are other poetic figures which indirectly signify death, such as the man's closed eyes being blind beneath his eyelids. We should also note further features which render this moment lyrical: the sound effects created by assonance are striking (sleep/deep). The 'what' of a fairly basic plot is emphasised in the 'how' of narration.

Such lyrical effects are combined with short and elliptical sentences ('Oh, so remote, so peaceful. He was dreaming.') which signify the rapid movement of mind and consciousness. For as Clare Hanson has argued, the lyrical short story was derived from two sources: the prose poem and the psychological sketch, which were prevalent in magazine publication in the 1880s and 1890s. The prose poem shaped the kind of poetic language which organises the symbolic prose of 'The Garden Party'. The psychological sketch influenced the lyrical short story, of which 'The Garden Party' is an example, towards representations of consciousness. As Hanson points out, the psychological sketch was especially favoured by late nineteenthcentury 'New Woman' writers such as George Egerton.[41]

We appear to have, then, two kinds of short story. In Hardy's epical 'The Withered Arm', recognition and reversal are foregrounded by the story. Recognition occurs in 'The Garden Party' as well (Laura recognises the superficiality of the garden party when confronted with death), but it is significantly different from Hardy's story in that the reader of 'The Garden Party' follows Laura's recognition through access to her inwardness, registered through her inner speech.

But inwardness poses interpretative problems for the reader because Mansfield's narrator is minimally present. For example, the object of recognition in Mansfield's short story is actually quite difficult to state with certainty. This is exemplified in the closing lines of 'The Garden Party': on her return from the house of the dead man, the crying Laura meets her brother Laurie:

> 'Isn't life' she stammered, 'isn't life –' But what life was she couldn't explain. No matter, he quite understood.
>
> '*Isn't* it, darling?' said Laurie. (p. 261)

We should note here that we have moved from Laura as focaliser, registered through her inner voice, to Laurie as focaliser, who 'understands' her unfinished enunciation about 'life'. Practically, however, such understanding would be difficult to conclude, because Laura's utterance is of indeterminate status, neither a statement nor a question and missing an adjective. Laurie, then, speaks for Laura to 'fill in' the gap: '"*Isn't* it, darling?"' This is a process that the narrative explores: we should remember that at the moment when Laura gazes at the corpse she also 'speaks' for it in her imagination: 'All is well, said that sleeping face. This is just as it should be. I am content.' The difficulty here is: how can Laura know?

Being able to read the story at one sitting enables the reader to locate parallel technical effects and interpretative questions in a focused manner. The question 'how can Laura know?' is one that the critical reader may transport to this moment after re-reading the very first paragraph of 'The Garden Party', where Laura is the focaliser and the image of the garden is recounted in her 'voice': 'As for the roses, you could not help feeling that they understood that roses are the only flowers that impress people at garden parties' (p. 245). Laura's sense of what the roses understood of themselves is as fanciful and as subjective as her conviction that she could be friends with the workmen who arrive to erect the marquee. The episode which ends with Laura's imagined sense of her ability to maintain easy-going, cross-class relations begins with the narrator reporting that Laura attempts to be authoritative with the workmen by unconvincingly 'copying her mother's voice' (pp. 246–7).

This is an important detail. For in Katherine Mansfield's handling of the lyrical or technically experimental short story, one could argue that voice and speech are actually 'objects' of recognition, presented to the reader dramatically by the narration. The extent to which Laura's 'voice' is permeated by her mother's discourse and its evaluations is something that becomes apparent to the reader. As the reader progresses with the story, it becomes clear that Laura's mother, Mrs Sheridan, is an authoritarian figure who is concerned with beautiful things but also with the pragmatic maintenance of her family's privileged position to afford them. When the idealistic and artistic Laura insists that the garden party be cancelled out of respect for the dead working man, Mrs Sheridan replies 'coldly' that '"People like that don't expect sacrifices from us."' Mrs Sheridan speaks for the maintenance of class differences and contractual obligation over social sympathy. But in contrast to conventional devices for constructing character, Mrs Sheridan's direct speech and its values not only defines herself: they permeate Laura's voice as well. The opening lines of the story are both focalised by Laura and rendered in her voice: 'And after all the weather was ideal. They could not have had a more perfect day for a garden party if they had ordered it' (p. 245). As Dominic Head points out, the language of idealism and that of pecuniary command are juxtaposed in these lines.[42] Mrs Sheridan's language conditions the mapping of social space in Laura's consciousness: when Laura thinks of the cottages where the dead man has resided she recalls that 'children swarmed. When the Sheridans were little they were forbidden to set foot there because of the revolting language and what they might catch' (p. 254). The point of the implied author's intense focus on Laura's voice and its unstable mix of artistic idealism and pragmatism would seem to be that it is language as well as disease that one catches: Laura, despite her best intentions, has caught her mother's.

It is clear that Katherine Mansfield's 'The Garden Party' is a lyrically rich narrative which places subjectivity and voice in the foreground. But this is to dramatise and interrogate social relations and interactions: indeed, it is precisely about the way in which these are registered in voices and images of speech. In acknowledging this, we are reminded of Stevenson's point about questions of emphasis and suppression in narration. Thus, even epical short stories raise questions about voice and subjectivity. If we look at Hardy's 'The Withered Arm' again, it is important to note that Rhoda's struggle with the incubus is of undecidable status given that the reader only sees it from Rhoda's highly subjective perspective. The abrupt shift to a subjective focus in an otherwise 'epical' and exteriorised act of story-telling suggests that the implied author poses a question: is it a visitation or a psychological projection arising from social and emotional exclusion? Accordingly, the source of the tragic action – supernatural or social? – remains open and ambiguous.

4.12 The experimental novel: reading for voice and consciousness in Virginia Woolf's *Mrs Dalloway*

The short story offers a particularly intensive reading experience. The narratives of Katherine Mansfield exemplify the kind of experimentation with voice which leads us to a consideration of the distinctive presence of voice in the experimental novel. We will explore these by first looking closely at the opening of Virginia Woolf's post-World War I *Mrs Dalloway* (1925), a

narrative about a middle-aged, middle-class wife of a Member of Parlia-
ment on the day she holds a society party. At the same time, we need to recall
H. G. Wells's anxiety about the collapsing distinction between the novel
and the short story (see section 4.8). Indeed, the unified focus and foregrounding of voice in both experimental short story and novel invite a
question: what distinguishes the experimental novel from the experimental
short story? We will explore this question before going on to set Virginia
Woolf's novelistic experimentation in cultural context.

Let us begin by looking at the opening of *Mrs Dalloway*:

Mrs Dalloway said she would buy the flowers herself.

For Lucy had her work cut out for her. The doors would be taken off their
hinges; Rumpelmeyer's men were coming. And then, thought Clarissa
Dalloway, what a morning – fresh as if issued to children on a beach.

What a lark! What a plunge! For so it had always seemed to her when, with
a little squeak of the hinges, which she could hear now, she had burst open the
French windows and plunged at Bourton into the open air. How fresh, how
calm, stiller than this of course, the air was in the early morning; like the flap of
a wave; the kiss of a wave; chill and sharp and yet (for a girl of eighteen as she
then was) solemn, feeling as she did, standing there at the open window, that
something awful was about to happen; looking at the flowers, at the trees with
the smoke winding off them and the rooks rising, falling; standing and looking
until Peter Walsh said, 'Musing among the vegetables?' – was that it? – 'I prefer
men to cauliflowers' – was that it? He must have said it at breakfast one morning
when she had gone out onto the terrace – Peter Walsh. He would be back from
India one of these days, June or July, she forgot which, for his letters were awfully
dull; it was his sayings one remembered; his eyes, his pocket-knife, his smile, his
grumpiness and, when millions of things had utterly vanished – how strange it
was! – a few sayings like this about cabbages.

She stiffened a little on the kerb, waiting for Durtnall's van to pass. A charming woman, Scrope Purvis thought her (knowing her as one does know people
who live next door to one in Westminster); a touch of the bird about her, of the
jay, blue-green, light, vivacious, though she was over fifty, and grown very white
since her illness. There she perched, never seeing him, waiting to cross, very
upright.

For having lived in Westminster – how many years now? over twenty, – one
feels in the midst of the traffic, or waking at night, Clarissa was positive, a
particular hush or solemnity; an indescribable pause; a suspense (but that might
be her heart, affected, they said, by influenza) before Big Ben strikes. There! Out
it boomed. First a warning, musical; then the hour, irrevocable. The leaden
circles dissolved in the air. Such fools we are, she thought, crossing Victoria
Street. For Heaven only knows why one loves it so, how one sees it so, making it

up, building it round one, tumbling it, creating it every moment afresh; but the veriest frumps, the most dejected of miseries sitting on doorsteps (drink their downfall) do the same; can't be dealt with, she felt positive, by Acts of Parlia- ment for that very reason: they love life. In people's eyes, in the swing, tramp and trudge; in the bellow and the uproar; the carriages, motor cars, omnibuses, vans, sandwich men shuffling and swinging; brass bands; barrel organs; in the triumph and the jingle and the strange high singing of some aeroplane overhead was what she loved; life; London; this moment of June.[43]

In common with 'The Garden Party', *Mrs Dalloway* opens *in medias res* with an air of expectation, preparations for a social gathering: flowers have to be purchased, workmen are due to arrive. Another similarity is that the reader is promptly introduced to Clarissa Dalloway's voice, registered in the idiom- atically distinctive 'For Lucy had her work cut out for her.' Otherwise, readers may experience some problems of orientation when beginning to follow Clarissa Dalloway's movements on 'this moment of June', finding the seemingly random detail difficult to place in order.

A term often used to explain the workings of early twentieth-century ex- perimental narration is 'stream of consciousness', a concept which was first coined in the late nineteenth-century subjectivist and pragmatist psychology of William James, and which was appropriated by novel criticism. 'Stream of consciousness' writing strives to represent the myriad and subjective random impressions, sensations, memories and thoughts that comprise the activity of mind in the course of its daily activities. Woolf claimed that the experimental novel should aim to capture such movements in her essay of 1919 entitled 'Modern Fiction'. 'Stream of consciousness' deliberately eschews the consistent use of those stabilising conventions which order prose narrative, making experience – even the experience of inner life and thought – into a coherent story like this:

Mrs Dalloway could see that Lucy had her work cut out so she told her servant that she would go out and buy the flowers herself. Stepping out, she began to remember her adolescence at Bourton, and the amusing sayings of her old friend Peter Walsh; when would he return from India, was it June or July? As she paused to let a van pass before crossing the road her neighbour Scrope Purvis caught sight of her, admiring her poise, but noting her paleness: Clarissa's attack of influenza had affected her. But Clarissa was oblivious to his gaze, hearing instead Big Ben as it boomed out, marking the passing of another hour.

The opening of *Mrs Dalloway* does not read like this: but neither is it, strictly speaking, 'stream of consciousness'. The best examples of that can be found

in other experimental writings from the period, such as Dorothy Richardson's multi-volumed novel *Pilgrimage* (1915–35) and the final chapter
('Penelope') of James Joyce's *Ulysses* (1922), in which the voices of Miriam
Henderson and Molly Bloom are represented through unpunctuated,
elliptical and ungrammatical verbal forms which really do create challenges
for our sense-making abilities. What my rewriting of the opening of *Mrs
Dalloway* demonstrates is the clarifying effect produced by a maximally
present third-person narrator.

Yet such a narrator is minimally present in Woolf's original, and even
evident in the very first sentence: 'Mrs Dalloway said she would buy the
flowers herself.' The difficulties of reading are generated by what this
narrator delays in explicitly announcing. Thus, whilst we are told that 'She
stiffened a little on the kerb, waiting for Durtnall's van to pass', it is not
immediately clear until the next sentence that we have switched to Clarissa's
neighbour as a focaliser, for though it is the narrator who mediates Scrope
Purvis's perception, his voice ('A charming woman') is encountered before
its source is identified.

The minimalist narrator is thus overshadowed by other voices. Scrope
Purvis's voice constructs Clarissa metaphorically as a bird: she is likened to
a jay, and she notably 'perches' on the kerb. Poetic awareness is thus seen
to reside in everyday impressions. The principal voice belongs to Clarissa,
whose impressions are represented in the form of an interior monologue.
Impressions impinge on Clarissa's senses. We have encountered an earlier
version of this in Dickens's opening to *Bleak House*: we might say that this
is the poetic prose of modern urban life. This prose is characterised by an
alliterative catalogue of impressions of the crowd and activity ('tramp and
trudge', 'shuffling and swinging'). Clarissa's impressions also establish two
conflicting senses of time: the first is the linear time measured and regulated
by Big Ben ('the hour, irrevocable': Woolf's working title for *Mrs Dalloway*
was 'The Hours'); the second is 'the moment' which resists the regulatory
discipline of linear time by grasping the complex simultaneity of 'the
moment' as it is experienced subjectively.

4.13   The novelistic scope of *Mrs Dalloway*

The foregrounding of voice, the lyricism and complexity of the moment,
and the fact that the action of *Mrs Dalloway* unfolds during a single day
bring Woolf's narrative close to the unifying effects of the experimental short

story. In this section, we shall explore how, nonetheless, it achieves the scope
of a novel. In doing this, we should first note that Woolf's idea began its life
as a short story entitled 'Mrs Dalloway in Bond Street' (published in 1923).
In order to draw some contrasts with the opening of *Mrs Dalloway* extracted
in section 4.12, let us look at the way in which Woolf opened her earlier
short story:

> Mrs Dalloway said she would buy the gloves herself. Big Ben was striking as she
> stepped out into the street. It was eleven o'clock and the unused hour was fresh
> as if issued to children on a beach. But there was something solemn in the
> deliberate sway of the repeated strokes; something stirring in the murmur of
> wheels and the shufle of footsteps …
>
>   A charming woman, poised, eager, strangely white-haired for her pink
> cheeks, so Scrope Purvis, C.B., saw her as he hurried to his office. She stiffened
> a little, waiting for Durtnall's van to pass.[44]

Obviously Woolf revised the opening of the final version of *Mrs Dalloway*.
In the short story Mrs Dalloway is going to buy gloves rather than flowers.
Scrope Purvis is clearly established as a focaliser, and Mrs Dalloway's stiff-
ening to allow the van to pass is, coming after his establishment as focaliser,
unambiguously what he sees; and he sees Mrs Dalloway prosaically as a
woman rather than poetically as bird-like.

Most significantly, the narrator uses Big Ben immediately to establish the
time. The time prompts Mrs Dalloway's thought that the 'unused hour was
as fresh as if issued to children on a beach', an image which is reused in the
opening of Woolf's later version. In the short story the image is followed by
a sense of the solemnity that the strokes of Big Ben register, which creates a
tension with the carefree image of childish pleasures. In *Mrs Dalloway*, by
contrast, we get an inward turn: Clarissa's sense of the morning being 'as
fresh as if issued to children on a beach' is followed by 'What a lark! What
a plunge!' The carefree image of the children on the beach takes Clarissa
back to her youth. The narration of *Mrs Dalloway* explores the way in which
impressions of the moment prompt associations which lead back to memory:
Clarissa's reflection on the fact that Rumpelmeyer's men are coming to take
the doors off their hinges recalls to her consciousness the squeak of the
hinges of the French doors at Bourton when she was eighteen, which in
turn recalls Peter Walsh, a companion and lover from her youth, which in
turn loops back to the present and the news of his return from colonial
India.

Memory is dramatised to evoke a complex sense of the connections between the past and present in characters' lives, and this is one of the main ways in which *Mrs Dalloway* achieves a breadth and scope which are novel-istic. Through fragments of Clarissa's memory and recollection the reader is returned impressionistically to the social and intellectual world of late Victorian middle-class England, and Clarissa's initial exposure to Peter Walsh's radical ideas and her subsequent conformist marriage to the conser-vative Richard Dalloway. Later in the narrative, when Peter Walsh visits Clarissa, he becomes a focaliser and voice in his own right. The reader encounters his own memories and bitter disappointment in Clarissa, but also his colonising attitude to women, which is dramatised through his 'piratical' pursuit of an anonymous woman in central London.

We should not underestimate the challenge involved in constructing significance through memories, parallels and dramatised detail. Readers of the opening pages of *Mrs Dalloway* have to keep asking: 'What is relevant here, whom will the story prioritise, whom do I need to invest in?' The initial process of reading the narrative is made difficult by the minimalist narrator, who eschews the hierarchies of discourse which were such a staple of the Victorian realist novel as practised by Eliot (see section 3.13). To begin with Peter Walsh is merely a name, one of Clarissa's memories: but he becomes central. Scrope Purvis is endowed with a voice and his own way of seeing, but then is never mentioned again and makes no contribution to the story. Septimus Warren Smith, the shell-shocked victim of trench warfare, becomes a major voice in the novel, dramatising recent history: namely the war, assumptions about 'appropriate' masculine responses to it, and the medical treatment of trauma. To begin with, however, he is a character whom the reader first encounters briefly during the opening sequence of the narrative, when the narrator, in tracing the slow progress of a grand motor car through the busy streets, orchestrates the distinctive focalisations and voices of a variety of individuals in response to it: Septimus's paranoid sense that he alone is blocking the car's progress is initially on a par with the response of the workman who thinks he has seen '"the Proime Minister's kyar"' (p. 15).

The reader works with the sustained weaving together of parallel perspec-tives and voices vested in the figures of Clarissa Dalloway, Peter Walsh and Septimus Smith. 'Character' is a complex and embedded entity which is realised in the connections between voices and focalisers. For instance, Peter Walsh recalls to memory a conversation with Clarissa in which she meditated on the problem of knowing other selves:

For how could they know each other? You met every day; then not for six months, or years. It was unsatisfactory, they agreed, how little one knew people. But she said, sitting on the bus going up Shaftesbury Avenue, she felt herself everywhere; not 'here, here, here'; and she tapped the back of the seat; but everywhere ... So that to know her, or any one, one must seek out the people who completed them; even the places. Odd affinities she had with people she had never spoken to. (p. 135)

Here Peter's inner voice voice mediates his recollection of Clarissa's voice. Peter's interior monologue actually performs Clarissa's theory. Perhaps the key phrase in the passage which guides the reading of the novel is 'odd affinities'. For the novel's weaving of perspectives and voices refuses a neat closure, instead inviting the reader to see emotional and impressionistic affinities between Clarissa and Septimus: both experience revelatory insights into the forms of subjection and repression that they experience in their respective and very different social worlds during a June day, which ends openly for Clarissa with her society party still in full swing, and for Septimus in his suicide. It could be said that *Mrs Dalloway* is novelistic in a way not unlike Dickens's *Bleak House*. Unity of effect may be built upon the foregrounding of voice and the subjective movement of mind, and coherent narrative closure may be resisted, but Woolf's novel is still expansive, embracing a multiplicity of voices, and ambitiously seeking to represent hitherto unseen connections between divergent social and cultural worlds.

4.14   Woolf's narrative experimentation in context

Clarissa Dalloway's reflections on the difficulty of knowing characters and other selves touch on a problem which many readers experience when reading *Mrs Dalloway*. The narrative method implicitly refutes H. G. Wells's view (see section 4.8) which argued that models of character should be transparently available through the novel, the 'discursiveness' of which could authoritatively guide its readers during times of cultural change. Of course, Woolf's novel does not make character unknowable, because with effort the reader can still come to know Clarissa Dalloway, Peter Walsh and Septimus Smith intimately. Yet it does reframe the terms for representing and reading 'character'. This can be linked to Woolf's view that, in a period of social and cultural transition, human character itself was changing. She claimed as much in her literary-critical essay 'Mr Bennett and Mrs Brown', contending that human character changed in December 1910. Woolf's essay also meditates on the relationship between narrative and power relations in ways which challenge Wells's theory and practice of novel writing.

'Mr Bennett and Mrs Brown' is a generically hybrid production, some-where between literary criticism and the short story. In the essay, Woolf recalls being on a train: sitting opposite her are a middle-aged man and an elderly lady; the latter is Mrs Brown. Woolf reports the dialogue that passes between these two figures, and goes on to try to imagine a resolution to the situation which she infers from the dialogue: at the centre of that resolution is Mrs Brown's life. 'What I want you to see in it,' insists Woolf, 'is this. Here is a character imposing itself upon another person. Here is Mrs Brown making someone begin almost automatically to write a novel about her.'[45] Woolf argues that, at an imaginative level at least, Mrs Brown has imposed herself on Woolf and that, as a novelist, it is imperative for Woolf to recipro-cate responsibly, using techniques to situate Mrs Brown at the centre of her own story. It is the concept of imposition that we need to focus on, for the novelist can use it irresponsibly as a tool of domination. The 'Mr Bennett' of Woolf's title refers to the novelist Arnold Bennett, a realist contemporary of Wells. Analysing one of Bennett's novels, and focusing on its central woman character, Woolf objects to the fact that 'we cannot hear ... [her] voice; we can only hear Mr Bennett's voice telling us facts about rents and freeholds and copyholds and fines.'[46] In other words, Bennett's narrator 'imposes' on the character, diminishing the significance of her subjectivity.

We can use this critique of Bennett and the narrative discursiveness advo-cated by novelists such as Wells to make a connection with *Mrs Dalloway*; for that narrative, in addition to seeking to dramatise the voices of its characters, also explores the social technologies of imposition and domination that can result in the marginalisation of voice. These technologies are embodied in the patriarchal psychiatry of Sir William Bradshaw and his treatment of Septimus Smith's mental crisis. They are also present in regulatory mechan-isms such as the clocks with which Bradshaw is associated, and which, led by Big Ben, symbolically impose their regime on the imperial capital ('the hour, irrevocable'). As we saw in our analysis of the opening of *Mrs Dalloway* (section 4.12), Woolf's narrative experiment seeks to perform versions of multi-layered subjective life experienced in the 'moment' precisely in opposition to this regime of linear time. Contemplating 'The Future of the Novel' in 1899, Henry James speculated that it might be a new generation of women novelists who would carry forward his hope for greater degrees of narrative experimentation.[47] Woolf and other narrative experimentalists such as Dorothy Richardson and May Sinclair were major innovators. Their gender was an important factor too: their innovations and experiments often took shape against social and cultural institutions which reinforced masculine authority while marginalising women.

Writing to James Joyce in 1928, H. G. Wells thought there was a price to pay as the prose of the novel became less concerned to make 'language and statement as simple as possible', and more innovatory, poetical and distinctive. Wells was certainly prepared to acknowledge the authority of 'the hour, irrevocable': 'Who the hell is this Joyce who demands so many of the waking hours of the few thousands I have still to live for a proper appreciation of his quirks and fancies and flashes of rendering?'[48]

It is not a negligible question, and it raises the issue of the cultural construction of the implied reader of this kind of narrative. Peter Keating has argued in *The Haunted Study* that the 'professional' reader is the most powerful legacy of this period of transition. Indeed, *Mrs Dalloway* implies a dutiful reader who is willing to be educated in its ways of constructing patterns, echoes and parallels from its detail. What we see, what we realise of ourselves as we read, is the emergence of new kind of implied reader: the academic reader and re-reader. It could be said that this reader was born not a moment too soon, given the challenges that the metafictional, postmodern and postcolonial narratives to be explored in the following and final chapter will pose. The paradox is that some of these narratives pre-date the birth of such a reader.

Notes

1. Edgar Allan Poe, review of Nathaniel Hawthorn's *Twice-Told Tales*, in Vassiliki Kolocotroni, Jane Goldman and Olga Taxidou (eds), *Modernism: An Anthology of Sources and Documents* (Edinburgh: Edinburgh University Press, 1998), p. 94.
2. See Kolocotroni *et al*, *Modernism*, xvii.
3. For a representative late Victorian assessment, see A.W. Ward, *Charles Dickens*, English Men of Letters (London: Macmillan, 1882).
4. Randall Stevenson, *Modernist: Fiction: An Introduction* (Hemel Hempstead: Harvester Wheatsheaf, 1992), p. 5.
5. Charles Dickens, *Bleak House* (Harmondsworth: Penguin, 1971): all further references will be to this edition, and will appear in parentheses in the main text.
6. See M. M. Bakhtin, *Dialogic Imagination*, trans. Caryl Emerson and Michael Holquist (Austin: University of Texas Press, 1981), especially in his reading

of the style of Dickens's *Little Dorrit* in the important essay 'Discourse in the Novel', pp. 300ff.

7. This is a term taken from the essay 'Art as Technique' (1917) by the Russian literary critic and theorist Victor Shklovsky: 'Art exists that one may recover the sensation of life ... The technique of art is to make objects "unfamiliar", to make forms difficult, to increase the difficulty and length of perception because the process of perception is an end in itself and must be prolonged. *Art is a way of experiencing the artfulness of the object; the object is not important*' (emphasis in original; extract from Kolocotroni *et al*, *Modernism*, p. 219).

8. A good introduction to Jakobson's work can be found in Terence Hawkes, *Structuralism and Semiotics*, New Accents (London: Methuen, 1977). David Lodge has systematically applied Jakobson's work on metaphor and metonymy to nineteenth- and twentieth-century prose narrative in *The Modes of Modern Writing: Metaphor, Metonymy and the Typology of Modern Literature* (London: Arnold, 1977).

9. See Chapter 16, 'Tom-All-Alone's', p. 272, in which the poor of a slum district are referred to as 'maggot numbers', and compare with 'On Duty With Inspector Field' when journalist and policeman stumble upon a scene of poverty: 'Men, women, children for the most part, heaped upon the floor like maggots in a cheese' (Charles Dickens, *American Notes and Other Reprinted Pieces*, London: Chapman and Hall, n.d., p. 258).

10. See Patrick Brantlinger, 'What is Sensational about Sensation Fiction?' *Nineteenth-Century Fiction* 37:1 (June 1982), pp. 1–28.

11. Peter Keating, *The Haunted Study: A Social History of the English Novel 1875–1914*, 1989 (London: Fontana, 1991), p. 296.

12. John Stokes, *In the Nineties* (Hemel Hempstead: Harvester Wheatsheaf, 1992), p. 19.

13. Peter W. Sinnema, *Dynamics of the Printed Page: Representing the Nation in the 'Illustrated London News'* (Aldershot: Ashgate, 1999), p. 13.

14. From an interview conducted by the journalist Edmund Yates for his newspaper the *World*; republished in *Celebrities at Home*, 3 vols (1877–9), III, p. 135; cited in Richard Salmon, *Henry James and the Culture of Publicity* (Cambridge: Cambridge University Press, 1997), p. 109.

15. Stokes, *In the Nineties*, p. 21.

16. Emerson, 'Works and Days' (1870), cited in Salmon, *Henry James and the Culture of Publicity*, p. 133.

17. Henry James, *The Spoils of Poynton*, World's Classics (Oxford: Oxford University Press, 1982); all references will be to this edition, and will be given in parentheses in the text.

18. James coined the phrase in the preface to his novel *The Tragic Muse*; R. P. Blackmur (ed.), *The Art of the Novel* (New York: Scribners, 1934), p. 84.

19. Henry James, 'London Notes', *Harper's Weekly*, June 1897, in Morris Shapira (ed.), *Selected Literary Criticism* (London: Heinemann, 1963), p. 172.

20. Conrad, letter to Edward Garnett, 13 February 1897, in Frederick R. Karl and Laurence Daines (eds), *Collected Letters of Joseph Conrad*, 3 vols (Cambridge: Cambridge University Press, 1983), I, p. 339.

21. John Goode, 'The Art of Fiction: Walter Besant and Henry James' in John Lucas, David Howard and John Goode (eds), *Tradition and Tolerance in Nineteenth-Century Fiction* (London: Routledge and Kegan Paul, 1966), p. 254.

22. Henry James, 'The Art of Fiction', in Shapira, *Selected Literary Criticism*, p. 54.

23. Henry James, 'Criticism' (1891), in Shapira, *Selected Literary Criticism*, p. 134.

24. Henry James, 'The Future of the Novel', in Shapira, *Selected Literary Criticism*, pp. 180–1.

25. Keating, *Haunted Study*, pp. 16, 344.

26. James, 'Future of the Novel', pp. 181, 185.

27. See Patrick Parrinder and Robert M. Philmer (eds), *H. G. Wells's Literary Criticism* (Brighton: Harvester Wheatsheaf, 1980), p. 185.

28. H. G. Wells, 'The Contemporary Novel', in Parrinder and Philmer, *Literary Criticism*, pp. 192–3.

29. See James, 'The Future of the Novel', pp. 186–9, and Wells, 'The Contemporary Novel', pp. 198–9.

30. Wells, 'The Contemporary Novel', p. 195.

31. H. G. Wells, *Ann Veronica* (London: Virago, 1980), pp. 129–30, 116.

32. Wells, 'The Contemporary Novel', pp. 193–4.

33. Keating, *Haunted Study*, p. 39.

34. Eileen Baldeshwiler, 'The Lyric Short Story: The Sketch of a History', *Studies in Short Fiction* 6 (1969), 483–53.

35. Clare Hanson, *Short Stories and Short Fictions: 1880–1980* (London: Macmillan, 1985); Dominic Head, *The Modernist Short Story: A Study in Theory and Practice* (Cambridge: Cambridge University Press, 1992).

36. Robert Louis Stevenson, 'A Humble Remonstrance', in Edwin M. Eigner and George J. Worth (eds), *Victorian Criticism of the Novel* (Cambridge: Cambridge University Press, 1985), p. 217.

37. The version that I refer to is the later one, published in *Wessex Tales*; the edition I have used is Thomas Hardy, *Outside the Gates of the World: Selected Short Stories*, Everyman (London: Dent, 1996).

38. Hardy, 'The Withered Arm', p. 257.

39. Walter J. Ong, *Orality and Literacy: The Technologising of the Word*, New Accents (London: Methuen, 1982), p. 67ff.

40. Katherine Mansfield, 'The Garden Party', *Collected Short Stories* (Harmondsworth: Penguin, 1981), p. 261; all page references will be to this edition and will be given in parentheses in the main text.

41. Hanson, *Short Stories and Short Fictions* pp. 12–18. 'New Woman' writers, such as Egerton, Mona Caird and Sarah Grand, were late nineteenth-century

128   Innovative stories and distinctive readers

novelists whose heroines challenged the codes and conventions which had dominated the representation of the domestic woman from the mid-Victorian period and before.

42. Head, *Modernist Short Story*, pp. 132–3.

43. Virginia Woolf, *Mrs Dalloway* (London: Triad/Grafton 1976), pp. 5–6; all future references will be to this edition and will be given in parentheses in the main text.

44. Virginia Woolf, 'Mrs Dalloway in Bond Street', in Stella McNichol (ed.), *Mrs Dalloway's Party: A Short Story Sequence* (London: Hogarth Press, 1973), p. 19.

45. Virginia Woolf, 'Mr Bennett and Mrs Brown', in *The Captain's Death Bed* (London: Hogarth Press, 1950), p. 96.

46. Woolf, 'Mr Bennett and Mrs Brown', p. 103.

47. James, 'The Future of the Novel', p. 188.

48. Parrinder and Philmer, *Wells's Literary Criticism*, pp. 176–7.

History, intertextuality and the carnivalised novel: postmodern conditions and postcolonial hybridities

5.1 Playful narratives

Virginia Woolf's early twentieth-century *Mrs Dalloway* (sections 4.12–14) poses interpretative challenges to its reader; Woolf claimed that the refined artistic rationale which shaped her experiments with narrative would take the novel beyond the tired and oppressive conventions of realism to grant the reader access to a deeper, more truthful account of life. Moving beyond this position to the later twentieth century, this concluding chapter will explore the 'metafictional' or 'postmodern' novel, which asks its reader to entertain instead more sceptical and playful questions about the relationship between narration and our knowledge of life, reality and history.

The chapter will focus substantially on Salman Rushdie's *Midnight's Children* (1981), a novel about post-Independence India which can be read as a postmodern metafiction. In focusing on *Midnight's Children* as a particular kind of reading experience, the chapter will question the extent to which the source of its narrative energy can be explained with exclusive reference to late twentieth-century theories of postmodern scepticism and playfulness. It will argue that *Midnight's Children* is an example of what M. M. Bakhtin calls the 'carnivalised' novel, and as such participates in a much longer cross-cultural history. Consequently, exploring *Midnight's Children* in this light will necessitate a reverse from the 'forward march' of cultural history that has characterised this book so far. The chapter will return to the eighteenth century, and Laurence Sterne's masterpiece of carnival literature, *Tristram Shandy*.

Sterne's novel will be the intertextual link to the other main topic which this chapter addresses in its discussion of *Midnight's Children*. Given that Rushdie's novel is about India and its modern history of decolonisation, it can be read to reflect on the relations of power, domination and resistance that are present in the cross-cultural encounters which inhere in colonialism. Postcolonial criticism addresses such relations and asks: what kind of aware-ness about contexts and intertexts do readers need to acquire to appreciate the way in which the narrative energy of *Midnight's Children* challenges and resists colonial power in the cultural field? Which cultural field do we mean? As we shall see, these are challenging but important questions.

5.2   The novel as history, and the postmodern novel as metafiction

When Henry James stated (in his essay on 'The Art of Fiction'; see section 4.5) that 'the novel is history. That is the only general description ... that we may give of the novel', he articulated something that novelists had long recognised.[1] Eighteenth-century novels often described themselves as 'histories' in their full titles (Richardson's *Clarissa*, Fielding's *Tom Jones*); and George Eliot's novels aspired to represent the 'incarnate history' embedded in the webs and relationships that comprised ordinary life (see section 3.12). Although Woolf's experimental *Mrs Dalloway* (see sections 4.12–14) rejected the realist conventions of narration that descended from Eliot, the recent events of World War I and the more distant past of the late Victorian world are senses of history that the reader can access and connect through the interstices between the orchestrated voices and perspectives.

If we look to the novel in the later twentieth century, a solid sense of the past is something that narrative can no longer guarantee to deliver. For instance, John Fowles's novel *The French Lieutenant's Woman* (1969) is ostensibly an historical romance set in mid Victorian England. By the end of Chapter 12 the narrator has established a detailed picture of the topography of the novel's setting, Lyme Regis, as well as a coherent characterisation of his hero, Charles Smithson. But at this moment the narrator poses a question about his enigmatic heroine Sarah Woodruff:

> Who is Sarah?
> Out of which shadows does she come?

At the beginning of Chapter 13, the narrator answers his own question:

> I do not know. The story I am telling is all imagination. These characters I create never existed outside my own mind. If I have pretended until now to know my characters' minds and innermost thoughts, it is because I am writing in (just as I have assumed some of the vocabulary and 'voice' of) a convention universally

accepted at the time of my story: that the novelist stands next to God. He may not know all, yet he tries to pretend that he does. But I live in the age of Alain Robbe-Grillet and Roland Barthes.[2]

The narrator is here engaging in metafictional commentary. 'Metafiction' names a practice that plays upon the conventional workings of fiction: 'meta' means above, so metalanguages are languages that 'comment' on an object language. 'Metafiction' refers to a strain of self-reflexivity in a fiction which comments on the workings of that fiction and reflects, often sceptically, upon its relations to the social and historical world it claims to represent. This metafictional strategy lays bare and questions the convention of nineteenth-century omniscient narration which 'knows' both character and history (see the discussion of George Eliot's omniscient narrative voice in section 3.13).

In naming Alain Robbe-Grillet and Roland Barthes, Fowles alludes to the later twentieth-century movements which have shaped his metafictional impulse. First, Alain Robbe-Grillet pioneered the French New Novel of the 1950s and 1960s, which experimented with, and radically subverted, orthodox narrative conventions for constructing time schemes, coherent focalisers, voices and characters. And second, the cultural theorist and semiotician Roland Barthes employed the methods of structuralism and poststructuralism to question the characteristically nineteenth-century epistemological foundations on which these conventions had been built. Barthes claimed that pre-structuralist literary criticism – of the kind that we have seen exemplified in Selden Whitcomb's early twentieth-century study of the novel (see sections 1.5, 1.8) – operated on the basis of these same epistemological foundations. An example of their shaping power on the realist novel can be found in the discussion of Eliot in section 3.5. Barthes argued against this epistemology by claiming that what we think we 'know' transparently as 'law'-governed social and material reality is always already encoded in sign systems and narratives.[3] Fowles's point is that his narrative can merely parody the conventions of the nineteenth-century realist novel because his writing has been shaped by discourses which question the authority and transcendence of the means at our disposal for gaining access to the 'depth' of character, or the 'truth' of the past. We could say that Fowles's narrative confronts consequences of the multi-faceted 'postmodern condition'.

The postmodern condition is conceived as, variously, the latest and even more intense episode in the long history of economic and social modernisation; a theory of the fragmentation of knowledge following a collapse of the strategies that have traditionally been used to legitimate it; and the theory and practice of art in contemporary culture which, in the field of narrative art, has been realised in fictions which share many of the self-reflexive features of metafictional narratives. It would be wrong to state that there is such a thing as the 'exemplary' postmodern novel or fiction. If post-modernism as a social and cultural phenomenon resists one single expla-nation, it follows that there must be many kinds of postmodern fiction.

These include, on the one hand, the multi-layered works of late twentieth-century American fiction writers such as Robert Coover and Paul Auster, which reflexively interrogate the terms in which written stories relate to life. For instance, in Paul Auster's *City of Glass* (1985), the central character, Daniel Quinn, is a New York-based writer of detective fictions who gets mistaken for a 'real' detective called 'Paul Auster'. Masquerading as 'Paul Auster' the detective, Quinn seeks to protect his client from the threat of murder by following and interpreting the actions of the elderly suspect, who wanders the streets of New York picking up and collecting unrelated objects and fragments, seemingly arbitrarily. Quinn literally 'traces' in a notebook the suspect's movements, which, when rendered graphically, could be read as alphabetical letters forming words which signal, in code, a possible intention to commit murder. However, Quinn could simply be writing significance into completely arbitrary movements, as the suspect 'had not left his message anywhere. True, he had created the letters by the movements of his steps, but they had not been written down … And yet, the pictures did exist – not in the streets where they had been drawn, but in Quinn's red notebook.'[4] This dilemma is impossible to decide definitively when set in the context of other narrative layers: the suspect is collecting objects in order to fashion a new theory of language which will re-establish the broken relationship between words and things. Moreover, when Quinn seeks the real 'Paul Auster' to help him with the baffling case Auster turns out not to be a detective, but another writer from New York. During their meeting Auster discusses his latest piece of writing concerned with the problem of who narrates Cervantes's early novel, *Don Quixote* (1605). This is a problem which the narration of *City of Glass* itself performs, given that 'Paul Auster' is just another character in the tale, 'disowned' by the narrator at its end: 'As for Auster, I am convinced he behaved badly throughout.' Auster's post-modern fictions pose questions about the relationship between writing and life, asking the reader to consider the extent to which significance, meaning and control may be established in either.

On the other hand, in another kind of postmodern novel which has come to be known as the historiographic metafiction, the authority of historical knowledge – the form of knowledge rendered most vulnerable by the collapse of legitimating strategies – is playfully scrutinised and questioned. In order to illustrate the complex of relations that I have started to outline in my initial approach to the postmodern condition, I shall move to a discussion of Salman Rushdie's *Midnight's Children*.

5.3 *Midnight's Children* as postmodern 'historiographic metafiction': sniffy incredulity towards metanarratives

In what sense can Salman Rushdie's *Midnight's Children* be read as a postmodern historiographic metafiction? The moment of birth of the novel's narrator and main character, Saleem Sinai, coincides precisely with the moment of Indian independence from England (midnight, 15 August 1947), a fact about time and chronology which he records haltingly ('spell it out, spell it out') making much of the clock-hands which 'joined palms in respectful greeting as I came'.[5] Saleem goes on to 'confide' chaotically his life story from the Bombay pickle factory where he works. The narrative framework incorporates devices that we have seen in early fictions such as *Pamela*; Padma is Saleem's narratee, but at this moment (Book 2, Chapter 4), she has abandoned Saleem, who confesses to a confusion and disorientation which are a feature of his narration:

> Reality is a question of perspective; the further you get from the past, the more concrete and plausible it seems – but as you approach the present, it inevitably seems more and more incredible. Suppose yourself in a large cinema, sitting at first in the back row, and gradually moving up, row by row, until your nose is almost pressed against the screen. Gradually the stars' faces dissolve into the dancing grain; tiny details assume grotesque proportions; the illusion dissolves – or rather, it becomes clear that the illusion *is* reality ... we have come from 1915 to 1956, so we're a good deal closer to the screen ... abandoning my metaphor, then, I reiterate, entirely without a sense of shame, my unbelievable claim: after a curious accident in the washing chest, I became a sort of radio.
>
> But today I feel confused ... a little confusion is surely permissible in these circumstances. Re-reading my work, I have discovered an error in chronology. The assassination of Mahatma Gandhi occurs, in these pages, on the wrong date. I cannot say, now, what the actual sequence of events might have been; in my India, Gandhi will continue to die at the wrong time. (pp. 165–6)

There are a number of points that we can make about this passage that place it in the context of contemporary positions which seek to articulate a sense of the postmodern and its relationship to narrative.

First, Saleem locates the story in the year 1956. Postmodernity has a social and economic frame of reference and for historical sociologists such as Daniel Bell, the postmodern era is a post-1945, or post-World War II, phenomenon. It is argued that postmodern economies are characterised by a shift from production and goods-based economics to those based on the supply of services and information. This has implications for the human subject's experience of everyday life, which becomes increasingly saturated by the effects of this transformation. Bell was writing at a time (1976) which permitted him to generalise about the artistic phenomenon which came to be known as 'Modernism', the experimental forms of which we explored in sections 4.11 and 4.12–14. Bell argues that Modernist art tended to create a cultural space in which individual perception and imagination were celebrated as minority forms of artistic resistance to the technological im- positions of modernisation. Under postmodern culture, the human subject's imaginative life is increasingly indistinguishable from the new forms of consumption.[6] It is notable that in reaching for metaphors to account for himself and his own curious powers – hiding in the laundry basket, Saleem has suffered an accident to his sinuses which is causing him to hear voices in his head – he draws upon the modern communication technology of the radio.

The other modern communication technology present here is, of course, cinema; cinema helps Saleem to understand his interpretative relationship to the present and the past (the story begins in 1915 with Saleem's grandfather, Aadam Aziz). But the cinematic metaphor is a comment on the way in which reality is perspectival and constructed: 'reality', when you get close up, is as illusory as the images which turn out to be nothing other than the grain of a projected celluloid frame. This brings us to a dimension of the postmodern condition elaborated by the French sociologist and philosopher Jean Baudrillard. Baudrillard argues that, in the light of a move from a production-based society to an information- and image-led society, the distinction between representations and things has blurred, and image or the 'simulacrum' has grown in power.[7] At this point postmodernism and metafictional practice conjoin: after all, if there are no longer clear-cut dis- tinctions between things and images, the whole idea of a fiction finds itself in an expanded empire of possibilities. Consequently, narrative is given licence to reflect not only on its own constructed and relative status, but also on the implications that this has for apparently 'real' domains of authority and knowledge.

History is, of course, a major domain of authoritative knowledge, and it is in respect of one of the events of public history – the assassination of Gandhi – that Saleem's narrative acknowledges itself to be subjective and fictional: chronologically, he gets the date wrong, but 'in my India, Gandhi will continue to die at the wrong time'. Linda Hutcheon describes gestures such as this as a 'historiographic metafiction', a concept which traces the generic similarities between narrative fictions and narrative histories (history as a form of knowledge exists primarily in written, narrativised forms, known as historiography).[8] 'Metafictions' of this variety prompt us to see the possibility that histories of a public, professional kind are, of their nature, as materially fictional or 'made' as novels. This is a perspective that has been brought to the debate about postmodernity by Hayden White's theory of the 'metahistorical' nature of historiographical narration. In White's view, there is always a linguistic dimension to historical narration, which makes the view of the past one narrates an effect of the combination of tropes, or figures of speech, one chooses to use, rather than the 'truth' of what happened.[9] Saleem actually reflects on the way in which such linguistic choices and combinations have determined his representation of himself as an 'agent' in history:

> How, in what terms, may the career of a single individual be said to impinge on the fate of a nation? I must answer in adverbs and hyphens: I was linked to history both literally and metaphorically; both actively and passively, in what our (admirably modern) scientists might term 'modes of connection' composed of 'dualistically-combined configurations' of the two pairs of opposed adverbs given above. This is why hyphens are necessary: actively-literally, passively-metaphorically, actively-metaphorically and passively-literally, I was inextricably entwined with my world. (p. 238)

Saleem's expression of his relationship to history in terms of a language game inspired by modern science links Rushdie's novel to another dimension of the postmodern condition, elaborated this time by the French philosopher Jean-François Lyotard. Lyotard has argued that postmodernity is characterised by the proliferation of specialised and incommensurable 'language games'; the consequent fragmentation of knowledge has resulted in a widespread 'incredulity towards metanarratives'. By 'metanarratives' Lyotard means those great, public, secular histories, or master narratives, which sustained faith in humanity's progress to freedom and liberation throughout the nineteenth century and the earlier part of the twentieth.[10] Such master narratives imply origins from which a linear movement develops, so the reader's 'incredulity' towards narrative in general in *Midnight's Children* is shaped by the digressive story of Saleem's origins. For these turn out to be bogus: or, at least, not explicable in terms of the story that the narration appears to establish, for the story continually turns back on itself.

Saleem has barely begun his narration before he is alluding to his nick-names, which include 'Snotnose' and 'Sniffer', and which indicate that Saleem has a very large nose. He owes his job in the pickle factory to his acute sense of smell. From the point of view of our reading tactics the nose is out in front, we might say. It remains out in front as Saleem returns to his origins by telling the story of his grandfather Aadam Aziz, a Western-educated Muslim doctor from Kashmir. Aadam Aziz's nose is prominent in two senses. First, and like Saleem's, it is very large. Second, it features in the events of public history with which Aadam's story is enmeshed: a timely sneeze throws him to the ground, saving him from death during General Dyer's brutal massacre of the Indian population of Amritsar in April 1919 (p. 36). In Aadam and Saleem's noses the reader is being invited to trace a narrative line which traces 'origins', 'heredity' and 'descent'. However, this code has effectively to be erased by the reader when Saleem reveals that he is not, biologically, from Aadam Aziz's family line at all. Instead, he has been planted in Aadam Aziz's daughter's arms when mischievously swapped at birth with the child of an accordion player, Wee Willy Winkie, and his wife. But the new story of Saleem's 'origins' is reversed again: Saleem reveals that Wee Willy Winkie is not actually his biological father, for he has been illegitimately sired by William Methwold, one of the last representatives of English colonialism in Bombay (who, to complicate matters further, is of Anglo-French extraction). The story about Saleem's origin and descent is undermined by a number of self-consciously staged narrative reversals. In a metafictional comment Saleem conceptually reverses the reader's core assumptions about our origins and the stories we tell of them when he speaks of his powers of invention in 'giving birth to fathers and mothers' (p. 108).

Saleem has, given his origins, a precarious hold on identity, and this returns us to the place where we started: Saleem's reflections on the illusory nature of reality. At this point in his narration his identity is made up of different characters and objects derived from an amalgam of modern and archaic narratives; he is not only India's Child of Midnight, the hope for the future validated in a letter from India's new prime minister, Nehru; but also a radio who 'receives' the sound of voices; and, in another version, the new prophet Mohammed, who hears voices and 'sought and received reassurance from wife and friends: "verily", they told him, "you are the messenger of God"' (p. 163).

Saleem hears voices and tells his father that archangels are speaking to him: his father takes him to be jesting in bad taste and knocks him to the ground, which he hits after falling through a glass-topped table. Saleem is of course cut: but readers who approach the text from the perspective of the postmodern may already have recognised Saleem's cuts and splits as being more than skin deep. Saleem is 'split' in the sense of being schizoid, a subject who is not at one with himself: 'Please believe me that I am falling apart' (p. 37). Theories of the postmodern argue that the human subject is, with varying degrees of acknowledgement, split, or pulled between multiple points of identification. If the narrated self is only ever a fiction, or something that is made – our analysis of Richardson's *Pamela* (Chapter 2) stressed the way in which Pamela 'makes' herself through writing – then Saleem's self parades its splits and contradictions, and has dispensed with the illusory fiction of 'coherence'.

5.4   The novel as national fiction: postcolonial concerns

How far should one pursue this postmodern reading of *Midnight's Children* as historiographic metafiction? Clearly there is a strong basis to it, but the difficulty with this reading is that whilst it can account for history and subjectivity as abstract problems, it has not said very much about the specifically Indian content of Rushdie's novel, for Saleem's story is interwoven with the history of India in the twentieth century, and is organised around actual events (even if it gets the chronology of some of those events wrong, like the assassination of Gandhi): the struggle for independence, the partition of the continent into India and Pakistan, the language riots, the India–Pakistan war. It should not be assumed that theories formulated in the West about social and economic development, the collapse of legitimating grand narratives, and split subjectivity can be grafted onto a narrative about quite different historical and cultural experiences. We need some additional tools and we shall, consequently, need to turn to a form of critical discourse which engages more directly with the 'fate of a nation' theme which Saleem's narration manifestly pursues.

Selden Whitcomb's 1906 book on the study of the novel (see Chapter 1) equated the development of the novel with the modern nation. For Whitcomb, the novel was an expression of 'national consciousness', and Whitcomb saw novelists who shared a language at particular moments of history, such as 'the eighteenth-century English realists', expressing 'the unity of a national school'. Whitcomb held that even 'in the individual novelist, national consciousness has often been pronounced'.[11]

Benedict Anderson and Timothy Brennan, writing in the late twentieth century, continue to see a vital connection between the novel and the nation: for these historians of culture the novel, along with the newspaper, was a central component in the powerful 'national print medias', a technology at the heart of developing European nation states in the nineteenth century (see section 4.4). Whereas for Whitcomb the novel was determined by, and an expression of, 'national consciousness', Anderson and Brennan argue that the influence ran in the opposite direction. They remind us that Germany, for instance, was a loose confederation of principalities in the early nineteenth century (Germany did not unify until 1870). They point out that the novel became a powerful cultural medium in the first decades of the nineteenth century, precisely the point at which German Romantic scholars were 'discovering' unifying national origins in folk traditions. It was the novel which played a strategic role in creating the nation in the form of an 'imagined community'. We saw the impact of this on a British context in the brief discussion of Scott's national-historical novel *Waverley* and its influence on Eliot's fiction, which itself attempted imaginatively to grasp the totality of the 'nation' (see section 3.13). As Brennan has argued, summarising Anderson's thesis, the novel was a print medium which assisted in this construction of a sense of continuity and belonging in that it:

> created the conditions where people could begin to think of themselves as a nation. The novel's created world allowed for multitudinous actions occurring simultaneously within a single, definable community ... Read in isolation, the novel was nevertheless a mass ceremony; one could read alone with the conviction that millions of others were doing so at the same time.[12]

In practice, the unity of the European nation states was as fictional – that is to say constructed – as the novel. The novel was a fiction in which readers pleasurably invested time and intellectual energy; it assisted in making imaginary European nations into politically and civically sustainable entities. In addition, the forms of 'national consciousness' which the novel engendered played a role in legitimating overseas colonial activity mounted in a nation's name. We saw in Chapter 3 how *Jane Eyre* concludes with Jane's allusion to the missionary zeal of St John Rivers 'hew[ing] ... down the prejudices of creed and caste' in colonial India (I shall return to this theme in section 5.7).[13]

A critical approach to a late twentieth-century novel about a territory releasing itself from the shackles of colonialism can take these observations as a starting point. Rushdie's novel is set in India: specifically, an India that is having to invent itself as an independent nation after almost three centuries of English colonialism. As a 'postcolonial' story, *Midnight's Children* was praised – as the cover-blurb tells us – by the *New York Times* for sounding 'like a continent finding its voice'. In what sense is Saleem the 'voice' of the Eastern subcontinent? Saleem's identification with the narrative traditions of the Orient is clear when he likens himself to Scheherazade, the inner-frame narrator of the ancient collection of tales comprising the *Arabian Nights*, who each night has to tell a new story to King Shahryar in an effort to defer her execution (pp. 9, 24). In addition, Saleem alludes to figures from Hindu myths and folklore throughout his narration (Shiva, Parvati, Ganesh) and the extent to which, even though a Muslim, he is 'well up in them' (p. 149). And Saleem's opposition to the linearity of chronological history may have less to do with the postmodernism of Lyotard than with the Indian concept of *Maya*, a dynamic 'dream-web' to which he alludes (pp. 406, 194), and which, in the emphasis it gives to the illusoriness of visible life, presents history in mythical terms, as rhythmic cycles of *Yugas* or vast aeons of time:[14]

> Think of this: history, in my version, entered a new phase on August 15th, 1947 – but in another version, that inescapable date is no more than one fleeting moment in an Age of Darkness, Kali-Yuga, in which the cow of morality has been reduced to standing, teetering, on a single leg! Kali-Yuga ... began on Friday, February 18th, 3102 B.C.; and will last a mere 432,000 years! Already feeling somewhat dwarfed, I should add, nevertheless that the Age of Darkness is only the fourth phase of the present Maha-Yuga cycle, which is, in total, ten times as long. (p. 194)

Finally, the novel presents Saleem as not only an internally 'split' subject, but also a subject caught between warring linguistic communities in an India that was paradoxically subdividing in order to maintain unity. Saleem recollects 1955, the year in which the new nation was divided into fourteen states and six centrally administered territories: 'But the boundaries of these states were not formed by rivers, or mountains, or any natural features of the terrain; they were, instead, walls of words. Language divided us' (p. 189). These reflections on India's linguistic heterogeneity, and before that on the mythic cosmology of *Maya*, are instructive moments which can take us into postcolonial criticism's quarrel with certain trends in postmodernist novel reading. Vijay Mishra and Bob Hodge argue that:

> For postmodernism, Rushdie's questioning of historical certainties is exemplary of its own project; for the post/colonial what is important is the way in which another, lost master/narrative recalled through the creative power of *maya*, of illusion, is used to free the colonized ... Whereas a postmodern reading of *Midnight's Children* would emphasise play and deferral, a fully post/colonial reading will locate the meaning of the untranslated words and the special, culture/specific resonances of the text.[15]

The most important point about a postcolonial criticism is that it insists on cultural specificity: words are walls, not in the sense that they erect in/surmountable points of resistance, but because they mark out a particular cultural territory. Whilst postmodern theories of language and subjectivity foreground splits, difference and heterogeneity, Mishra and Hodge imply that in being assimilated into a particular style of novel criticism, these theories have tended to emphasise a repetitive sameness in the texts they address: metafictional playfulness, a questioning of history, and narrative deferral and reversal. Accordingly, one might read Rushdie's *Midnight's Children* in much the same way as one might read Graham Swift's *Waterland* (1983), a complex, convoluted, first/person narrative about family history and historical knowledge, though in this instance set in the fens of eastern England. Against this levelling out of experience, Mishra and Hodge propose that the novel shaped by colonial experience and location, and the postcolonial criticism that practices upon it, should aim to support one another towards advancing a political end: 'free the colonized.' The post/colonial novel may begin to achieve this through its specific and alien range of cultural reference, which halts the Western reader's easy assimilation of the usual range reference which makes a novel, in Raymond Williams's phrase, a 'knowable community'.

Do such cultural specificities as the magical narrative of *Maya* account for the 'narrative energy' of *Midnight's Children* as Mishra and Hodge claim? In part of course they do, but we need to remember that it is written in English by an author who, although of Indian/Muslim origin, was also educated in England, and who is familiar with Anglo/European fictional traditions. One of the features of postmodernism is a raiding of the past for things to appropriate in the present. We need to bear this in mind when we think about the particular novelistic discourse and intertextual affiliations which Rushdie has used to fashion Saleem's 'voice'.

5.5   The discourse of *Midnight's Children* in 'long' cross-cultural history: Laurence Sterne's *Tristram Shandy* as eighteenth-century metafiction

Consequently our approach will need to do more than supplement a postmodern reading with a corrective postcolonial range of reference. We shall also need to think intertextually about the particular novelistic discourse in which Rushdie's *Midnight's Children* is written. It belongs, as we shall see, to a discourse with a long cross-cultural history, for it is not the case that metafictionally self-referential and self-reversing narratives are exclusively a feature of the postmodern condition of the later twentieth century. What is the nature of this discourse? Saleem, in telling the reader that he is 'falling apart', qualifies his remark: 'I am not speaking metaphorically ... my poor body ... has started coming apart at the seams' (p. 37). We will need to come back to Saleem's body, and there will be no escaping his nose. To do this we shall explore Bakhtin's history of the novel, which foregrounds the body as a figure of discourse with powerful and long-established comic-grotesque resonances. This will entail our own 'reversal' from the 'forward' movement of literary and cultural history that we have been pursuing so far in this book: we shall return to the eighteenth century, to Laurence Sterne's *Tristram Shandy* (1760–7), as well as to some of its precursors. This can help us to understand *Midnight's Children* as a carnivalised, parodic novel. Such a 'digression' can help to provide an intertextual context which can assist in shaping a revised postcolonial reading of the novel.

The full title of Sterne's novel is *The Life and Opinions of Tristram Shandy, Gentleman*; it began to appear just twenty years after Richardson's *Pamela*. The narrator is Tristram Shandy, and his ostensible aim is to tell his life story. This aim remains hilariously unfulfilled because the narrator's 'opinions', indeed opinions in general, keep interrupting and deferring the events of the life that the narrator strives to recount. The narrative begins with strict chronological propriety, the narration of the first 'event' of Tristram's life being his conception. Yet this is plagued by interruption: first Walter Shandy's act of *coitus* is interrupted by his wife's observation that he has forgotten to wind the clock. The narration of this event is then interrupted by Tristram, who offers an opinion as to the problem which his mother's interruption caused to his own development from the 'homunculous' state, a reflection which leads Tristram to 'tremble to think what a foundation had been laid for a thousand weaknesses both of body and mind'.[16] Tristram's bodily infirmities are most immediately evident in his damaged nose, which, as the reader discovers in volume III of his narrative (there are nine volumes in all), was flattened by forceps during his birth. This becomes an occasion for a long digression into Walter Shandy's obsession with physiognomical theories of noses and all they imply about the decline in fortunes that his family has experienced. This is Walter's 'hobby horse'. Tristram's uncle Toby's 'hobby horse' is the groin wound inflicted on him at the Battle of Namur, and his subsequent efforts to reconstruct the event on his bowling lawn: this comes to occupy a greater part of the narrative than Tristram's story. The narration of Tristram's subsequent history is further deferred by Tristram's metacommentary on the justification for beginning his narrative with his conception:

> right glad I am, that I have begun the history of myself in the way I have done; and that I am able to go on tracing every thing in it, as Horace says, *ab Ovo*. [trans. 'from the egg']
>
> Horace, I know, does not recommend this fashion altogether: But that gentlelman is speaking only of an epic poem or a tragedy; – (I forget which) – besides, if it was not so, I should beg Mr Horace's pardon; – for in writing what I have set about, I shall confine myself neither to his rules, nor to any man's rules that ever lived. (p. 38)

The allusion is to Horace, the Roman classical literary critic, who praised Homer for beginning the epic *Iliad in medias res*. The precise meaning of the allusion is less important than Tristram's attitude to the 'rules' of critical propriety: he declares that he will not be bound by rules.

Indeed, Tristram's narration operates as a kind of metafictional commentary which breaks rules in order to lay bare and question generic conventions. When he offers an opinion on biography, he argues that only biographies of an imagined race of people from the intensely hot planet Mercury might actually be possible because, reasoning on the basis of efficient causes and final causes, only their bodies could be sufficiently transparent to reveal what is inside them. This is a parody which has two objects. The first object is eighteenth-century scientific rationalism, the reasoning processes of which are mockingly imitated. This leads to the second and main object, which questions the expectations associated with prose which claims to show the reader the 'truth' of character. For Tristram argues that 'our minds shine not through the body, but are wrapped up here in a dark covering of uncrystallized flesh and blood' (pp. 96–7). Sterne may not be writing in the age of Robbe-Grillet and Barthes, but we could say that this anticipates Fowles's late twentieth-century metafictional questioning of the conventions for 'revealing' character in narrative (see section 5.2).

Tristram also writes a metacommentary on the representation of time. Recalling the ever-deferred events leading up to his birth, he writes:

> It is about an hour and a half's tolerable good reading since my uncle Toby rung the bell, when Obadiah [servant] was ordered to saddle a horse, and go for Dr Slop, the man-midwife; – so that no one can say, with reason, that I have not allowed Obadiah enough time, poetically speaking ... both to go and come; – though morally and truly speaking, the man, perhaps, has scarce had time to get on his boots.
>
> If the hypercritic will go upon this; and is resolved after all to to take a pendulum, and measure the true distance betwixt the ringing of the bell and the rap at the door; – and after finding it to be no more than two minutes, thirteen seconds, and three-fifths, – should take upon him to insult me for such a breach in the unity, or rather probability, of time; – I would remind him, that the idea of duration and of its simple modes, is got merely from the train and succession of our ideas, – and is the true scholastic pendulum, – and by which, as a scholar, I will be tried in this matter, – adjuring and detesting the jurisdiction of all other pendulums whatever ... and that whilst Obadiah has been going those said miles and back, I have brought my uncle Toby from Namur, quite across all Flanders, into England ... (pp. 112–13)

This metacommentary is concerned again with time, and the relationship between duration in narrative and duration in life. In our very first reading of narrative (*Emma*; see section 2.4), we saw that duration was a category of analysis, in the sense that narration regularly and conventionally condenses chronological time into summaries. *Tristram Shandy* foregrounds duration as a problem here and elsewhere: famously, Tristram, upon reaching the middle of his fourth volume, reflects that, in terms of lived composition time, it has taken him a year to narrate the first day of his life and, consequently, there are three hundred and sixty-four more days to narrate than there were when he started to write: 'the more I write, the more I shall have to write' (p. 286). Recalling when *Tristram Shandy* was written (the middle of the eighteenth century), at one level Sterne is parodying Richardson's concern with writing 'to the moment' (see section 2.9). At another level, according to the early twentieth-century Russian Formalist literary critic Victor Shklovsky,

Tristram Shandy has universal importance as a novel in that it 'lays bare' the devices of conventional narrative.[17]

But there is another way of reading the passage above which highlights the different domains of knowledge that the narrative brings together for the reader to experience and judge between. Tristram's metacommentary concedes that there are different epistemological conventions for accounting for the passage of time. His allusion to the unity of time can be read as a reference to Aristotle's theory of the unities as applied to mimetic arts (Aristotle argued that time systems need to be internally consistent to support dramatic effect). But Tristram also has recourse to the more scientific notion of probability, which measures the passing of time mechanically and objectively. The 'pendulum' which Tristram proposes to take as his standard is from the domain of philosophical speculation. It derives from the seventeenth-century empirical philosophy of John Locke, who argued, in the *Essay Concerning Human Understanding* (1690), that our knowledge is derived from sensations which the mind receives as ideas (see section 2.12). These ideas, initially simple, are named, conventionally but otherwise arbitrarily, by language and combined into more complex ideas and associations of ideas: our sense of the passage of time is, then, shaped by the associated ideas we have of it, and their 'train and succession' in the subjective shifting movements of mind: a mental process which the narrative deferrals and digressions of *Tristram Shandy* dramatises.

If this sounds like a narrative effect more suited to Modernist experimentation or postmodern scepticism then we should bear in mind that, although seventeenth- and eighteenth-century empiricist philosophies sought to advance the spread of reason and universal understanding, they could also be pushed into positions of extreme subjectivism and scepticism. For instance, the eighteenth-century philosopher David Hume, starting from Locke's theories, entertained the possibility that there was no transcendent entity called 'the self' which was independent of the bundle of sensations that an individual subject was receiving through the senses. 'Coherent' experiences of selfhood in time are maintained by conventions which produce fictions of continuity in the form of memory. Thus, in addition to its parodic metafictional questioning of conventions for knowing character, Tristram's narration also questions the basis on which the events of history can be definitively known and linked, and the truth of the past accessed and agreed upon.

Tristram Shandy exposes the reader to a comic sense of the vibrant philosophical and rhetorical disputation which characterised eighteenth-century culture. Moreover, it should be apparent that features which we initially marked out as distinctive characteristics of the postmodern condition of the late twentieth century in sections 5.2–3 – the incoherence of the self or subject, scepticism about history, incommensurable language games – were concerns too for Sterne, who also responded to them through parodic and metafictional narrative strategies.[18] Sterne's novel is highly allusive, and among his allusions are citations of even earlier writers such as the Greek satirist Lucian and the French Renaissance humanist François Rabelais (p. 201). These writers – especially Rabelais – have been significant for Mikhail Bakhtin's subversive account of the development of the novel; it is to Bakhtin's work that we should now turn.

5.6   Bakhtin's 'carnivalised' narrative: a 'second line of development' for the novel

Bakhtin argues that the novel has a long cross-cultural history: his account of the nineteenth-century Russian novelist Fyodor Dostoevsky explains features of his narratives by tracing them to antiquity and their origins in very different cultural settings. Bakhtin argued that the novel developed in antiquity 'in an epoch of intense struggle amongst numerous and heterogeneous religious and philosophical schools and movements, when disputes over "ultimate questions" of world view had become an everyday mass phenomenon among all strata of the population'. In other words, the results, such as Lucian's satires, were 'full of overt and hidden polemics with various philosophical, religious ... and scientific schools'.[19] Lucian's narratives satirised contests between warring knowledges much in the way that Sterne's *Tristram Shandy* would in eighteenth-century England.

Rabelais, the other author frequently cited by Tristram in Sterne's novel, is centrally important to Bakhtin's account. Rabelais's *Gargantua and Pantagruel* was published in France in the 1530s but became widely known all over Europe. Gargantua and Pantagruel are not realist 'individual' characters but are instead fantastical grotesques who link together a multiplicity of comic narrative episodes: they are father-and-son giants whose stories parody royal genealogies, theological education, medical discourse, travel writing and much besides. For Bakhtin, the main significance of Rabelais's work was the very reason why it is often viewed as a work in bad taste: its recognition of the body's dependence on food, its need to deposit excrement, its desire to reproduce, and the laughter that these and the body's various related protuberances and orifices can generate.

Bakhtin traces this poetics of the body to ancient and irreverent traditions of folk culture. According to him, grotesque humour has been shaped by the peasant culture of festivals in which authority relations were reversed and there were no divisions between performers and spectators. For Bakhtin this tradition became the essence of 'carnival' in Christian medieval Europe, where, although it was licensed by the church, it subverted the church's seriousness and dogmatic authority. According to Bakhtin, Rabelais fashions this deeply ambivalent but life-affirming humour into prose which parodies serious and authoritarian knowledge. In a reading of the prologue to *Pantagruel* Bakhtin notes how the prose is double-edged, located at once in 'low' and 'high' culture:

> Therefore, to make an end to my prologue, I offer myself, body and soul, tripe and bowels, to a hundred thousand basket-loads of fine devils in case I lie in so much as a single word in the whole of this History. And, similarly, may St Anthony's fire burn you, the epilepsy throw you, the thunder-stroke and leg ulcers rack you, dysentery seize you, the erysipelas, with its tiny cow-hair rash, and quicksilver's pain on top, through your arse-hole enter up, and like Sodom and Gomorrah may you dissolve into sulphur, fire, and the bottomless pit, in case you do not believe everything that I tell you in this present *Chronicle!*[20]

We should note that this is a prelude to the history of Pantagruel, thereby raising the question of truth, untruth and belief, in common with all the narratives we are examining in this chapter. The language is excremental and bodily ('tripe' and 'arse-hole'), at once replete with insults and oaths reminiscent of the marketplace (a form of language known as 'billings-gate'), whilst being also 'a parody and travesty of the ecclesiastical method of persuasion'. Bakhtin's point is that Christian dogma and the 'historical' narratives which legitimised it are the objects of this parody: 'behind the "Chronicles" stands the Gospels ... the exclusiveness of the church's truth'.[21]

But how does a Bakhtinian reading get from here to a reconsideration of the question of the long, cross-cultural history of a certain practice of novel writing? Bakhtin sees 'carnivalised' narrative of the kind performed in *Tristram Shandy* as a frequently overlooked yet powerful generic tradition in its own right in the history of the novel and prose narrative. Bakhtin acknowledges that the best-known line of development in the novel is the tradition which focuses on realism, sentiment and bildung (essentially that of the novels which we examined in Chapters 2 and 3 – *Pamela, Emma, Jane Eyre, Mill on the Floss*). Bakhtin's view of the novel is not primarily mimetic: it is discursive, arguing that the novel is not a reflection or 'picture' of its times but, instead, a representation of all the social and cultural voices of its era.[22] Bakhtin called the multiplicity of voices that made up a language 'heteroglossia'. In emphasising language, his account of the novel finds parallels with the work of Nancy Armstrong (see sections 2.14–15), who argued that the novel of sentiment and domestic desire developed in part out of a displaced political struggle and, linked to that struggle, debates about the cultural propriety of certain kinds of language use. Bakhtin also conceives of the novel of sentiment and bildung as belonging to a tradition which has a specific relationship to heteroglossia. As we have seen in our discussion of *The Mill on the Floss* (sections 3.13), the novel of bildung has been capable of representing dialects and forms of demotic speech (the speech of the provincial Tullivers and the Dodsons), but it organises them into a clear hierarchy, and according to Bakhtin this amounts to an approach to heteroglossia from 'above'. In this kind of novel authoritative literary language 'descends' upon the variety of voices, dialects and jargons that comprise a given culture.

Novels of the 'second' line of development adopt a different relationship to heteroglossia. Bakhtin argues that these narratives approach heteroglossia from 'below': 'out of the heteroglot depths they rise to the highest spheres of literary language and overwhelm them.'[23] We can see the point he is making if we think about texts that we have been reading. Rabelais's prose provides the most pointed example: we have seen the way in which the 'billingsgate' of the marketplace rises to inhabit and parody a high ecclesiastical genre. And in *Midnight's Children* there is Padma, the common-sensical narratee who just wants Saleem to tell his story in a straightforward manner, demanding 'what is so precious to demand all this writing-shiting?' (p. 24). In using a comic and pretension-crushing language of excrement, Bakhtin would say that Padma's voice refuses 'to acknowledge … poetic, scholarly or otherwise lofty and significant labels' which are always aligned, however subtly, with forms of social and political power.[24]

Bakhtin's conception of 'lines of development' has a real but limited usefulness; after all, the kinds of narrative that we are looking at in this chapter are very good at exposing them as spurious fictions of coherence. It is perhaps more useful to think in terms of intertextual borrowings and inflections, the point of intersection and recognition being the implied readers and the 'heteroglossia' that shapes their horizons. Whatever, Bakhtin's notion of an approach to 'heteroglossia' from 'below' does help us to comprehend a mode of intertextuality which can direct its comic energies to oppose the 'scholarly … lofty and significant labels' which organise the cultural practices of colonial domination. However, in arguing this through an exploration of the intertextual affiliations between *Midnight's Children* and *Tristram Shandy* we shall have to negotiate debates at the heart of postcolonial criticism.

5.7   Carnivalised narrative, postcolonialism and the debate about 'hybridity': *Midnight's Children* revisited

In section 5.4 I cited Vijay Mishra and Bob Hodge, who claimed that the 'narrative energy' of *Midnight's Children* derives from the way it incorporates Indian cultural concepts such as *maya*, which relativise Western notions of historical time by highlighting their illusory status. Yet the 'narrative energy' of *Midnight's Children* is surely attributable to postmodern Western cultural sources as well (see section 5.3). Moreover, in my account of the long cross-cultural history of carnivalised narrative, readers will have noted parallels and intertextual affiliations between *Tristram Shandy* and Rushdie's *Midnight's Children*. Both Tristram and Saleem are preoccupied with time – both narratives begin with clocks – yet neither is able to keep his digressive narrative on course. In a direct echo of Tristram, Padma (the narratee in *Midnight's Children*) urges Saleem to 'get a move on or you'll die before you get yourself born' (p. 38). Both narrators are preoccupied with their noses: in Tristram's case, his lack of a nose prompts a digression into his father's obsession with physiognomical theories of noses. In Saleem's case his huge nose as good as names him ('Sniffer') and appears – falsely – to indicate his descent from his grandfather, Aadam Aziz. Aadam Aziz's powers of smell also prompt a narrative digression, leading Saleem to deliver 'a brief paean to dung' during his narration of the most stern and murderous assertion of English colonial discipline, the Amritsar massacre of 1919 (p. 32). English colonial control is cut down to size in its comparison with the life-affirming 'brotherhood of shit' which levels humans and beasts in the city, and which can be linked to Rabelaisian bodily humour.

These rich veins of cross-cultural intertextuality provide us with a perspective on a phenomenon that Selden Whitcomb (see Chapter 1) noted when he remarked in 1906 that 'there are few great novels which do not show the influence of more than one nationality', and that, consequently, 'the history of fiction is largely a study of international relations' (p. 189). Whitcomb's observation is borne out by the fact that, during the eighteenth century, Samuel Richardson's fictions (see sections 2.7–10) had a powerful impact on the development of sentimental and epistolary fiction in France. At the end of the nineteenth century, Henry James (see sections 4.5–8) was an American who wrote novels about English life which were influenced in their method by the experimental techniques of the French novelist Gustave Flaubert. We began this chapter by looking at the influence of the French Robbe-Grillet on the British John Fowles. And in the long cross-cultural history of the carnivalised novel that we have traced in this chapter, we have established that Sterne's *Tristram Shandy* absorbed aspects of a comic French tradition through Rabelais's *Gargantua and Pantagruel*; it also alludes to a Spanish tradition through Cervantes's *Don Quixote*. We have seen how Sterne's novel is connected to classical Greek and Latin satiric narratives; and how, in turn, *Tristram Shandy* has been absorbed into Rushdie's novel about India, *Midnight's Children*. This is not to mention the other international affiliations which *Midnight's Children* registers through its intertextual echoings of so-called 'magic realist' narratives from different cultures: the German Günter Grass's *The Tin Drum* (1959), and the Latin American García Gabriel Márquez's *One Hundred Years of Solitude* (1967).

But we have to ask what kind of critical enterprise we are involved in when extending Whitcomb's claims about the 'internationalism' of fiction by drawing attention to the intertextual echoes in *Midnight's Children*. It is important to be aware that artistic transactions between imperial nations such as England and France have a somewhat different status to transactions between a nation and a colony, even a new nation in the process of decolonisation (such as India). Edward Said's thesis on the nature of 'Orientalism' argues that the imperial European nation states in the nineteenth century developed a powerful colonial discourse which shaped artistic practices such as novel writing and literary criticism. This discourse was rooted in the scholarly and intellectual archives of philology (a 'racial' history of language development), lexicography, history, political and economic theory, and biology and anthropology. A good example of the literary-critical results would be Selden Whitcomb's book. Whitcomb thought that the novel 'reflected' the conflicts between races and creeds thrown together by empire, but he viewed empire as a 'moral unity' (implying that what it colonised was chaos). Such colonised races and creeds were, for Whitcomb, essential types which could be known and classified according to a 'semi-scientific spirit' (pp. 134–5). This 'semi-scientific' discourse about the East ('the Orient') rendered it, from the point of view of civilization and race, inferior to the West ('the Occident'), and was used as a form of intellectual domination over colonial subjects. As Said points out, novelists such as George Eliot, Charles Dickens and Gustave Flaubert shared the assumptions of this discourse, which promulgated the 'indisputable truth that Occidentals are superior to Orientals'.[25]

The difficulty is that this archive of Orientalist scholarship may continue to assert itself unconsciously in the present. As Dipesh Chakrabarty notes, when Linda Hutcheon writes on *Midnight's Children* as a postmodern novel she names its Western intertextual sources, such as *The Tin Drum* and *Tristram Shandy*, whilst simply referring to the nameless 'Indian legends, films and literature' which it incorporates.[26] In foregrounding the intertextual affiliation between *Midnight's Children* and *Tristram Shandy* it could be argued that I am simply assimilating Rushdie's novel about India to a European 'tradition' of novel writing and criticism which is its yardstick, the standard to which it must aspire. Am I thereby continuing to participate in an Orientalist practice of colonial domination?

This takes us to a debate in postcolonial criticism which addresses the cultural politics of colonialism in general. The debate reflects on, first, the relationship between first culture, language and subjectivity; and, secondly, practices of colonial domination and the role that the novel and prose narrative play in the shaping of colonial subjectivities. On the one hand, Ngũgĩ wa Thiong'o, an African writer and intellectual, has started from a premise which links an historical materialist politics to the argument which proposes that culture is communitarian and coterminous with language. For Ngũgĩ, the mode of productive life which has shaped cooperation and communication during the course of a community's long history gives rise to a sophisticated and distinctive language and, thereby, an equally distinctive culture: 'culture is a product of the history which it in turn reflects.'[27] Ngũgĩ goes on to argue that under colonial administration, indigenous languages are outlawed through the education system: he describes, autobiographically, the subjective scars that this inflicts: namely, the profound sense of alienation he experienced in leaving his village and its language (Gĩkũyũ), and attending school to learn English, where those who continued to use the language of the 'home culture' were punished and humiliated. Ngũgĩ's arguments about the relationship between language, culture and subjectivity lead him to insist on the imperative facing indigenous writers to write in the language of their own people, rather than the language of the coloniser. Ngùgì is critical of the audience implications of what he calls 'hybrid traditions', that is to say writing about a particular colonial experience in the language of the coloniser.[28] This is one context for assessing the political and cultural relations in which *Midnight's Children* is embedded: the number of indigenous Indian people who have a good command of English is around thirteen million – a large number, yet it amounts to only 2 per cent of the total population.[29]

Ngùgì sees 'hybrid traditions' as a stage that postcolonial writing must pass through before intellectuals start to write in their indiginous languages: as we shall see in section 5.8, Ngùgì's own career as a writer of the novel of colonial experience passed through such a stage. But what if 'hybridity' is more than just a stage? It can be argued that *Midnight's Children* performs and dramatises the inescapability of 'hybridity'. Saleem contends that 'things – even people – have a way of leaking into each other' (p. 38). Indeed, the concept of hybridity actually constitutes another strategy of postcolonial analysis, and Rushdie's novel reflects on this strategy at a number of levels. Beginning with character, many people and traditions (Hindu, Muslim, Anglo-French) have, of course, 'leaked' into Saleem to make him what he is, a facet of self-knowledge which is performed in his digressive narration.

Before specifying the other levels, we need to address the conceptual coordinates of this strategy. For postcolonial theorists such as Homi K. Bhabha, the concept of hybridity articulates the divided condition of language, culture and identity. Instead of seeing language, culture and identity as rooted in one location, static and imbued with essences, this approach acknowledges the divisions, fluid boundaries and diasporic mobility which renders them permeable, and leaking all the time. Bakhtin's theory of the heteroglot nature of language (see section 5.6) and its implications for the subject have provided points of departure for postcolonial critics.[30] Bakhtin argued that the subject can become an object of its own perception through pre-existing categories that evolve in the discourses of social life. Such categories are formed by discourses which are made up of the common material of signs, or the currency of 'inner' and 'outer' speech, which shape identity while enabling participation in dialogue and social interaction. But the signs of a supposedly 'national' language, such as English or Russian, are themselves accented in a variety of ways according to the social position from which they are articulated. The process of dialogue is constantly modifying and inflecting the accents and significance of these signs. Magnified, and transported to more radically divergent cross-cultural encounters – say, English meets Gìkùyù, or Urdu meets English – this model enables an understanding of languages, cultures and subjectivities in variable hybrid states. From this perspective it is possible to theorise colonial situations in which the languages, cultures and identities of colonised and colonisers are 'leaking' into one another to effect symbolic and psychic shifts against the grain of the presumed structure of power relations.

Of course, this model can never override the attention we must pay to Ngùgì's political analysis of the enforced erasure of an indigenous language by systematic force through beatings and humiliation in colonial schools. But what it can do is to provide Western academic readers with ways of interpreting the intertextualities of 'hybrid' fictions such as *Midnight's Children* which use the language and indeed the fictional traditions of the West, while yet appropriating these traditions to generate new, carnivalised forms of resistance to the colonial structures of thought embodied in Orientalism and colonial ideologies.

Clement Hawes provides us with a way of thinking about how Rushdie does this, and this is where we bring *Tristram Shandy* back into the frame. We have seen how postcolonial critics such as Mishra and Hodge have objected to postmodern readings of *Midnight's Children*. Hawes is in turn critical of postcolonial readings which approach the novel as a 'staged' confrontation between Western and Eastern modes of knowledge. Focusing on the way in which *Midnight's Children* allows *Tristram Shandy* to 'leak' into it, Hawes contends that 'Rushdie's novel exemplifies the potential of a more nuanced politics of literary affiliation and periodisation ... Rushdie's gesture in reaching back to *Tristram Shandy* can be seen as a fitting strategy of reappropriating the European past for the emerging political and cultural project of postcoloniality.'[31]

How, in Hawes's view, does Rushdie achieve this? Hawes focuses on the figure of the nose, which is a feature of both novels. Hawes argues that in *Tristram Shandy*, Sterne's representation of Walter Shandy's obsession with noses, character and their relationship to family fortunes is a parody which is directed at class-based codes of physiognomical knowledge (for nineteenth-century manifestations of this see section 3.5). As Hawes points out, the parody is made effective through a metafictional reflection on the role of narrative in constructing knowledge. Tristram's nose has actually been flattened at birth by forceps, but Walter Shandy is convinced that Tristram's shortcomings in nasal proportions have been 'caused' by descent from his grandfather's own inferior proboscis: Walter Shandy arbitrarily constructs a given feature as a 'cause' or origin of something to which it is unrelated.

Hawes argues that Sterne's eighteenth-century parody of origins is appropriated by Rushdie's novel, for it is remarkably similar to the narrative of origins and descent that the reader of *Midnight's Children* is drawn into when following the nasal similarities between Saleem and his grandfather, Aadam Aziz, before experiencing its metafictional reversal. However, it is important to be aware that the metafictional parody works differently in the postcolonial context which Rushdie's novel addresses. This is because the structures of knowledge and power, which Rushdie's carnivalised humour of the body mobilises the reader's laughter against, are themselves different. Hawes argues that in allowing Saleem to 'give birth to parents', *Midnight's Children* parodies and refuses the scientific, classificatory theories of racial types and essences which became increasingly powerful in the nineteenth and twentieth centuries through Orientalist discourses, and such narrative forms as the nationalistic historical novel, which frequently represented characters fashioned from discourses which defined national and racial types. Of course, Hawes is fighting on a Western academic front, but from the perspective of an academy which was once at the heart of the production of Orientalist scholarly discourse, knowledge and power, this is still significant. The intertextualities of *Midnight's Children* can be read as a productive and challenging performance of postcolonial 'hybridity'.

5.8   Conclusion: long live postcolonial realism, the bildungsroman – and leakage

I began this final chapter by reflecting on the late twentieth-century novel's postmodern scepticism about historical knowledge. From the discussion of intertextuality that followed, it is clear that, far from seeing no further need for history, late twentieth-century novels such as *Midnight's Children* playfully internalise and reinflect both a sense of history and the history of the novel in order to issue complex invitations to the reader. In being invited to reflect on the experience of colonialism and decolonisation, the implied reader of *Midnight's Children* laughs, puzzles over narrative digressions and reversals, and is urged by the novel's intertexts to consider other narrative traditions, some perhaps familiar, others perhaps alien: but always to consider them in fresh ways.

What are the implications of this discussion of the carnivalised novel for the history of the novel, and the novel in history? As Bakhtin's insistence on two lines of novelistic development should remind us, not all late twentieth-century novels are either metafictional or carnivalised novels (see section 5.6). For some writers, the politics of colonialism and decolonisation can still be addressed within the frame of the historical novel. For instance, Ngũgĩ wa Thiong'o, before taking his stand against the use of the English language in his artistic work, made his own contributions to the tradition of the Anglo-African novel: *Petals of Blood* (1977), which dramatises the process of decolonisation in Kenya, is shaped by the form of the European historical novel. Indeed, the narrative voice articulates a strong commitment to the reconstruction of an authoritative and liberating history of native origins, once the partialities of colonial ideologies have been swept aside:

> For there are many questions about our history which remain unanswered. Our present day historians, following on similar theories yarned out by defenders of imperialism, insist we only arrived here yesterday. Where went all the Kenyan people who used to trade with China, India, Arabia long before Vasco da Gama came to the scene …? But even then these adventurers of Portuguese mercantalism were forced to build Fort Jesus, showing that Kenyan people had always been ready to resist foreign control and exploitation. The story of this heroic resistance: who will sing it?[32]

Ngũgĩ's answer to this question is to find the resistance in a complex narrative web which, in a diverse medley of prose genres, weaves the intersecting memories and lives of his characters, who centre on the village of Ilmorog. The village mediates, and stands as a microcosm for, the developing tensions between the urban centres and the localities, both of which, despite decolonisation, continue to be controlled by international capital. Ngũgĩ's narrative is governed by an historical-realist frame. The narrative is shaped by the time-space coordinates of national history and territory, and the bildungsroman or novel of education is an important sub-genre for exploring the process of political and personal enlightenment.[33]

Bakhtin saw the bildungsroman as part of the 'first' line of novelistic development, and this narrative framework continues to hold appeal for contemporary diasporic writers in English such as Hanif Kureishi, albeit inflected in new ways. Kureishi's novel *The Buddha of Suburbia* (1990) is a first-person, autobiographical bildungsroman about Karim's hybrid upbringing in south London, as the son of an Indian father and English mother. Like Wilhelm Meister, the subject of Goethe's original bildungsroman, Karim becomes an actor (see section 3.1). Such a contemporary novel of formation is complex, given the melting pot of late 1970s cultures, identities and conflicts that the narrative traces: the repressions and longings for freedom experienced in the suburban family; émigré recollections of Bombay and its customs in a grocer's shop under siege from right-wing racists; left-wing avant-garde theatre in the city; and the anarchic phenom-enon of punk music. There is a heterogeneity and an inventiveness that are emblematic of both the postmodern condition and postcolonial hybridity, vested in characters who cast off an old self to appropriate a new version which turns out to be a parody: Karim's father, a civil servant, reinvents himself as a parody of a Buddhist guru; his uncle Anwar, a shopkeeper, reinvents himself as a parody of Ghandi as he goes on hunger strike to protest at his daughter's initial refusal to agree to an arranged marriage. Karim's progress through this urban and suburban landscape is based on a narrative momentum reminiscent of that which we saw in *Jane Eyre* (see Chapter 3). At the end of his story Karim, surrounded by his family at a celebratory gathering, narrates in the language of the classical bildungs-roman 'about what I'd been through as I'd struggled to locate myself and learn what the heart is. Perhaps in the future I would learn to live more deeply'.[34] At other times Karim's progress is comic and grotesquely Rabelaisian. In a parodic, suburban imitation of the balcony scene in *Romeo and Juliet*, Karim tries to get the attention of his girlfriend whilst bypassing her racist father; he fails, is verbally abused by the father, and succeeds only in arousing the sexual interest of the family's Great Dane. Thus, in Kureishi's hands the tradition of bildung and sentiment is 'leaked' into by the comic-grotesque. It is perhaps appropriate that we should conclude this study of the novel — a form which promiscuously defies generic regularity — not with Bakhtin's 'two lines of development' running parallel to one another and at arm's length, but instead merging, leaking into one another.

Notes

1. Henry James, 'The Art of Fiction', in Morris Shapira (ed.), *Selected Literary Criticism* (London: Heinemann, 1963), p. 51.
2. John Fowles, *The French Lieutenant's Woman* (London: Triad/Panther, 1977), pp. 84–5.
3. See Roland Barthes, 'Criticism as Language', 1963, in David Lodge (ed.), *Twentieth-Century Literary Criticism: A Reader* (London: Longman, 1972); and 'Introduction to the Structural Analysis of Narrative', 1966, in Susan

Sontag (ed.), *Barthes: Selected Writings* (London: Fontana/Collins, 1983).

4. Paul Auster, *City of Glass*, in *The New York Trilogy* (London and Boston: Faber and Faber, 1988), p. 71.

5. Salman Rushdie, *Midnight's Children* (London: Vintage, 1995), p. 9; all further references will be to this edition and will appear in parentheses in the main text.

6. Daniel Bell, *The Cultural Contradictions of Capitalism*, 2nd edition (London: Heinemann, 1979), pp. 53–4.

7. Baudrillard makes this case in *Simulacra and Simulations*, trans. Paul Foss, Paul Patton and Philip Beitchman (New York: Semiotext(e), 1983).

8. See Linda Hutcheon's *A Poetics of Postmodernism: History, Theory, Fiction* (London: Routledge, 1988), and *The Politics of Postmodernism* (London: Routledge, 1989).

9. See Hayden White, *Metahistory: The Historical Imagination in Nineteenth-Century Europe* (Baltimore: Johns Hopkins University Press, 1973).

10. J.-F. Lyotard, *The Postmodern Condition: A Report on Knowledge*, trans. Geoffrey Bennington (Manchester: Manchester University Press, 1984).

11. Selden L. Whitcomb, *The Study of a Novel* (London: D. C. Heath, 1906), p. 188. All future references to this text will be to this edition and given in parentheses in the main text.

12. See Benedict Anderson, *Imagined Communities* (London: Verso, 1983), and Timothy Brennan, 'The National Longing for Form', in Homi K. Bhabha (ed.), *Nation and Narration* (London: Routledge, 1990), pp. 48, 52.

13. Edward Said has examined the ways in which the nineteenth-century European novel was both implicitly and explicitly implicated in colonialism in *Culture and Imperialism* (London: Chatto and Windus, 1993).

14. For a more detailed account of these concepts, see Aruna Srivastava, '"The Empire Writes Back": Language and History in *Shame* and *Midnight's Children*', in Ian Adam and Helen Tiffin (eds), *Past the Last Post: Theorising Post Colonialism and Post Modernism* (Hemel Hempstead: Harvester Wheatsheaf, 1991), pp. 65–78.

15. Vijay Mishra and Bob Hodge, 'What is Post(-)Colonialism?', *Textual Practice* 5:3 (1991), 399–414, reprinted in Patrick Williams and Laura Chrisman (eds), *Colonial Discourse and Post-Colonial Theory: A Reader* (Hemel Hempstead: Harvester Wheatsheaf, 1993), p. 282.

16. Laurence Sterne, *The Life and Opinions of Tristram Shandy* (Harmondsworth: Penguin, 1967), p. 37; all future references will be to this edition and given in parentheses in the main text.

17. Patricia Waugh, *Metafiction: The Theory and Practice of Self-Conscious Fiction*, New Accents (London: Methuen, 1984), p. 70.

18. Lyotard approaches the postmodern in terms which reject the 'idea of linear chronology' and its sense of 'post-' as a new departure, 'the hands of the clock ... put back to zero'. Instead Lyotard sees a cyclical quality to postmodern 'expressions of thought' which are performed in particular acts of analysis

(Sterne's writing may be seen in this light). See Lyotard's 'Note on the Meaning of "Post"', in Thomas Docherty (ed.), *Postmodernism: A Reader* (Hemel Hempstead: Harvester Wheatsheaf, 1993), pp. 48–50.

19. See M. M. Bakhtin, *Problems of Dostoevsky's Poetics*, 1963, trans. C. Emerson (Minneapolis: University of Minnesota Press, 1984), Chapter 4; taken from Pam Morris (ed.), *The Bakhtin Reader* (London: Arnold, 1994), p. 192.

20. François Rabelais, *Gargantua and Pantagruel*, trans. J. M. Cohen (Harmondsworth: Penguin, 1955), pp. 168–9: the translation of this passage which appears in Bakhtin's *Rabelais and His World* (1965) is different at points; 'belly and bowels' for 'tripe and bowels', and 'bumgut' for 'arse-hole'.

21. M. M. Bakhtin, *Rabelais and His World*, trans. H. Iswolsky (Bloomington, IN: Indiana University Press, 1984), from Morris, *Bakhtin Reader*, pp. 216–17.

22. Bakhtin, *Dialogic Imagination*, trans. Caryl Emerson and Michael Holquist (Austin: University of Texas Press, 1981), p. 411.

23. Bakhtin, *Dialogic Imagination*, p. 400.

24. Bakhtin, *Dialogic Imagination*, p. 402.

25. Edward Said, *Orientalism* (London: Routledge and Kegan Paul, 1978), pp. 14–15.

26. Dipesh Chakrabarty, 'Postcoloniality and the Artifice of History: Who Speaks for the "Indian" Pasts?', in H. Aram Veeser (ed.), *The New Historicism Reader* (London: Routledge, 1994), p. 343; Chakrabarty is referring to Hutcheon's *The Politics of Postmodernism*, p. 65.

27. Ngũgĩ wa Thiong'o, *Decolonising the Mind: The Politics of Language in African Literature* (1986), extracts reprinted as 'The Language of African Literature' in Williams and Chrisman, *Colonial Discourse and Post-Colonial Theory*, p. 441.

28. Ngũgĩ, *Decolonising the Mind*, in Williams and Chrisman, *Colonial Discourse and Post-Colonial Theory*, p. 450.

29. See Richard Cronin, 'The Indian English Novel: *Kim* and *Midnight's Children*', *Modern Fiction Studies* 33:2 (summer 1987), 201–13, 201. Cronin's point is that the 'Indian English' novel is the only possible 'Indian' novel, given the linguistic and cultural diversity that characterises the territory.

30. See for example Mae Gwendolyn Henderson's use of Bakhtin in 'Speaking in Tongues: Dialogics, Dialectics and the Black Woman Writer's Literary Tradition', in Henry Louis Gates, Jr. (ed.), *Reading Black, Reading Feminist: A Critical Anthology* (1990); reprinted in Williams and Chrisman, *Colonial Discourse and Post-Colonial Theory*, p. 259.

31. Clement Hawes, 'Leading History by the Nose: The Turn to the Eighteenth Century in *Midnight's Children*', *Modern Fiction Studies* 39:1 (winter 1993), 147–68, 148.

32. Ngũgĩ wa Thiong'o, *Petals of Blood*, African Writers Series (Edinburgh, Melbourne, Auckland, Singapore, Kuala Lumpur, New Delhi: Heinemann International, 1986), p. 67.

33. Ngùgì, *Petals of Blood*; see for example the story of the character Karega's education, pp. 197–200.

34. Hanif Kureishi, *The Buddha of Suburbia* (London: Faber and Faber, 1990), p. 284.

Select bibliography and suggested further reading

This is not a full bibliography of all the secondary texts referred to in the notes, though it does include many of the works cited there. Its purpose is to facilitate additional and in some cases more advanced reading and study. For reasons of space, entries are restricted to general works about the novel, prose narrative, and related critical themes and movements.

General guides to the novel

General histories and evaluations of the English novel can be found in Walter Allen, *The English Novel* (London: Phoenix House, 1954), and Arnold Kettle, *An Introduction to the English Novel*, 2 volumes (London: Hutchinson, 1951). Kettle's work continues to offer valuable insights. Jeremy Hawthorn's *Studying the Novel* (London: Arnold, 1985) remains an excellent introductory work. Lennard J. Davis, *Resisting Novels: Ideology and Fiction* (London: Methuen, 1987), offers a more challenging introduction to the novel which looks at the basic elements of the novel – location, character, narrator, reader, plot – from the perspective of theories of ideology.

Literary theory: general guides

Perhaps the most accessible introduction to the main positions and 'schools' comprising literary theory is Terry Eagleton, *Literary Theory: An Introduction*, 2nd edition (Oxford: Blackwell, 1996). A helpful general introduction to reading through theory can be found in Raman Selden, *Practising Theory and Reading Literature: An Introduction* (Hemel Hempstead: Harvester Wheat-sheaf, 1989); another good introduction to reading through theory is Julian Wolfreys and William Baker (eds), *Literary Theories: A Case Study in Critical*

159

Performance (London: Macmillan, 1996), which has the advantage of using a variety of critical approaches to read the same short narrative (by Richard Jefferies). Stuart Sim (ed.), *The A/Z Guide to Modern Critical and Cultural Theorists* (Hemel Hempstead: Harveter Wheatsheaf, 1995), contains brief introductory essays on major theorists. Michael Payne (ed.), *A Dictionary of Cultural and Critical Theory* (Oxford: Blackwell, 1996), provides entries on movements and concepts as well as theorists. There are two useful anthologies on the New Historicism which provide more detailed and nuanced accounts of the movement. They are Kiernan Ryan (ed.), *New Historicism and Cultural Materialism: A Reader* (London: Arnold, 1996), and H. Aram Veeser (ed.), *The New Historicism Reader* (London: Routledge, 1994). Both anthologies reprint representative pieces of criticism; the Ryan is particularly useful because it provides extracts from the 'founding' theoretical positions which have contributed to New Historicism and cultural materialism – though there is nothing from the important works of Mikhail Bakhtin. Pam Morris (ed.) has assembled a valuable selection from Bakhtin's writings in *The Bakhtin Reader* (London: Arnold, 1994), framed by good commentaries. The same can be said for Simon Dentith (ed.), *Bakhtinian Thought: An Introductory Reader* (London: Routledge, 1995).

Approaches to narrative practice: general

Erich Auerbach's *Mimesis: The Representation of Reality in Western Literature*, 1946 (translated into English in 1953 by Willard R. Trask) (Princeton, NJ: Princeton University Press) is an ambitious and wide-ranging work which embraces writings from Homer to James Joyce; essential reading for under-standing 'realist' narrative conventions and their relations to the 'everyday' as well as the tragic. Cleanth Brooks and Robert Penn Warren, *Understanding Fiction* (New York: Appleton-Century-Crofts, 1943), was an important guide to the study of fictional and non-fictional narrative which under-pinned the American New Critical tradition, an approach emphasising form and artistic autonomy. For a rhetorical approach to narrative see Wayne C. Booth, *The Rhetoric of Fiction* (Chicago and London: University of Chicago Press, 1961). Seymour Chatman, *Story and Discourse: Narrative Structure in Fiction and Film*, 1978 (Ithaca, NY, and London: Cornell University Press, 1993), and Shlomith Rimmon-Kenan, *Narrative Fiction: Contemporary Poetics*, New Accents (London: Methuen, 1983) are compre-hensive and accessible books which synthesise some of the most demanding work on structuralist narratology, including Gérard Genette's influential *Narrative Discourse*, 1972 (translated into English in 1980). Ian Reid's *Narrative Exchange* (London: Routledge, 1992) is a challenging work which uses poststructuralist and linguistic theories to go beyond the categories of narratology, especially the category of the 'event'.

The rise of the novel

The best-known contributors to this debate are Ian Watt's *The Rise of the Novel: Studies in Defoe, Richardson and Fielding*, 1957 (London: Hogarth Press, 1987), Lennard J. Davis's *Factual Fictions: The Origins of the English Novel* (New York: Columbia University Press, 1983), Michael McKeon's *The Origins of the English Novel 1600–1740* (Baltimore: Johns Hopkins University Press, 1987), and Nancy Armstrong's *Desire and Domestic Fiction: A Political History of the Novel* (Oxford: Oxford University Press, 1987). All are substantially discussed (with full citation) in Chapter 2. It is important here to highlight the revisionary feminist work of Jane Spencer, *The Rise of the Woman Novelist* (1986), and Ros Ballaster's *Seductive Forms: Women's Amatory Fiction from 1684 to 1740* (Oxford: Clarendon Press, 1992).

The most recent and boldly revisionary contribution to the debate is Margaret Anne Doody's *The True Story of the Novel*, 1997 (London: Fontana, 1998); it refutes the critical orthodoxy which holds the novel to be an exclusively Western European phenomenon of fairly recent origins. Doody has instead focused on the popular 'romance' narratives of classical Graeco-Roman culture, which have tended to be regarded as unworthy forerunners of the novel. Doody makes a powerful case for these narratives of the classical age as sophisticated precursors of the modern novel, on which their modern descendants continue to draw. Doody emphasises the complex hybrid origins of these classical narratives by tracing African and Eastern influences: her account of the rise of the novel is shaped by both postcolonial and feminist concerns.

Postcolonial orientations have broadened perspectives on the question of the origins of the novel. For instance, Nancy Armstrong and Leonard Tennenhouse argue that, in addition to originating in English conduct manuals, *Pamela* suggests affinities with colonial American 'captivity narratives' (Puritan confessional narratives by settler women who had been captured by native Americans) which were being exported across the Atlantic to England in the later seventeenth century; 'The American

Origins of the English Novel', *American Literary History* 4:3 (fall 1992), 386–410. Turning to a Marxist theorist who is critical of certain positions in postcolonial theory, Aijaz Ahmed's 'Jameson's Rhetoric of Otherness and the "National Allegory" in *In Theory: Classes, Nations, Literatures* (London: Verso, 1992) conducts an argument against Frederic Jameson's theory of the Third World novel as 'National Allegory', and in doing so offers a fascinating account of the rise of the Urdu domestic-realist novel as an important facet of an emergent indigenous print culture and civil society in nineteenth-century colonial India. Ahmed's perspective – which draws out the liberatory energies of such publishing practices – offers a counterpoint to Nancy Armstrong's work on the function of the domestic novel in England.

The work of Raymond Williams initiated an early British exploration of the relationship between the rise of the novel, literacy, and the struggle to develop a democratic culture. *The Long Revolution* (London: Chatto and Windus, 1961) accounts for the relationship between the development of literacy, cultural forms and political institutions in England from the late eighteenth century to the present. Williams published *The English Novel from Dickens to Lawrence* in 1970 (London: Chatto and Windus). This work follows from, and is a revision of, Leavis's somewhat reactionary account of the same network of relations. Leavis's influential work on the English novel, *The Great Tradition*, was published in 1948 (London: Chatto and Windus). Richard D. Altick's history of popular reading trends in England, *The English Common Reader: A Social History of the Mass-Reading Public* (Chicago and London: University of Chicago Press, 1957), remains an important source of reference.

Prose narrative (biography, autobiography)

Roger Pooley's *English Prose of the Seventeenth Century, 1590–1700* (London: Longman, 1992) contains valuable chapters on Elizabethan fiction, biography and the spiritual autobiography, as well as important seventeenth-century prose forms such as the sermon. Elspeth Graham, Hilary Hinds, Elaine Hobby and Helen Wilcox have edited *Her Own Life: Autobiographical Writings by Seventeenth-Century English Women* (London: Routledge, 1989). This is a collection of primary texts, and the editors have written a valuable introduction outlining contexts for reading these writings, as well as reflections on the theory of autobiography in relation to the concept of the gendered self. Felicity Nussbaum's *The Autobiographical Subject: Gender and Ideology in Eighteenth-Century England* (Baltimore: Johns Hopkins University Press, 1989) explores the gender of autobiographical discourse in eighteenth-century England. George P. Landow (ed.), *Approaches to Victorian Autobiography* (Athens, OH: Ohio University Press, 1979), contains a variety of useful essays. Reginia Gagnier's *Subjectivities: A History of Self-Representation in Britain, 1832–1920* (Oxford: Oxford University Press, 1990) explores the shared and divergent conventions that writers of different genders and from different classes used to represent themselves in the nineteenth century. David Vincent's *Bread, Knowledge and Freedom: A Study of Working Class Autobiography* (London: Methuen, 1981) is a ground-breaking study of working-class autobiography in the nineteenth century. Carol Jenkins addresses a gap in Vincent's work in 'The Major Silence: Autobiographies of Working Women in the Nineteenth Century' in J. B. Bullen (ed.), *Writing and Victorianism* (London: Longman, 1997). Ira Bruce Nadel's *Biography: Fiction, Fact and Form* (London: Macmillan, 1985) contains some valuable chapters on the similarities between biography and fiction, and biography as a literary and cultural institution. The latter theme is pursued further in David Amigoni's *Victorian Biography: Intellectuals and the Ordering of Discourse* (Hemel Hempstead: Harvester Wheatsheaf, 1993). Trev Lynn Broughton's *Men of Letters, Writing Lives: Masculinity and Literary Autobiography in the Late Victorian Period* (London: Routledge, 1999) makes valuable links between autobiographical and biographical genres, gender and the workings of late nineteenth-century literary culture. For a perspective on women and autobiography in the twentieth century see Linda Anderson's *Women and Autobiography in the Twentieth Century: Remembered Futures* (Hemel Hempstead: Harvester, 1996).

Eighteenth-century and Romantic period fiction

Frederick Karl's *A Reader's Guide to the Development of the English Novel in the Eighteenth Century*, 1974 (London: Thames and Hudson, 1975) is a detailed, readable and highly informative guide to the major eighteenth-century novelists. Clive T. Probyn's *English Fiction of the Eighteenth Century* (London: Longman, 1987) covers similar ground and can be seen, in a sense, as an alternative to the discourse-system explanations of origins by critics such as Lennard J. Davis and Michael McKeon (see 'The rise of the novel' above): for Probyn 'the novel is the most recalcitrant of forms, resisting all attempts to follow any single development' (p. 12). John J. Richetti (ed.), *The Cambridge Companion to the Eighteenth-Century Novel* (Cambridge: Cambridge University Press, 1996), contains a number of valuable essays on major themes and individual novelists, including Margaret Doody on Richardson. Gary Kelly's *English Fiction of the Romantic Period 1789–1830* (London: Longman, 1989) is probably the definitive study of this period: it includes probing chapters on Sir Walter Scott and Jane Austen; the chapter on Austen situates her writing in the context of other fictional trends in the period. Kate Ferguson Ellis's *The Contested Castle: Gothic Novels and the Subversion of Gender Ideology* (Urbana: University of Illinois Press, 1989) is a study of the gothic movement and its relations to gender ideology. E. J. Clery's *The Rise of Supernatural Fiction 1762–1800* (Cambridge: Cambridge University Press, 1995) is a highly original study of gothic fiction as a site of convergence for the struggles which surrounded discourses of the supernatural and commerce in the later eighteenth century.

Nineteenth-century fiction

Michael Wheeler's *English Fiction of the Victorian Period, 1830–1890* (London: Longman, 1985) is a useful survey which provides accounts of the major trends in Victorian fiction. In addition to contributing to the debate about the rise of the novel, Nancy Armstrong's *Desire and Domestic Fiction: A Political History of the Novel* extends her account of the gender politics of domestic discourse into a reading of the English nineteenth-century novel, particularly novels published around 1848. Mary Poovey's *Uneven Developments: The Ideological Work of Gender in Mid-Victorian England* (Chicago and London: University of Chicago Press, 1988) extends this feminist work on the relationship between the novel and gendered discourses.

Catherine Gallagher has produced a major work of New Historicist scholarship in *The Industrial Reformation of English Fiction: Social Discourse and Narrative Form* (Chicago and London: University of California Press, 1985). Gallagher's work constructs relations between discourses of social and industrial reform and the narrative strategies employed by Victorian novelists. A similar approach is adopted by Mary Poovey's more recent *Making a Social Body: British Cultural Formation 1830–1864* (Chicago and London: Chicago University Press, 1995). Poovey's account reconstructs a pervasive discourse of the body which was common to the great documents of sanitary reform and social management, and the novels of Disraeli,

Dickens and Gaskell. D.A. Miller's *The Novel and the Police* (Berkeley, CA, and Los Angeles: University of California Press, 1987) is another influential New Historicist approach to the nineteenth-century novel, which takes its lead from the work of Michel Foucault. Miller's work contends that the novel is a form of discourse which 'polices' subjectivity: though his readings of the mechanisms and strategies by which such processes are performed stress sophistication and complexity. Jenny Bourne Taylor and Sally Shuttleworth's *Embodied Selves: An Anthology of Psychological Texts 1830–1890* (Oxford: Clarendon Press, 1998) assembles a rich selection of hitherto inaccessible material, which provides the means for making connections between nineteenth-century theories of psychological moral management and narrative strategies in a wide range of Victorian texts, especially sensation fiction. An exemplary study is Jenny Bourne Taylor's *In the Secret Theatre of the Home: Wilkie Collins, Sensation Narrative and Nineteenth-Century Psychology* (London: Routledge, 1988). For a more general intro duction, see Lyn Pykett, *The Sensation Novel*, Writers and their Work (London: Northcote House, 1994).

Transitional and Modernist fiction

Peter Keating's *The Haunted Study: A Social History of the English Novel 1875–1914*, 1989 (London: Fontana, 1991) is an essential starting point, and is particularly good on the social history of publishing and reading trends. Clare Hanson's *Short Stories and Short Fictions: 1880–1980* (London: Macmillan, 1985) offers an account of the development of the short story form in the period. Dominic Head's *The Modernist Short Story: A Study in Theory and Practice* (Cambridge: Cambridge University Press, 1992) is more theoretically challenging and focuses on the Modernist short story. David Trotter's *The English Novel in History, 1895–1920* (London: Routledge, 1993) is a wide-ranging examination of high Modernist and popular fictions (such as the detective and imperial adventure novels); it is also a revisionary reading of Modernist stylistics. Lyn Pykett's *Engendering Fictions: The English Novel in the Early Twentieth Century* (London: Arnold, 1995) is a feminist reading of developments in the early twentieth-century novel centred on gender ideology and late nineteenth-century theories of degeneration. Randall Stevenson's *Modernist Fiction: An Introduction* (Hemel Hempstead: Harvester Wheatsheaf, 1992) examines Modernist narrative practice in relation to historical shifts in perceptions of time, space and value:

Stevenson's account is influenced by Bakhtin. Malcolm Bradbury and James McFarlane (eds), *Modernism, 1890–1930* (Harmondsworth: Penguin, 1976), situates Modernism in a wider European context, and contains essays on fiction. Vassiliki Kolocotroni, Jane Goldman and Olga Taxidou (eds) have produced a wonderful resource in *Modernism: An Anthology of Sources and Documents* (Edinburgh: Edinburgh University Press, 1998). It contains much of relevance for the study of fiction. Patricia Waugh's *Practising Postmodernism, Reading Modernism* (London: Arnold, 1992) provides a postmodern approach to the reading of Modernist fiction which is premised on the argument that there is no substantial aesthetic break between Modernist and postmodernist narrative practice.

Metafiction and postmodern fiction

Steven Connor, *The English Novel in History, 1950 to the Present*, (London: Routledge, 1995), surveys the post-war period. Patricia Waugh's *Metafiction: The Theory and Practice of Self-Conscious Fiction* (London: Methuen, 1984) is an excellent introduction to the many facets of self-conscious narrative. Patricia Waugh goes on to chart debates within postmodernism in her *Postmodernism: A Reader* (London: Arnold, 1992). Thomas Docherty provides similar but perhaps wider-ranging guidance in his *Postmodernism: A Reader* (Hemel Hempstead: Harvester Wheatsheaf, 1993), which assembles a range of writings on topics as diverse as fiction and architecture. Major studies of postmodern fiction can be found in Brian McHale's *Postmodernist Fiction* (London: Methuen, 1987) and in Linda Hutcheon's *A Poetics of Postmodernism: History, Theory, Fiction* (London: Routledge, 1988), in which Hutcheon coins the concept of 'historiographic metafiction'. The relationship between postmodernism and postcolonialism is explored in Ian Adam and Helen Tiffin (eds), *Past the Last Post: Theorising Post Colonialism and Post Modernism* (Hemel Hempstead: Harvester Wheatsheaf, 1991).

Postcolonialism

Edward Said's *Orientalism* (London: Routledge and Kegan Paul, 1978) is the important starting point. His *Culture and Imperialism* (London: Chatto and Windus, 1993) updates and expands his thesis. There is a (slightly unfair) tendency now to regard Said's early theory of Orientalist discourse as 'monolithic' in the claims that it makes about the West's scholarly and intellectual will to power over the East. This is reflected in the title of Bill Ashcroft, Gareth Griffiths and Helen Tiffin's joint work, *The Empire Writes Back: Theory and Practice in Post-Colonial Literatures* (London: Routledge, 1989) a useful introduction to the field of postcolonial literary studies which draws many of its examples from novels and fictions. However, Vijay Mishra and Bob Hodge in their essay 'What is Post(-)Colonialism?' have asked whether postcolonial criticism of the kind performed by Ashcroft, Griffiths and Tiffin perhaps places too heavy a reliance on the presumed 'subversiveness' of the heteroglot novel (p. 280). Their essay can be found in Patrick Williams and Laura Chrisman (eds), *Colonial Discourse and Post-Colonial Theory* (Hemel Hempstead: Harvester Wheatsheaf, 1993), along with a rich variety of sources which map the major critical and intellectual directions in the field. Homi K. Bhabha (ed.), *Nation and Narration* (London: Routledge, 1990), contains many valuable essays on the relationship between narration and 'location'. Bhabha is one of the leading post-colonialist theorists and critics; his challenging work on subjectivity, mimicry and diasporic movement is exemplified in his *The Location of Culture* (London: Routledge, 1994). Gayatri Chakravorty Spivak is another major voice in postcolonial theory: an overview of her challenging corpus can be found in Donna Lendry and Gerald McLean (eds), *The Spivak Reader: Selected Works of Gayatri Chakravorty Spivak* (New York: Routledge, 1995).

Index